This book belongs to

_____

_____

So sod off
and get your
own copy

Sports Banger:
Lifestyles of the Poor,
Rich & Famous

Sports
BANGER

T
&H

BANGER

CONTENTS

Introduction
Jonny Banger   6

BEDKNOBS AND BOOTLEGS   18   THE KNOCKING SHOP   58

Rent   20   724 Seven Sisters Road   60
Jonny Banger   Jonny Banger

Free Tulisa   26   Under the Counter   70
Phone Thieves   30   Slazenger Banger   86
Team Nigella   34   Free Party Is Not a Crime 96

'Why Bootlegging Will Never Die' 38   106
by Anastasiia Fedorova   Sumitra Upham   109
                                           Chunky   110

Totally Enormous Extinct Dinosaurs 50
Anna Lomax   51   THE T-SHIRTS   114
Klose One   52
Artwork   55

VIVA LA BOOTLEG	130	MAISON DE BANG BANG	234
Knocking Down the Wall Jonny Banger	132	Making the Maison Jonny Banger	236
My First Fashion Show	142	HERAS Records	252
Classics Never Die	156	The People Deserve Beauty	256
Fuck Boris	164	MAX Banger	276
Pop Culture Is Trash	174		
		'Seven Sisters Is Burning'	282
'Modern Metal Is Trash'	196	by Jeremy Deller	
by Nathalie Khan			
		The Final Act	284
In Pigeons We Trust	198		
Paranoid London	202	Ami Benton	298
Mega Aid	210	Celeste Kennedy Doig	299
Banger Pirates & The Covid Letters	214	Neil Landstrumm	300
		Jeanie Crystal	302
Caro Howell	226	Holly Harris	303
Eloise Smyth	227		
Jaime Winstone	228		
Emanuelle Soum	229	Contributors	305
Dom Ridler	230	Picture Credits	306
Max Allen	232	References	307
		Index	308
		Thanks	310

999

INTRODUCTION
by Jonny Banger

I was born in Colchester. Parents divorced when I was four. It was a single-parent family, seeing our dad every other weekend to go watch Aldershot Town FC. My mum was a mental health nurse, and my dad worked for the London Federation of Boys' Clubs, organizing inner-city boxing and football for kids from disadvantaged areas. For my 10th birthday, my brother got me a tape pack of live recordings from the Mindwarp raves in Essex – it was all UK hardcore, parts of it bordering on happy hardcore. It was the most exciting thing I'd ever heard. Long before either of us ever went to a rave, both our rooms were covered in flyers we got from Rapture Records in town. Our mum got ill when I was 13 and my brother was 16. We got split up and had to go live at different friends' houses, just seeing each other at school. At 15, my mum died, and I started work experience at a local record shop called Lost Wood. I was the youngest person there, so they called me Newborn. My brother and I stayed in the house; now he was 18, he could be my legal guardian. I don't know if the people at the shop knew my situation, but it was quite a mad environment for a kid. They really looked after me. This was where I got exposed to DIY culture. The people around me were making their own zines and T-shirts, putting on their own nights, DJing, dealing, everything. I saw some of the older kids who worked at the shop go to college, get student loans and get the fuck out of town. This was my escape route.

Bootlegging has been around since forever. People bootleg for all different reasons. I've been selling bootlegs since I was 10, when I started selling counterfeit clothing with my dad at car boot sales and markets. You can go to any market in the world, and you'll find knockoffs. I found a load of wicked knockoff Lacoste tracksuits on holiday in Morocco – the market seller asked what I did for a living, and I said, 'Same as you.'

Since I started Banger, I've had 10 cease and desists from the government, three PayPal accounts and two Big Cartel accounts shut down, one merchant account closed, and gotten a bunch of solicitor's letters in the post. Working on this book, we realized there was a copyright infringement on almost every page.

Everyone always asks: What is Sports Banger? It's hard to answer, and I love that. Clothes are one thing, but it's the people and the music that bring it all to life. We are 100% independent, and for the last decade have operated without investors, agents, management, or PR. It's about as DIY as you can get. It means we can make T-shirts, couture pieces, and books, throw raves, put out records, and put on exhibitions and fashion shows. Although it can look like chaos, there is a thread that joins it all together.

When we started working on this book, I went into a slump and didn't leave my bed one morning until Dom sent me a video of a pigeon that had wandered into the studio. I rushed down there, but she had gone. An hour later, she returned, and I wrote the first words for this introduction. One of our friends and collaborators, Emma Brewin, told me that you get sent a bird when you need one the most. We named the pigeon Billie, and she has visited us every day since. On a sunny day at Maison de Bang Bang, the giant double-height wooden doors swing wide open, and we work with our pigeons watching over us.

This book is a celebration. Ten years of Sports Banger. The work has found a home. If I'd come across a book like this when I was at school or college, I would have lost my shit. It's for kids who feel like they have no power to change the situation they're in. It's a DIY cookbook that I hope will inspire others to get shit done.

Big up.

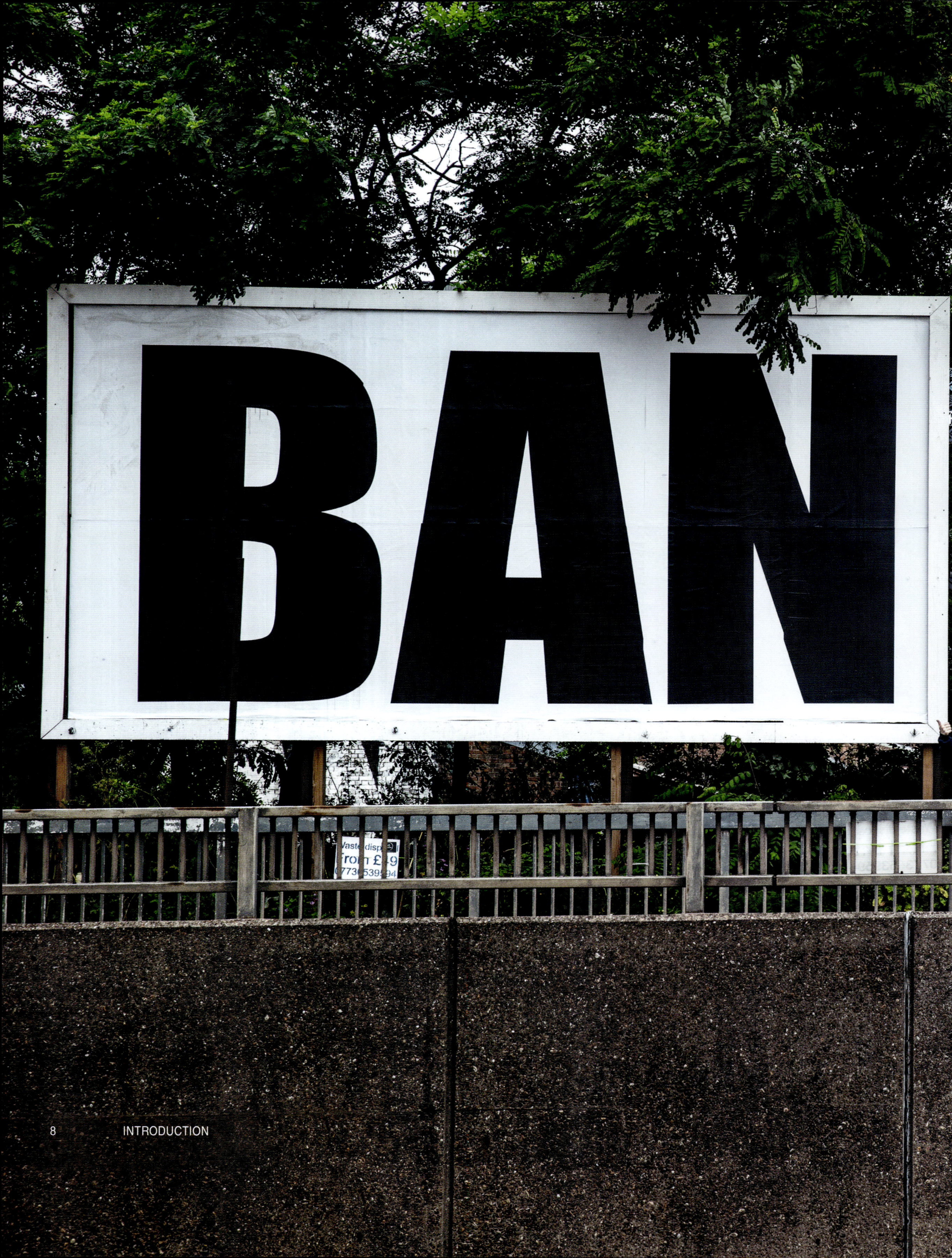
BAN

Previous, left: Young Jonny in his favourite jumper.
Above: Jonny and his BANGER billboard on the Bow roundabout.

Above: GIZ A FIVER. A £5 note sellotaped by Jonny to a traffic sign on Belfast Road.
Opposite: Musician and DJ Eliza Rose wears the Sports Banger Lucozade 'NRG!' dress from 'The People Deserve Beauty' collection in a London off-licence.

INTRODUCTION

DJ and vocalist Josh Caffé in head-to-toe Banger, performing with Paranoid London at Mega Rave 4 in Tottenham, 2021.

Another quality product from the **OXFORD** range of accessories

OXFORD
Balaclava *Eyes* ©

Essential Cotton 'Eyes' Balaclava

'Yeux' Coton Balaclava
Baumwolle 'Blick' Balaclava
Balaclava 'Ojos' de algodón
cotone 'Occhi'
bawełniana "Oczy"

Moisture wicking

Universal Size

OXFORD
Balaclava *Eyes*
Essential Cotton 'Eyes' Balaclava

Above: Discarded balaclava packaging fortuitously found outside Sports Banger's old studio on Seven Sisters Road. *Opposite:* A bouquet at the knocking shop, wrapped in bootlegged Polo Ralph Lauren ribbon.

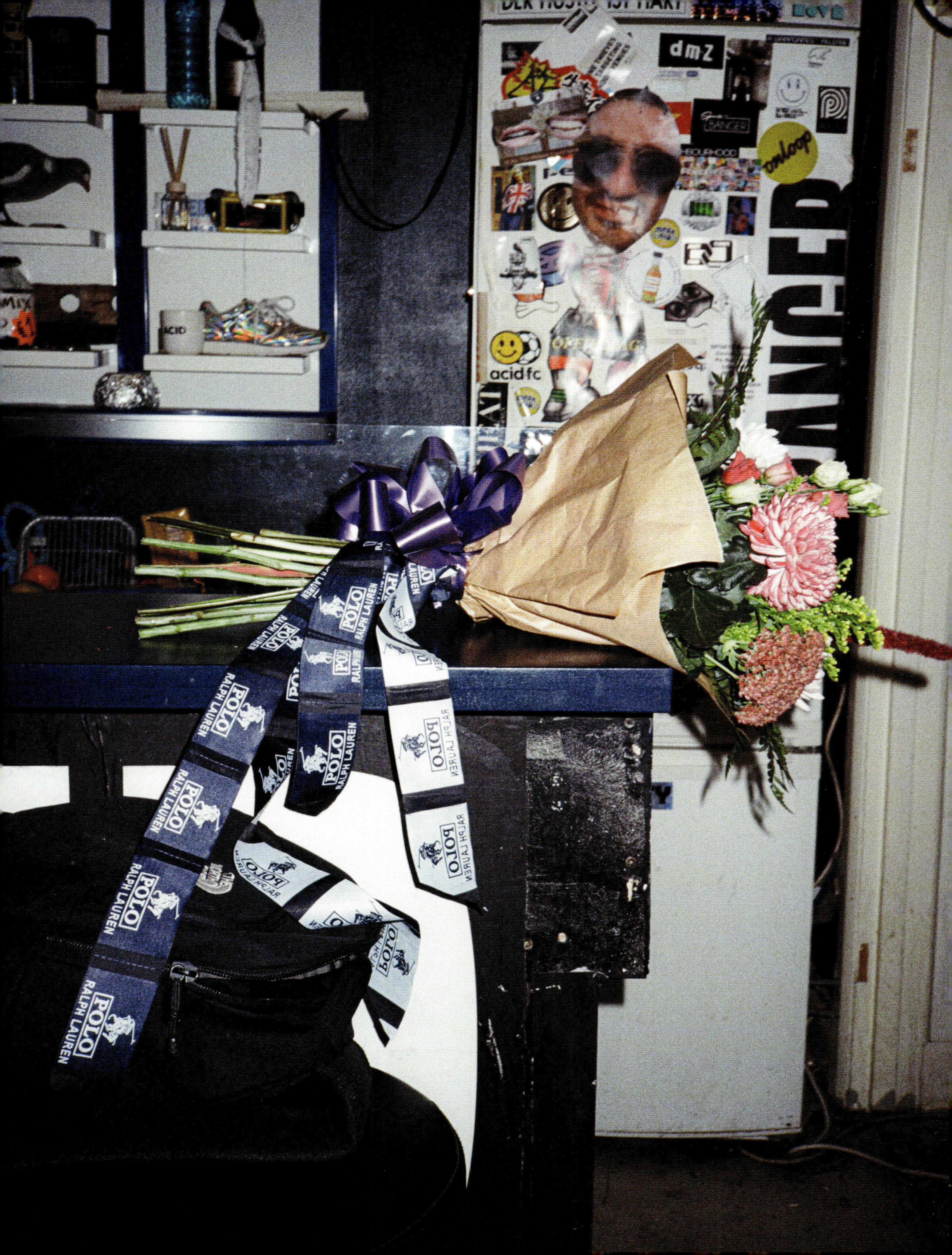
dmz
onloop
acid fc
ACID
POLO
RALPH LAUREN

Make-up artist Becca Wordingham backstage with
actor Eloise Smyth (interviewed on page 227) and dancer
Maëva Berthelot at Sports Banger's 'Pop Culture is Trash'
runway show.

BEDK
AR
BOOT

NOBS
NOD
LEGS

RENT
by Jonny Banger

In 2010, I moved with a few other mates into an old warehouse. The place had just been raided (the previous tenant used it as an illegal grow), so we painted it, built beds and stuck our decks and speakers in. Its location was pretty inconspicuous, behind a giant metal gate. Perfect for making noise. We had friends living next door and mates round the corner, and we used to go out to raves in big numbers. At the end of the night, we usually had half the crowd and all the DJs back to ours.

At the time, I was working at Vibe Bar on Brick Lane, where I'd started off as the flyer boy. There was a wicked crew down there, Norris 'Da Boss' Windross was my boss, and it was still run like old clubland. Brick Lane started changing big time, and so did the management, so I quit when it all turned to shit. I was skint, unemployed, depressed, and couldn't afford rent. This was the start of Sports Banger.

It's hard to describe the first five years of Banger. It was budget DIY chaos. There was no pot to piss in. My bedroom was full of stock, and every surface was a packing table. The first T-shirts were heat pressed at a spot on Bethnal Green Road that had its own range called BMC (Big Money Clothing). I got the first 'FREE TULISA' T-shirt printed there for my birthday. I thought the case was a load of bollocks. A working-class girl being dragged through the mud by the tabloids. Everyone ended up wanting one. I'd never seen anything like it – people stopping me, asking for photos. It made people talk, and the support for her was real.

I was in the printers every few days, usually before a rave. Friends would request a T-shirt, and I'd get a handful pressed until I had enough money to screenprint a load. Rinse FM was just round the corner, and I was hosting on the mic for School Records, a label started by Loefah and Jan 'Aset' Francis (RIP), who both brought a lot of people together. Loefah's dance music label Swamp 81 was a big inspiration for us all. There was a whole community of people producing and playing tracks with everyone trying to ID all the unreleased sounds. The T-shirts all came out of these raves and worked their way up into pop culture, politics and fashion.

Sports Banger began with a hand-me-down smartphone, no laptop, an internet cafe and a local post office. I was in the post office a couple of times a week sending out T-shirts and knew the whole family who ran it. Faisal always greeted me with 'Mr Banger' and if there were queues, he would open a separate till at the front to process my orders. You'd meet other regulars with big sacks who'd all quiz each other about their businesses. There was one guy selling hundreds of knock-off designer slippers, another sending out packs of protein powder, another selling crypto hardware wallets, and another who had a roaring trade in candles. Everyone wanted to be the top seller. I asked Faisal who was number one, and he said, 'Banger, you'd be top seller, but you go missing for weeks, and we don't see you.' I think this probably sums up the business of Sports Banger.

The T-shirts are usually spinning round in my head and I scribble notes on any scrap of paper going or collage stuff on my phone. My friend Tom Proper has artworked all the designs for print from day one. Shout out Tom.

You can map the T-shirts against a timeline of the country. They kinda document a feeling or what you might hear on the bus or in the smoking area at a club. Some see my work as political. I just say what I see. It's rave, resistance, and eccentric British iconography. Rave and politics have always been arch nemeses, so I suppose this is what you get when you smash it all together.

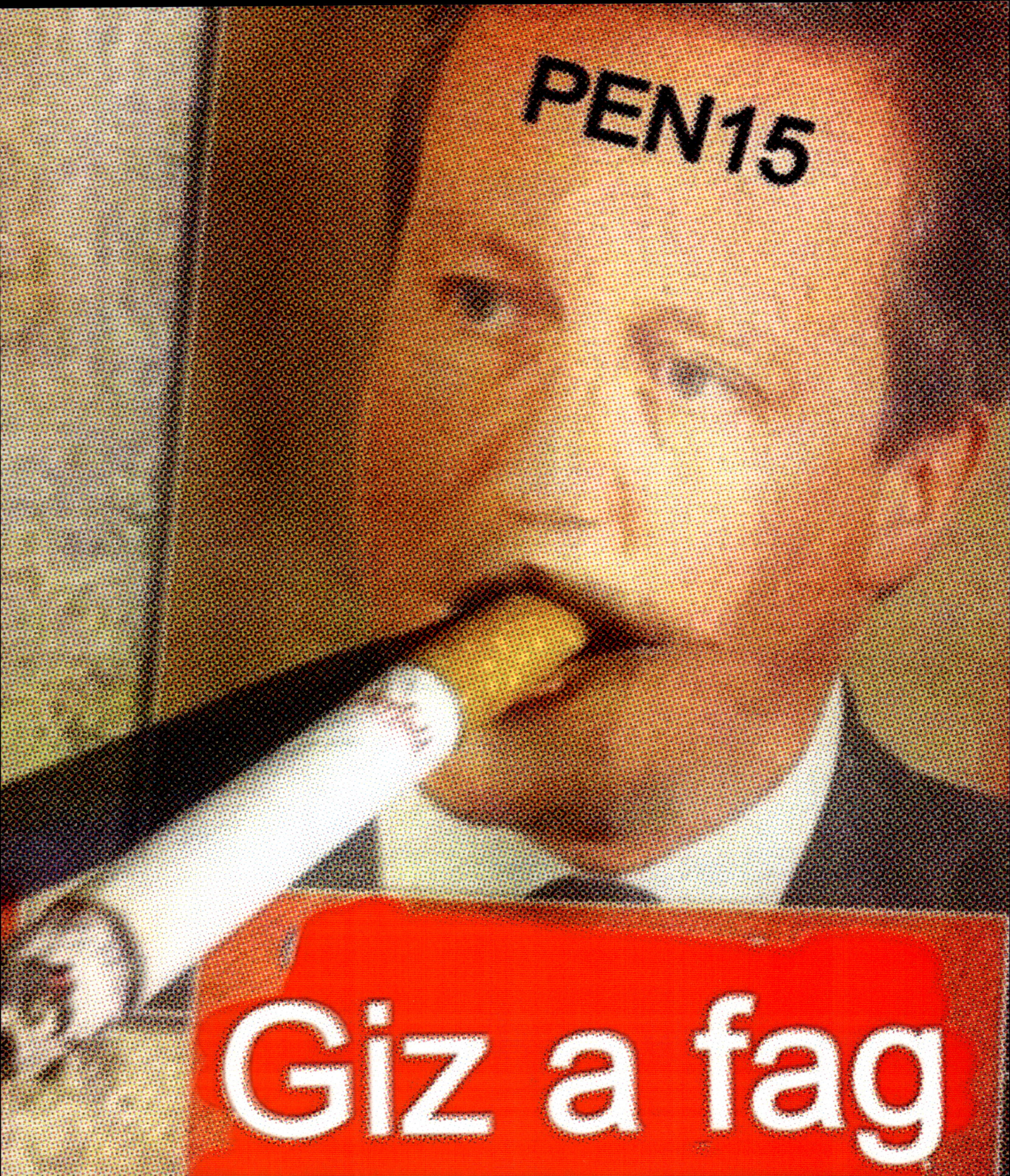

PEN15

Giz a fag

Previous, left: EARLY DAYS. Jonny packs 'FREE TULISA' T-shirts at home.
Above: A newspaper cutting of David Cameron, modified by Jonny.

Jonny and Artwork (aka Arthur Smith) (interviewed on page 55) with a GOLF SALE sign at an anti-austerity march in London in 2016.

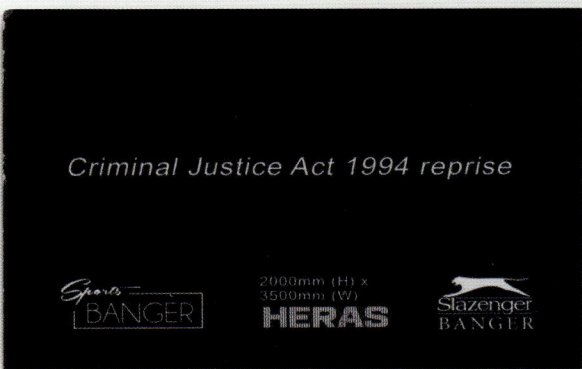

Opposite: Jonny in a hi-vis 'ACID' Banger hoodie.
Above: Sports Banger's original 'hotline' business cards.

FREE TULISA

In 2013, a tabloid sting led to the N-Dubz star and *X Factor* judge Tulisa
Contostavlos being arrested on false drug charges. The UK tabloids plastered
her across every front page. The whole thing was a fucking disgrace. Tulisa
is a homegrown working-class queen. The 'FREE TULISA' T-shirt was
the beginning of Sports Banger.

BEDKNOBS AND BOOTLEGS

Previous, left: An original 'FREE TULISA' T-shirt signed by
the artist herself.
Previous, right: SPREADING THE MESSAGE. 'FREE TULISA'
spotted in the crowd at a UK festival.
Above: THE FEMALE BOSS. A cardboard cut-out Tulisa mask.

Mazher Mahmood, the self-titled 'king of the sting' who entrapped Tulisa was jailed for tampering with evidence in the collapsed drug trial. As the verdict was read out, someone in the public gallery shouted, 'Your turn now, Mazher.'

Above, left: Courtroom sketch of Tulisa and rapper Mike GLC, who was also wrapped up in the trial.
Above, right: Courtroom sketch of the judge delivering the verdict – Mahmood and his driver were both found guilty of tampering with evidence.
Below: Stills from a 2018 episode of ITV's *Don't Hate the Playaz*, showing host Jordan Stephens giving Tulisa his 'FREE TULISA' T-shirt.

PHONE THIEVES

Phone thieves made the headlines in 2013, when phones were being nicked left, right and centre. One guy in a Manchester nightclub was caught with over 40 phones stashed down his trousers. There was a newspaper story about a florist falling in love with a phone thief that read, 'He stole my phone and with it my heart.' Clubs started sticking up signs, and bar staff wore T-shirts saying, 'IS YOUR PHONE SAFE?'

This weekend 25 phones will get stolen in Hackney venues

Please look after your belongings

KEEPING IT OUT OF SIGHT
WON'T RUIN YOUR NIGHT.

AVOID
~~PLAYING~~

DON'T LEAVE
HANDBAGS
OPEN

KEEP
YOUR PHONE
IN A SECURE
PLACE

INFORM OUR
SECURITY TEAM
IF YOUR PHONE
IS MISSING

fabric

PHONE THIEVES
ARE TARGETING
LONDON VENUES

BEDKNOBS AND BOOTLEGS

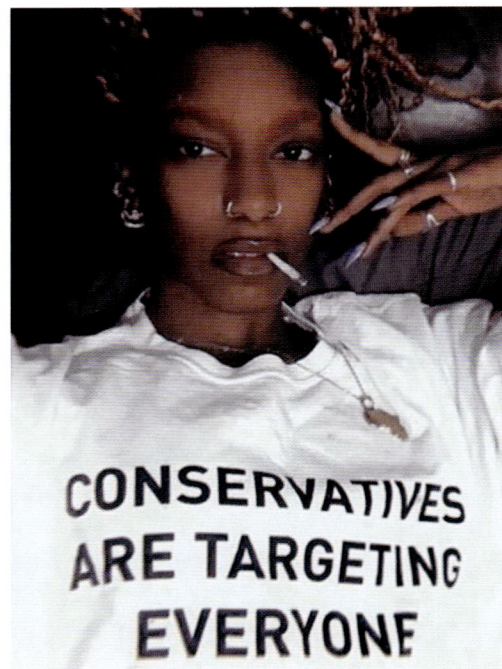

Previous, left: An original 'Phone Thieves' T-shirt.
Previous, right: A 2013 poster from former Hackney club
Dance Tunnel (RIP).
Above: A 2013 flyer from London's Fabric nightclub, which
inspired the 'Phone Thieves' T-shirt.

Below: A trilogy of T-shirts based on the flyer:
Below, left: Jonny wears the original;
Below, centre: Film-maker Bafic wears the second version
at Notting Hill Carnival (made when the Met closed Fabric
and put their licence up for review);
Below, right: Meme Gold wears the final edition.

98   4   11737 +44 7527 14! +44 7597 92 +44   :6:7991 654657   NE THIEVES AF +44 7
S ARE TAR(ONE THIEVES , PHONE THIEV PHONE THIEV PHONE THIEV e thieves are ta DON VENUES PHON
ES ✷   NDON VENUES LONDON VEN(LONDON VEN LONDON VENes.   LOND

92   4   86290 +44 7   7723 99 +44 7821 64   7 004369   7597 005428   +44 7
S ARE TAR(ONE THIEVES , PHONE THIEV PHONE THIEF PHONE THIEVNE THIEVS ARE NE THIEVES AF Phone
ES #ellom8NDON VENUES LONDON VENI LONDON VEN LONDON VENDON VENUES DON VENUES ; venues

17   7829 79972 +44   7985 48 +44 7   7955 6518   7723 007001   +44 7
S ARE TAR(ONE THIEVES , PHONE THIEV PHONE THIEV PHONE THIEV e thieves are ta NE THIEFS ARI PHON
S   NDON VENUES LONDON VENI LONDON VEN LONDON VENes   DON VENUES LOND

05   4   76300 +44 7   7411 49 +44   7825 274   7985 481   +44 7
S ARE TAR(ONE THIEVES , PHONE THIEV PHONE THIEV PHONE THIEV e thieves are ta NE THIEVES AF PHON
    NDON VENUES LONDON VENI LONDON VEN LONDON VENes   DON VENUES LOND

69   7821 64792 +44 7   44 7983 36 +44   32   2 390372   7411 492518   +44 7
S ARE TAR(ONE THIEVES , PHONE THIEV PHONE THIEV PHONE THIEVNE THIEVES AF NE THIEVES AF PHON
    NDON VENUES LONDON VENI LONDON VEN LONDON VENDON VENUES DON VENUES LOND

16   4 7   94777 +44   44 7825 56 +44 7703 36   762889   7983 365   +44 7
S ARE TAR(ONE THIEVES , PHONE THIEV PHONE THIEV PHONE THIEVNE THIEVES AF NE THIEVES AF PHON
    NDON VENUES LONDON VENI LONDON VEN LONDON VENDON VENUES DON VENUES LOND

63   4   27343 +44 7   44 7917 61 +44   :774   696   78   681   +44 7
S ARE TAR(ONE THIEVES , PHONE THIEV PHONE THIEV PHONE THIEVNE THIEVES AF NE THIEVES AF PHON
ES   NDON VENUES LONDON VENI LONDON VEN LONDON VENDON VENUES

33   PHONE THIEVES

Above: Customers texted in 'PHONE THIEVES ARE TARGETING LONDON VENUES' to score a free T-shirt during a Banger giveaway.
Below: Ravers with their Sports Banger stickers.

We love Nigella. She's the unofficial queen of our house and beloved by the nation. In 2013, she was at a Mayfair restaurant with her then-husband Charles Saatchi and he was snapped grabbing her by the throat. Within days the papers ran an all-out smear campaign against her. Bastard media and men of power.

I didn't have a drug problem. I had a life problem

THE DAY NIGELLA UNBURDENED HER SOUL IN COURT

BRUTAL
SAATCHI

DENIAL Nigella
yesterday and,
inset, choke row

Mino wears a dress by **Andreas Kronthaler for Vivienne Westwood**, top by **Sports Banger**, shoes by **MSGM**, gloves by **Sarah Balmont** and earring by **D'heygere**. Her belt is custom by the stylist.

Previous, left: An original 'TEAM NIGELLA' T-shirt.
Previous, right: Twenty times a goddess, Nigella boldly faced the tabloid dogs.
Opposite: The 'Nigella newsprint' velour top in *TANK* magazine.
Above: Courtroom sketch of Nigella Lawson giving testimony, 2013.
Below: DJ/Producer Skream is Team Nigella at Boiler Room in London, 2014.

WHY BOOTLEGGING WILL NEVER DIE
by Anastasiia Fedorova

A brand is a shortcut. This is perhaps the most straightforward way to describe what happens when we come into contact with Nike, Gucci or Coca-Cola. A brand is like any other representational symbol, but embedded in the capitalist landscape.

The time it takes to decode a brand is incredibly brief. For most of us, there is no need to verbalize what Apple or BMW stand for. A brand is a fast track not only into consumers' choices but also their aspirations, memories and emotions. Most of us have grown up surrounded by branding. It's on the clothes on our bodies, the packaged food on our kitchen tables, in our cityscapes and dreams. Marketing experts estimate that a contemporary Western consumer is exposed to between four and ten thousand branded messages a day. In this increasingly branded reality, being a bootlegger carries an overtly political meaning. Bootleggers remind the rest of us that it's possible to engage with reality creatively and critically – to shake off the torpor of simply being a consumer.

In 2020, I curated 'The Real Thing', an exhibition at London's Fashion Space Gallery that explored the potential of bootlegged fashion as a creative language and disruptive political power. Alongside work from other collectives, artists and designers, Sports Banger's T-shirts and NHS-logo-printed garments hung on a HERAS fence at the centre of the gallery. Also featured in the exhibition were Hassan Kurbanbaev's photographs of counterfeit goods at markets in Uzbekistan, a T-shirt from local queer collective 'Nite Dykez', artist May Hands' concrete-filled luxury shopping bags, and documentation of Harlem couturier Dapper Dan.

When I spoke with Jonny Banger about his work, it turned out that his involvement in bootlegging is rooted in childhood memories, much like it is for me. I've been obsessed with bootleg fashion for years because I grew up surrounded by it. My dad used to take me to flea markets in post-Soviet Russia – colourful landscapes of counterfeit Gucci belts and knock-off Adidas tracksuits. This is how I learnt about the desire and joy that fashion brands can create – and how fashion intersects with money, power and social hierarchy.

When I asked Jonny about the origin of his interest in bootlegging, he remembered working weekends at his dad's best friend's sports shop as a pre-teen, 'printing football shirts for local teams and selling counterfeit sportswear out of a wholesale warehouse in Farnborough.' And yet one of his most impactful designs, the Nike 'NHS' T-shirt, has an even more personal story. As Jonny recalled, 'I got given a flyer at the train station that said: "HACKNEY SUPPORTS JUNIOR DOCTORS". It kind of hit me in the face like a sledgehammer. I read [it] and remembered all my personal experiences with the NHS. My mum was a mental health nurse at Severalls Hospital in Colchester. She got ill with leukaemia when I was 13 and died when I was 15. I'd buried that whole part of my life, and then the junior doctors flyer brought it right up front.' Describing how he came up with the design for the T-shirt, Jon says, 'I thought the N [in NHS] looked like NIKE, and the NHS is good – tick. Some said it was a comment on the commercialization and privatization of the NHS. NHS is free. NHS with a NIKE tick is £19.99. Read it however you want. I wanted to show support to my junior doctor peer group as the government began to demonize them in the media.'

Today, the power of brands is reinforced by marketing and design agencies, and their presence is inescapably intertwined with our lives. One way of pushing back against this is to reclaim or undermine their power. With the onset of the pandemic in 2020, Sports Banger's 'NHS' T-shirts and hoodies helped raise roughly £100,000 for the delivery of healthy meals to ICU workers and community centres across London. In 2022, Sports Banger released a new edition of the design to support striking NHS workers. When I asked Jonny why he kept using the NHS logo despite problems with the government, he simply said, 'Because I'm a bootlegger.' Being a bootlegger is not just what you do; it's a way of existing.

In the mid-2010s, Sports Banger emerged alongside a handful of other independent labels that embraced political bootlegging. For a brief moment, the wider fashion industry seemed to follow: Demna Gvasalia made the Vetements logo visually rhyme with Champion, Balenciaga did the same with Bernie Sanders's presidential campaign logo, and Gucci collaborated with Dapper Dan and graffiti artist GucciGhost. As the grand fashion houses were enlisting counter-culture talents, it was a good moment for subversive moves. From 2016 to 2020, philanthropic streetwear brand HYPEPEACE bootlegged the Palace logo to raise money for Palestine. Citizens of Nowhere, a small-scale, London-based operation, created bootlegged garments with a name reclaimed from Theresa May's infamous Brexit speech. Bootlegging can be a perfect way to create a political banner to provoke, challenge and drive change.

But what is the future of bootlegging as a creative language in our increasingly digital culture? The more time we spend online, the more exposed we are to branded content. And beyond this, internet culture is gradually distorting and eroding the very meaning of authenticity. We enthusiastically create AI-generated versions of ourselves, surf alongside deepfake videos and ponder luxury digital skins for avatars in video games. Branding has permeated everything around us, and the effect of its omnipresence is yet to be determined.

For me, the true meaning of bootlegging has always been its spirit of inclusivity. This is the world of Sports Banger, as we see on the runways at their fashion shows – where nurses, ravers, drag queens, rude boys and Tottenham teenagers all come together. In an excessively branded world, bootlegging has a rare ability to create an experimental, political and deeply inclusive space.

BEDKNOBS AND BOOTLEGS

Above: Bought at a market in Turkey, Jonny's favourite
bootleg T-shirt from his extensive collection, featuring counterfeit
Gucci branding, a two-tone fade, and the ghost mascot from
Judgement Day, a '90s hardcore rave held in Newcastle.
Opposite: Jonny wears bootleg Tommy Hilfiger bought
from Deptford Market.

My old Rinse FM show was right after Julie Adenuga's. She gave me her brother's address and told me to send him some stuff. Skepta went on tour pushing the UK sound stateside. It was a really important and exciting time for UK music and our 'Upside-Down Reebok' T-shirt flew as a flag of do-it-yourself independence.

After a long weekend of raves in Liverpool and Nottingham I got a call asking me to bring down a load of T-shirts to the 'Shutdown' video being filmed the next day. Now I'm in a Skepta video awkwardly sitting on a wall next to him in a Banger Mr Freeze hoodie, chain-smoking menthol fags wondering how the fuck I ended up here. Skepta wears an iconic all-white Cottweiler tracksuit and cap – the video is full of independent UK fashion and young artists. In the opening shots of the video, you see our bootleg 'Adidas M25' T-shirt. He bigged everyone up.

WHY BOOTLEGGING WILL NEVER DIE

Skepta in the Sports Banger 'Upside-Down Reebok' T-shirt with the A$AP Mob at Art Basel Miami Beach, 2014.

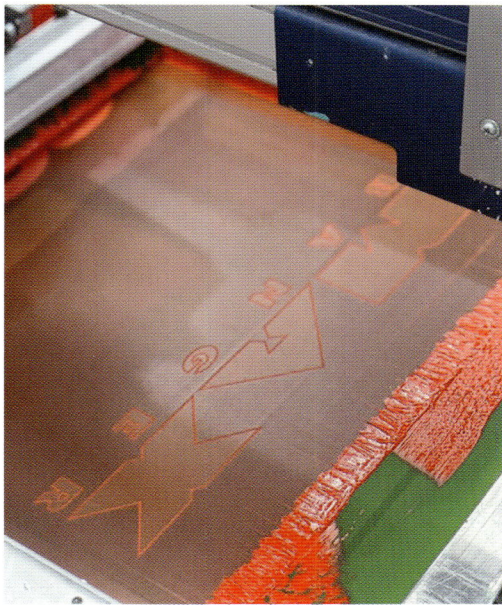

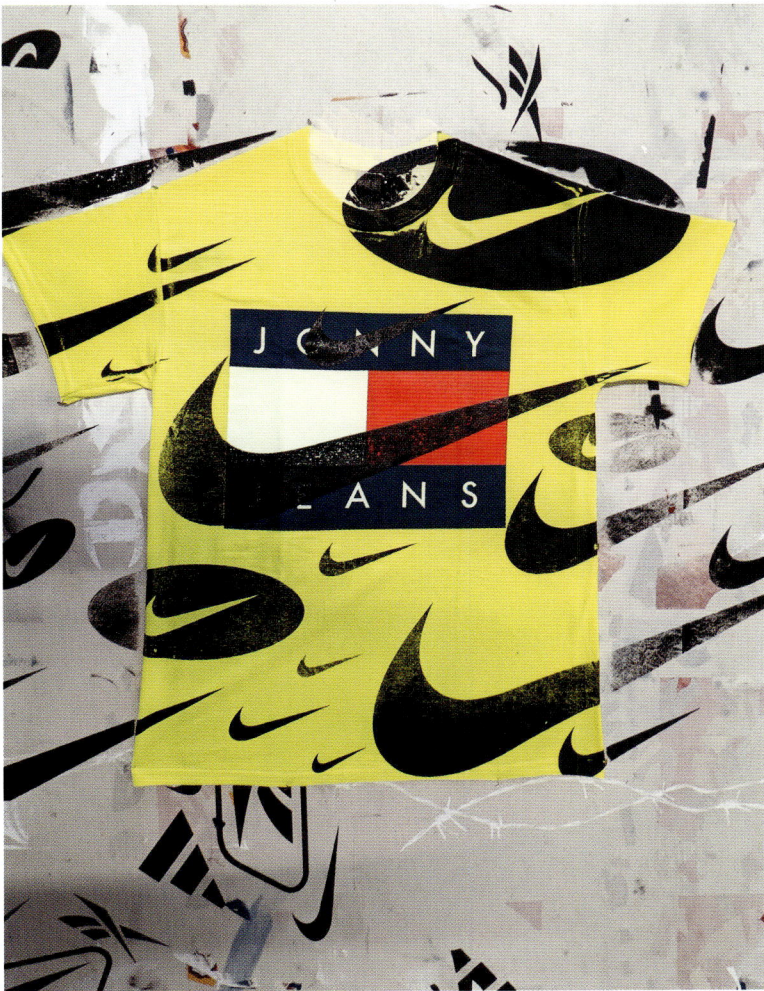

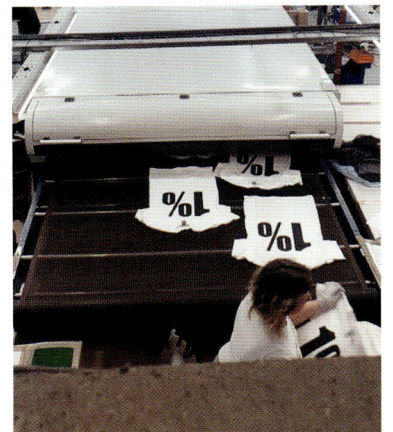

WHY BOOTLEGGING WILL NEVER DIE

Opposite: Detail of 'Shocker' overprinted hood, featuring velcro and 3M appliqué.
STRICTLY SCREEN PRINTS. Always have a good relationship with your local screen printer. *Above (clockwise from top left):* The 'MAX Banger' T-shirt in production; the Banger overprint jumpers ready to go; '1%' T-shirts rolling off the press; 'Jonny Jeans' over-branded T-shirt commission for dystopian Netflix film *The Kitchen.*

WHY BOOTLEGGING WILL NEVER DIE

Opposite: Holographic counterfeit Reebok labels bought by
Jonny from under the counter at a dodgy supplier in Istanbul.
Above: White hoodie adorned with counterfeit Reebok swing tags.
Overleaf, left: Where's my T-shirt? Assortment of photos from
Sports Banger supporters.

20:36

Tuesday 6 March

We got approval from the Bank of England!! 👍🏻
slide to reply

I refer to your application of ⬛⬛⬛⬛⬛

Consent under Section 18(1) of the Forgery and Counterfeiting Act 1981 is hereby given to reproduce the Bank of England banknotes in the manner indicated on the material submitted for the specific purpose requested in your application of ⬛⬛⬛⬛⬛. This consent will expire on ⬛⬛⬛⬛⬛.

The Bank of England also hereby grants to you a non-exclusive, non-transferable, royalty free, 12 month licence to reproduce the Bank of England copyrighted materials as indicated on the material submitted and limited to the specific purpose requested.

Amazing, thank you! The kids are really excited to receive some bits and they absolutely loved defacing the letter in the name of art!

Keep doin what you're doin at sportsbanger, there's something really rebellious and liberating about you guys.

Also, I'm a midwife and just wanna day thanks for all the shit you're doing for the NHS atm.

Stay safe ✌🏻 x

🖤 🤟

From Joe. 12. 👍🏻

((He REALLY loved doing this. Thank you for organising the competition. We spoke about how the gov is putting the NHS at risk for the sake of politics. It really sparked his imagination and it's now up on his bedroom wall. Thank you. 🖤 .))

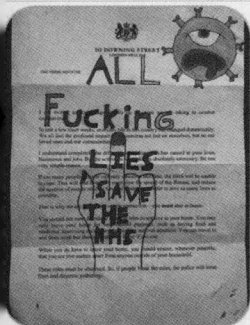

⚜ DJ Pitch ⚜
@Dee_Jay_Pitch

There's a guy doing yoga in a Slazenger Banger tracksuit in the departure lounge

03/12/2018, 11:26

1 Retweet 5 Likes

Was at the talk tonight at the design museum and I think you did so great! Talked v eloquently about important matters. When you asked the question to be simpler me and my friend laughed our heads off as we had absolutely no idea what that lady was asking either! For a self proclaimed recluse you were sick 👍🏻

Sonia – Best of 2018
1. Wally Badarou – Echoes [Music On Vinyl]
"I remember this album released as a kid and treasured it ever since, Endless Race is a cutie, together with the 12" of Chief Inspector with Novela Das Nove on the flip – both serious tunes. Wally played a crucial part in The Compass Point studios, Bahamas and all the sessions, Level 42, Sly & Robbie, Grace Jones etc. I'm so pleased it has been re-pressed. I'm holding it in the photo alongside SPORTS BANGER's Eddie Grant's Ice Records label for good measure ◆▶ "

CASTLEMORTON
Worcestershire
Please drive carefully

During the hearing, members of Spiral Tribe were ordered to cover up T-shirts bearing the controversial ravers' slogan 'Make Some F—ing Noise'.

To: jonsportswright@hotmail.com
Add to contac

PLEASE REPLY ABOVE THIS LINE

AUG 22, 2014 | 11:00AM MDT
Hi there,

We received a complaint from one of your customers that, along with their package, they received a a somewhat threatening note because they had filed a PayPal dispute after not receiving their package in a timely manner.

We don't like to get between store/customer complaints, but we do need some sort of explanation from you so we can confirm that there is no really threat, and that you aren't in the habit of threatening your customers who purchase through ⬛⬛⬛. While how you handle your own customers is your business, making threats (even as a joke) is a serious matter so we'll need your assurance that you'll be a bit more cautious going forward.

Can you let us know your side of the story please?

Thanks so much,

≡ **DAZED** +

London bootlegger Sports Banger threw the vibiest show of fashion week

≡ **DAZED** +

SPORTS BANGER PRESENTED THE VIBIEST SHOW AT LFW (AGAIN)

▶ Photo

Hello Jon. This is Pedro from Mexico City. I'm thrilled, my white fiverz arrived after 4 days and they're the sickest sneakers that I've seen in a while. Mate, huge congrats and please keep up the amazing work! Cheers from Mexico.

👊 👊 👊

---

here.is.sam
@SamStockham

When two tweets were just destined to be together @BangerJonny

Lord Sugar ✓ @Lord_Sugar · 1m
Aaron if you lose to the girls you might feel like what my dentist says to me when I am having a procedure . You may feel a little prick
💬 5   🔁   ♡ 23

Jonny Banger @BangerJonny · 1m
The Apprentice is so basic they still have girls and boys teams lol

Totally Enormous Extinct Dinosaurs (aka Orlando Higginbottom)

Musician, Los Angeles

DID YOU HEAR ABOUT SPORTS BANGER FIRST, OR DID YOU MEET JONNY FIRST?

I think the two things happened at the same time. I met him face-to-face for the first time at a music festival. I was rolling around with Arthur Artwork, and we had an afternoon hanging out with him. I immediately clicked with him. I've got to say, I mean, he's a lovely charming man, but there were things that he was saying and jokes he was making, where I was just like, 'Alright, this is my guy.' His passion for rave intertwined with mine – he definitely revered the dance floor and rave culture and partying, but also took the piss out of the whole thing. I saw him do that straight away, and I was like, 'Oh, yeah, wicked. Love this guy.'

That was the summer that the 'FREE TULISA' T-shirts came out. We both lived locally at the time, so we started hanging out and getting fish and chips on a Sunday and stuff. It was the beginning of a lovely friendship.

DID YOU HAVE MUCH OF A SENSE OF WHAT JON WAS UP TO WITH SPORTS BANGER AT THE TIME?

He didn't really communicate big plans for it – he didn't know what it was going to become. It was just sort of, like, rent money, and I think he'd probably be honest about that, too. At the beginning, it was rent money … and party money.

THINGS HAVE COME A LONG WAY SINCE THOSE TULISA T-SHIRTS.

Jon's decision-making and execution are almost like true north for me. He's so true to his vision and to doing everything in a way that's fair to everybody. I'm slightly lost for words about it, but he keeps it incredibly real. He won't do anything if it's not heart-first, you know? If he can't back it with his heart and say, 'Yeah, I fucking love this idea. It brings me joy', he won't do it. How many people can I say that about? Like, the artists from our generation? I'm not even going to try – I'll start insulting people. But it's so rare and so beautiful. So to see it work, and to see these moments where, you know, he gets institutional praise from editors and *Vogue* people and stuff, is so wonderful because he's so anti-institutional. He's a people's hero. He's not somebody who's craving fame. He's not going to suddenly whack his prices up and be untouchable. I just admire him so much as an artist, really.

DO YOU FEEL LIKE THE DIY ELEMENT OF SPORTS BANGER HAS INFLUENCED WHAT YOU DO?

Yeah, I mean, at many points in my career when I was feeling a bit lost, I'd chat to Jon about it and describe a situation, and he'd be like, 'Well, that's bullshit.' He'll call out the bullshit straight away. His encouragement to do things my way has pushed me forward. I'm not sure he really knows that. I don't know if I would have self-released my new album – or I certainly wouldn't have been so sure about it – without people like him around. Again, it's his sense of listening to your gut and your heart. When younger artists come to me asking for guidance, I find myself saying things that Jon has said to me. I'll be like, 'You're a pirate. Go out there and cause some trouble.' Essentially, be naughty, and people will come to you.

Anna Lomax

Visual artist, London

YOU USED TO SHARE A STUDIO WITH JON, DIDN'T YOU? HOW DID THAT COME TOGETHER?

It was ages ago – around the time when he'd just done the 'Upside-Down Reebok' T-shirt. He'd quit his job and was in a bit of a pickle. I said, 'Why don't you come and take half the studio space?' It was just somewhere to go so that he wasn't sat at home feeling miserable. Sometimes you just have to help a mate out, and I think that's what Jon's always done for others.

HOW WAS IT SHARING A SPACE WITH HIM BACK THEN?

He usually only came in at night, just as I was leaving – we were like passing ships. He basically used it as storage. He had loads of crap and clothes hung up. I remember that. And he'd break all the rules, like, he'd smoke inside. It was nice when our paths did cross, as we'd share ideas and plot things together, but funnily enough, we didn't collaborate until last year. He's always such a good sounding board and so enthusiastic about stuff – he gives you confidence. It's refreshing to speak to someone who doesn't really see boundaries or barriers … someone who laughs at the system.

YOU AND JONNY SHARE A LOVE OF KNOCK-OFFS. CAN YOU TALK A LITTLE BIT ABOUT THAT?

Yeah, we're both big fans of markets and second-hand stuff, dodgy things that don't quite hit the mark. Like really good, bad fakes. I've got a fascination with the luxury market and the idea that if it has a logo on it, it becomes luxury. I think we both quite enjoy playing around with that.

WHAT DO YOU THINK IT IS ABOUT SPORTS BANGER THAT GIVES IT SUCH WIDE APPEAL?

It's accessible, it's not elitist, and he's come at it in a very organic and personal way. Jon's a likeable character who really stands for what he believes in, and I think people relate to that. Obviously, a lot of big fashion brands try to emulate that kind of approach, and they will have somebody at the helm, but Sports Banger really is a personal project.

Sports Banger is about backing your mates and doing something that feels right in your gut. I think Jon approaches things almost like *this is what must be done*. I don't think he necessarily intends to go about it that way, but even if he tried to do something different, it's always going to come out in that authentic way – it's just him.

Klose One

HERAS label manager, Sports Banger

YOU'VE KNOWN JONNY SINCE HIS PIRATE RADIO DAYS, RIGHT? BEFORE SPORTS BANGER WAS EVEN A THING.

Yeah, we met paying subs on Itch FM, when Jon was doing his Beer & Rap show. We were around the same places a lot but really connected through mutual friends when he was working at Vibe Bar. He started hosting my radio shows on Rinse, and that's where 'Jonny Banger' was essentially born. I set up a Twitter account for him in the back of a taxi, and that was the name we settled on.

SO YOU'VE WITNESSED THE EVOLUTION OF SPORTS BANGER FROM DAY ONE.

It's really mad how much it's grown. I don't know if anyone really saw it coming. I mean, the first T-shirt was the 'FREE TULISA' thing he just made for himself to wear to a Swamp 81 night he has hosting. Everyone was going mad about it, so he made a couple more. But it was all very rough and ready – he was on a borrowed phone from one mate and a borrowed laptop from another.

He was part of the crew, hosting at Swamp 81 events, and I think that's probably where it really started to make waves. People were noticing it and wanting to buy the T-shirts. I remember there was one point where it changed. Me, Paleman and Benton were playing at a big warehouse party in Liverpool, and Jonny came up with us to host and brought a big bag of T-shirts with him. He ended up selling them over the front barrier of this rave and there was a big queue. The party essentially turned into a Sports Banger pop-up shop. At that point, it was like: Hang on, something's really happening. Everywhere we went, we'd see more and more people wearing his clothes; we'd look out to the crowd and see 10 or 15 people wearing the T-shirts. At the same time, you couldn't even buy a T-shirt if you wanted one! Even if you paid for it, the chance of actually getting it was quite unlikely because he was so disorganized and overwhelmed. So it had this sort of, like, unachievable thing, a kind of exclusivity – like, you couldn't actually get hold of them. Then people started turning up to the raves wearing T-shirts they'd made themselves that said: 'WHERE'S MY FUCKING T-SHIRT?'

CAN YOU TALK US THROUGH THE PROCESS OF SOUNDTRACKING THE FASHION SHOWS?

A normal fashion show will usually have an overall soundtrack or one piece of music. With us, Jon tends to have several key looks and moments in the show. So it's more about each section having its own sound and music. There are usually six to eight moments, and each moment will be between two and 10 minutes. And then, each of the dancer's routines is also accompanied by its own mix, which will be like four or five tunes mixed together very, very quickly. All those tracks will be mixed live to allow for shifts and changes like something overrunning or not quite being as choreographed as it might want to be. There's room for the music to stop or for me to react and ad-lib if need be. There are also the moments of silence, like when the lights go off between looks, and everyone regroups backstage. There's quite a lot of me shouting down the stairs like, 'Where's the next look? Where the fuck is Jon?!' while the audience is sitting in darkness, wondering what the fuck is going on. But that's what creates the magic.

AND NOW YOU ALSO WORK WITH BANGER AS A&R AND LABEL MANAGER FOR HERAS?

Well, when Jon started a record label, he needed someone to actually run it. Tell you what, though, just try to get Jon to relinquish control … ha ha. He's a busy man! I'm like, 'You can't run a fashion empire *and* a record label …' plus whatever else he's up to.

WHAT WOULD YOU SAY IS THE SOUND OF SPORTS BANGER?

It all comes under the UK rave banner – and that goes right from hardcore through to techno, house and garage. I don't think there's really a specific sound, but we're all ravers, and Sports Banger was kind of born in the rave for the rave. It's more about an ethos than a specific sound. Even with HERAS, the releases range from door slamming techno to four-to-the-floor driving bangers. It's just got to fit in with the sound of what we're all into.

WHAT ABOUT HOW THE MEGA RAVES COMPARE TO OTHER RAVES THAT YOU PLAY AT?

I mean, one thing that separates it is that there are no egos or hierarchy; there's no 'I want a better set time' or 'I want my name bigger on the flyer' or 'I want more money'. Essentially, we're all in it together. Anyone who comes and plays with us is always a bit blown away by the family vibe of it.

Glastonbury was a massive one for us this year – it was one of the biggest things we've done. When we opened up the area, there were thousands of people waiting to get in. Everyone was playing back-to-back for hours and hours, and we were all just like, 'Let's have a good time together.' Jon asked anyone who works for the NHS and is also a DJ to send us a mix. We got hundreds sent in and we picked two people to join us, so now you had a couple of care workers fulfilling their life-long dream and DJing at Glastonbury to thousands of people. I think that's a really nice way to be, and the crowd responds to that because they can see everyone on stage having as much fun as they're having. There's a real sense of camaraderie at the Mega Raves – of friends and family all being together.

HOW DOES HERAS FIT IN WITH THE REST OF THE SPORTS BANGER PROJECT?

It's another creative outlet for Banger. Each release has an item of clothing or object that comes with it, and the artwork and the way the record looks is very important – we keep it very in line with Sports Banger. That's something Jon quite enjoys, keeping that spirit of Sports Banger in the label, with cheeky little bits of bootlegging; we're always like, 'Are we gonna get away with this?'

It's amazing all the interest we've had so far, and it's still quite a small label – we've only done three releases. Not massive numbers, but it seems to be making little waves, and a lot of people are listening and excited by it, which is cool. We're just about to step it up as well – putting out more regular releases, and we've got some quality music signed. We're not just trying to sign a record because it's a hot record or because it's going to sell; it's about working together and building a timeless body of work.

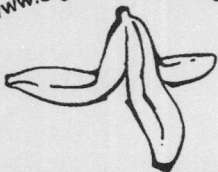

ARTWORK

SIDE 1

RED E.P.
1. RED   2. ROLEX RIDDIM

Written and produced by A. Smith for Artwork Ltd.
Published by Ministry of Sound Music

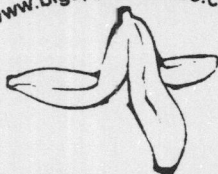

BENGA

SIDE 1

BAM 002

SKANK

Written and produced by B. Adejumo
Published by Copyright Control

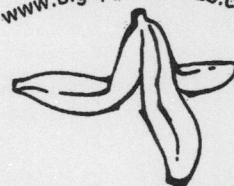

BENGA & SKREA

BAM 003

THE JUDGEMENT

Written and produced by B. Adejumo & O. Jones

GITAL MYSTIKZ

SIDE 1

A1: PATHWAYS   A2: UGLY

A1 Written and produced by M. Lawrence
A2 Written and produced by D. Harris
Published by Copyright Control

For all enquiries contact: 0208 688 1668

BENGA

BAM 005

SIDE A

A1: HYDRO   A2: WALKIN' BASS

A1 Written and produced by B. Adejumo
A2 Written and produced by B. Adejumo
Published by Copyright Control

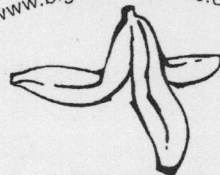

LOEFAH

BAM 006

A1: JUNGLE INFILTRATOR
A2: JAZZ LICK

Written & Produced By - P Livingston
Published By Copyright Control

For all enquiries contact: 0208 686 8786

SKREAM

07

SIDE A

A1: ACID PEOPLE
A2: GET MAD

Written & Produced By O. Jones
Published By Copyright Control

Info: apple@bigapplerecords.co.uk

BIG APPLE RECORDS

BENGA

ASIDE: FLAME
BSIDE: LIVE DRUMZ
BSIDE2: WOBBLERS

BAM 008

ALL TRACKS WRITTEN PRODUCED AND MIXED BY B. ADEJUMO. ALL RIGHTS OF THE MANUFACTURER AND OF THE RECORDED WORK RESERVED UNAUTHORISED PUBLIC PERFORMANCE BROADCASTING AND COPYING PROHIBITED

BIG APPLE RECORDS

COKI

A1: RED EYE
A2: BEEP

B1: THE SIGN
B2: HIDDEN TREAS

BAM 009

37 SURREY STREET
CROYDON, CR0 1RJ

Artwork
(aka Arthur Smith)

Music producer and DJ, New York

HOW DID YOU FIRST MEET JONNY?

I was at Snowbombing, playing a DJ set at the top of a mountain. I saw this fella in some random outfit, which really wasn't appropriate – no ski boots on or nothing, no gloves, no hat – and he was running along the top of the mountain trying to fly a kite. And I thought, 'Shitting hell!' He was clearly off his head. So I went over to try and help him, holding one end while he ran backwards, trying to get it up in the air. So, yeah, that's how we met, and we've been mates ever since.

DID YOU MANAGE TO GET THE KITE UP IN THE AIR?

No, it was dreadful. Total failure.

WORD HAS IT THAT YOU CONTRIBUTED FINANCIALLY TO GET JON UP AND RUNNING?

Jonny used to have these mad parties at his house that were like three-day events that just didn't stop. At one point, he had a bar with turntables on it and a fish tank in the bar.

Tulisa had been arrested as part of that sting operation by ~~████~~ They'd done the dirty on her, and he was very upset about the whole thing, and he was like, 'I'm gonna make these T-shirts saying "FREE TULISA"'. So I gave him the money to help get it off the ground.

So he printed up a load of T-shirts, then came along to all the festivals I was playing at in London and started handing them out to other DJs and selling them in the crowd for a tenner. I remember driving into a festival with him trying to flog them out the car window. Nobody wanted these T-shirts, you know. But then a couple of famous people wore them on stage somewhere, and that was it.

WHAT WAS IT THAT STRUCK YOU ABOUT JON (BESIDES THE AUDACITY OF TRYING TO FLY A KITE ON THE TOP OF A MOUNTAIN)?

Everybody's good at sitting around at an after-party and coming up with a mad idea. Anyone can sit down and say, 'I'm going to do this nutty thing', and everyone else goes, 'Yeeeaaahhhh, brilliant!' And, 99.9% of the time, nothing happens. But when Jon comes up with some nutty idea, he actually does it. And that's the difference with him. He's just one of those people where it doesn't matter how much effort it's going to take – he's going to do it. Like, 'I'm going to start a fashion brand', and you're like, 'Yeah, you are, Jon – I know you are.' He's just one of them, a very rare character.

YOU PLAYED THE MEGA RAVE AT FABRIC, DIDN'T YOU? HOW WAS IT?

The hardest night of the year to sell club tickets is the Friday before Carnival, and Jon took it on at Fabric and sold it out. It was amazing. I mean, that's the thing, Jon's always got this sort of stunned look, like, 'It's actually happening!' He's just pissing himself laughing. That's the great thing; where most people have got to this point, they suddenly get completely serious, and it suddenly turns into a massive business and stuff like that. For him, it's still taking the piss, and he's getting away with it, and he's really laughing about it.

THE PEOPLE WHO ARE INTO SPORTS BANGER SEEM TO BE UNIFIED BY THIS WAY OF THINKING, WHICH IS JUST NOT TAKING LIFE TOO SERIOUSLY AND LAUGHING AT THE SYSTEM.

Everything you see advertized to you on your phone every five minutes has a huge company behind it. There's a marketing plan that has millions pumped into it to sell you this thing that you 'want'. When you look at what Jonny's doing, it's *real*. You know he's just sat down and written an idea on the back of a fag packet and then started making it. He's doing it purely because he thinks it's brilliant, not because it's what people want – it's what he thinks is great. Rather than a big company thinking, 'Right, what do people want? What do we think they need? Let's make something that will make us loads of money' – it's exactly the opposite, which is so refreshing. The messages that he's putting across are what the world needs the most right now. Every single thing is terrible, apart from Sports Banger.

WHERE DO YOU IMAGINE IT ALL GOING?

I have no fucking idea. That's why me and Jon get on so well. There's never been any plan. It's just like, you do something until you find something more interesting to do. And then you do that until something else comes up to replace it. Again, it's not a business. There's no plan. So, unfortunately, I can't help you there.

Clockwise from top left: Banger studio crew Holly Harris (interviewed on page 303) and Dom Ridler (interviewed on page 230) at Mega Rave 4; Meme Gold and Jonny in Paris with Emanuelle Soum (interviewed on page 229) for her show Venus 555; Celeste Doig (interviewed on page 299) and Jonny at Fabric

T

KNOC

SH

THE FUCKING KING OP

BANGER

724 SEVEN SISTERS ROAD
by Jonny Banger

724 Seven Sisters Road was a dirty, magical place. A chance meeting led us to Barry the landlord's phone number. We called him 'Barry's Plumbs', not sure why. The previous tenants had been thrown out with a banning order placed on the premises. The door – which had a warrant taped to it – had been kicked in by SO15 counter-terrorism squad and was still off its hinges. Inside, the place was painted a dark mauve, and the walls were covered with shelves of books, trophies, and a couple of shrines to fallen Kurdish fighters. The water-damaged laminate floorboards were peeling up. We signed a straight-off-the-internet tenancy agreement with paintings of Che Guevara and Tito watching over us. I didn't have a clue what I was doing, but I knew I needed a space. After we signed the lease, Matt Harriman turned to me and said, 'another fine mess you've dragged me into.' The shop sat directly opposite Sid the Snail, an icon of north London; the Mona Lisa of Tottenham. I definitely saw this as a sign.

We managed to reunite the previous tenants with all their stuff and everyone chipped in to help sort the place out. We painted it all, stripped the floor, hung a HERAS fence from the ceiling and built a DJ booth in the kitchen. The microwave was under the decks, sink to the right. On the shelf behind was a 'shit mix jar'. Any dodgy mixes and you had to stick in a £1 penalty. Some DJs came for a mix and just stuck £20 in the jar straight away. We spent the money on booze and fags. We were there for five years. The space barely had any light, no air, and for the most part, it was constantly dirty and full of cigarette smoke. The buzzer outside had four buttons – ours, which said 'BANGER', was the only one that worked. This was slightly awkward when a brothel moved in upstairs.

The studio operated mainly for us to work in and store stock. Shop day was Saturdays, but people popped in all the time, coming from all over. One visitor was a 10-year-old lad who'd been terrorising the local area for the last year; he was part of the traveller community and had been banned from every shop on the road. He would come in asking for T-shirts, cigarettes, money, a job. We'd sit him down in front of old rave flyers and get him to redraw them, so he'd draw them all with dicks on. His best was a guy pissing on the Nike swoosh. We stuck it on a hoodie and gave him 40% of all sales. After his first payment, I asked his cousin what he did with the money. Apparently, he'd taken all his mates swimming. A local called round one day and warned us about the young lad and his gang, but we got on fine; it was sad they had nothing else to do. I recently bumped into one of the other kids from that group who ended up working with us in the shop. He'd just come out of prison. He was now old enough to have a pint, so we went to the pub, and he remembered his time at the shop so happily.

We were short on space after the Slazenger deal, so we stored a load of stock out the back crudely padlocked up. I noticed the boxes were gradually getting emptier until we found out a homeless guy had been taking the stock and selling it on to traders at the local market, which was funny. Loads of people sent us pictures of our clothes for sale alongside DIY tools. Seemed quite perfect. There were lots of good times at Seven Sisters Road. We built our own sound system, we built a team, we built everything – and it all came from a single T-shirt and a shared love of rave.

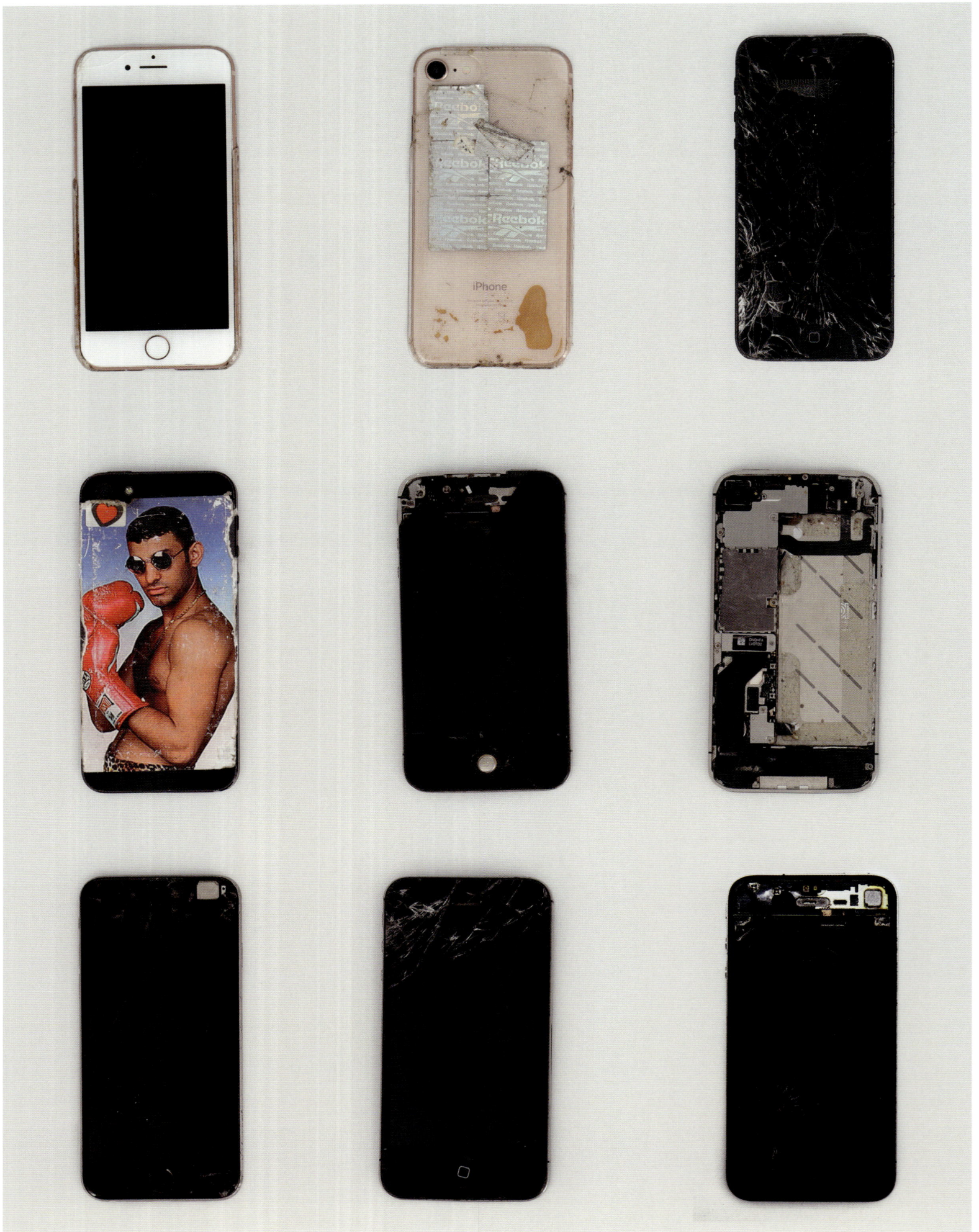

THE KNOCKING SHOP

Previous, left: The buzzer at the Seven Sisters Road studio.
Above: TOOLS OF THE TRADE. Jonny's old iPhones, used
to sketch up designs.
Opposite above: THE MONA LISA OF TOTTENHAM. Painted
in 1976, Sid the Snail sits directly opposite the old studio.
Opposite below: Left by the previous tenant, the studio's
signage translates as 'YOUR MONEY' in Polish.

Handwritten on whiteboard:

monday 14th
STUDIO

monday
email propose

A BELOVED SHITHOLE. Jonny at his desk in the Seven Sisters Road studio.

THE KNOCKING SHOP

Above: Anyone who clanged a mix on the studio turntables
had to donate £1 to the jar.
Opposite: An acid monolith made using studio materials:
an inflatable pool wiggle, Softcore ecstasy pill, smiley lamp
and shop display plinth.

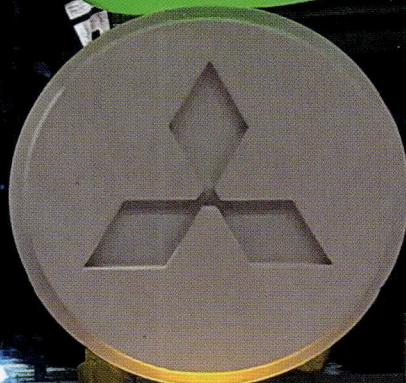

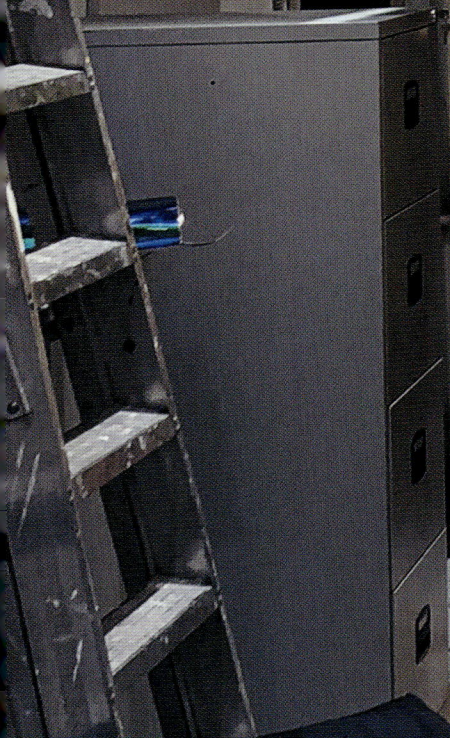

THE KNOCKING SHOP

Above: The shop shelves at the Seven Sisters Road studio.
Opposite: The 'Under the Counter' hoodie featured
in *L'Officiel Hommes*, September 2016.

Sweat-shirt à capuche en jersey de coton, **SPORTS BANGER.** Chemise en popeline de coton, **DIOR HOMME.** Pantalon en laine, **MONCLER.** Sac à dos en velours et cuir, **SAINT LAURENT.**

I first made the 'Under the Counter' T-shirt in 2015 when the junior doctors went on strike. The media were vilifying workers, and I wanted to show our peer group support. I was taken aback by the conversations the T-shirt started. The youth are the future workers and patients of the NHS, and it's been amazing to see young people taking ownership of it before it's gone.

i was born in the NHS
my mum worked for the NHS
the NHS tried to save my brother's life
the NHS saved my life
the NHS saved my dad's life
the NHS tried to save my mum's life
the NHS saved my best friends life
the NHS saved my other best friends life

● Save our NHS ● Defend the welfare state

Support the junior doctors

Junior doctors are in the front line of the government's aim to completely smash the welfare state; and teachers are not far behind. For that is what the imposition of contracts on the doctors, and the transfer of every school in the country to academies, is all about.

The Tories are lying when they say they want a 24/7 NHS, for doctors already work every day of the week. The contract removes safeguards on how long doctors work, and cuts their payments for working unsocial hours.

What the government really wants is to lower staff conditions across the NHS in preparation for even more privatisation. It is a ploy that also explains its plan to transfer every school in the country to academies.

It isn't only doctors who are under attack. Student nurses are

A junior doctor writes:
'We are under attack. The gove ing a new contract that threate NHS. We are not asking for mo fighting for the NHS and all wh it. We are in the front line.'

Junior doctors' rally, 1.00pm, Thursday 7 April Hackney Town Hall, Mare Street. Strike: 6-7 and 26-27 April

being threatened with the removal of burseries and instead having to pay £50,000 for a three-year course – a plan that will inevitably

discou ing a tals a

So surge due t phar gove of m deliv

A trust facin putti inev prov

The government can be stopped

The government is weak. The Budget fiasco last month, Ian Duncan Smith's resignation, the declining fortunes of chancellor George Osborne and internal arguments over the EU show what a shambles it has become.

This means junior doctors could force the government to back down from its attack. And

teachers too could stop the privatisation of education.

But in order to continue their fight, the doctors need to know the public supports them. Post a message of support to the facebook address below, and make an effort to get to their picket lines at Homerton Hospital on 6-7 and 26-27 April.

WH
● V
line
de
● F
on
● sh
Fa
● te
in

HACKNEY SUPPORTS JUNIO
● Facebook: Hackney Supports the Junio

Hackney supports Junior Doctors

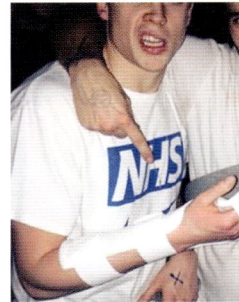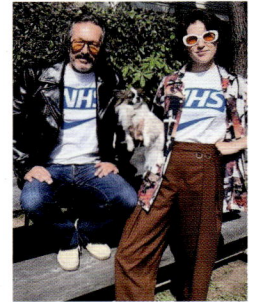

Previous, left: The 'Under the Counter' T-shirt.
Previous, right above: A short story written by Jonny Banger.
Previous, right below: Original flyer supporting junior doctors
in 2015, which inspired the 'Under the Counter' T-shirt.

Opposite, above left and below: The people in 'NHS' T-shirts.
Opposite, above right: Scottish midwife, trade union leader and abortion rights activist, Dame Cathy Warwick DBE after receiving her honour at Buckingham Palace.
Above: A Sports Banger poster wheat-pasted onto a billboard in Seven Sisters, London.

Dear Sir/Madam,

I am writing to you again because I have not received a response to my email below, dated 11/01/18.

As outlined in my email dated 11/01/18, the letters 'NHS' and the NHS logo are UK trade marks registered to the Secretary of State for Health and Social Care by the Department of Health and Social Care in England. These trade marks cannot be used by other organisations without the Department of Health and Social Care's authorisation. Unauthorised use or adaptation of the NHS trade marks is taken very seriously.

As previously requested, please provide evidence that you have been given permission to use the NHS trade marks or confirm that you will cease using them immediately.

Please respond to this email by 26/01/18. We reserve any rights to pursue such legal remedies as are available to us, including referring this to the Department of Health and Social Care.

Best,
Ursula

Department of Health & Social Care

Identity Team

E:

This e-mail and any attachment
unauthorised use, disclosure

11/01/

Department of Health & Social Care

Identity Team

E: ⬛⬛⬛⬛gov.

From: ⬛⬛⬛ On Behalf Of identity@dh.
Sent: 11 January 2018 11:07
To: '⬛⬛⬛⬛'
Subject: Possible Infringement of NHS Trademarks

Dear Sir/Madam,

I work for the team which is responsible for mana
Department of Health and Social Care in England

Your website (www.sportsbanger.com) has recent
is being used on multiple products being sold on t

The letters 'NHS' and the NHS logo are UK trade
and Social Care by the Department of Health and
Intellectual Property Office website at www.gov.u
organisations without the Department of Health an

The NHS Identity (letters and logo) generates high
the public. Therefore, use of the NHS Identity is
the NHS

Re: NHS Trademark Misuse [<⬛⬛⬛>]

nhs⬛⬛⬛⬛gov.uk <⬛⬛⬛⬛gov.uk>
Fri 06/05/2016 13:35

To: ⬛⬛⬛@hotmail.com <j⬛⬛⬛@hotmail.com>

Dear Sir,

Thank you for pixelating the national NHS logos on you website and advising users that the item is no longer for sale; http://www.sportsbanger.com/product/not-for-sale

Can you please provide your proposals and timelines regarding all resources/items that carry the NHS logo, such as marketing including the large poster on Holloway Road, and any exist items of clothing (tees and hoodies).
Can you include whether you have plans to have the entire NHS logo(s) removed from your website, or whether you intended to keep this pixelated as it is currently.

Kind regards

⬛⬛⬛ (colleague of ⬛⬛⬛)
NHS Brand and Identity Team
⬛⬛⬛gov.uk
020 7⬛⬛⬛

11/01/2023, 16:19

FW: NHS Trademark Misuse [<⬛⬛⬛>]

Jon ⬛⬛⬛ <j⬛⬛⬛@hotmail.com>
Fri 02/08/2019 23:40

To: ⬛⬛⬛@hotmail.com <⬛⬛⬛@hotmail.com>

From: ⬛⬛identity⬛⬛gov.uk <⬛⬛⬛gov.uk>
Sent: 04 May 2016 13:45
To: ⬛⬛⬛@hotmail.com <jonsportswright@hotmail.com>
Subject: NHS Trademark Misuse [<⬛⬛⬛>]

Dear Sir

I work for the NHS Identity team which is responsible for managing and protecting the NHS trade mark on behalf of the Department of Health in England.

Your website http://www.sportsbanger.com/product/nhs http://www.sportsbanger.com/products has recently been brought to our attention because it is advertising products (tee shirts and hoods) which feature the NHS logo. We also, note that you use the NHS logo on marketing posters which are also shown on the Sportsbanger Twitter and Facebook accounts.

The letters 'NHS' and the NHS logo are UK trade marks registered to the Secretary of State for Health by the Department of Health in England. For further details visit the Intellectual Property Office website at www.gov.uk/ipo. These trade marks cannot be used by other organisations without the Department of Health's authorisation.

---

https://outlook.live.com/mail/0/id/AQMkADAwATY3ZmYAZS1

To: ⬛⬛⬛Wright⬛⬛⬛wright@hotmail.com>
Subject: Fwd: Possible infringement of NHS trade

call me

Begin forwarded message:

From: Identity ⬛⬛⬛gov.uk>
Subject: **Possible infringement of NHS tra**
Date: 6 June 2019 at 11:21:36 BST
To: "sportsbanger⬛⬛@gmail.com" <sp⬛⬛

To whom it may concern,
I work for the Department of Health and Social
managing and protecting the NHS identity.

Your company has recently been brought to o
the NHS logo on a t-shirt.

The NHS logo and the letters 'NHS' are registe
Secretary of State for Health and Social Care
adapted without the Department of Health an
Similarly, the Secretary of State owns the copy
reproduced without permission from the Depa
more information visit the Intellectual Property

The NHS identity generates high levels of trus
the public and NHS staff. Therefore, use of the
and unauthorised use or adaption of the NHS
seriously.

We do not have any record of the Department
you to use the NHS letters or logo. We approv

Opposite: A selection of thank you letters from the Department of Health & Social Care :)
Above: An artwork gifted to Sports Banger by artist Ruby Rose.

Disguised in a Sports Direct jumper purchased on ebay, Jonny pastes up a poster on Holloway Road in support of junior doctors in 2015.

THE KNOCKING SHOP

Skepta in the full look performing 'Shutdown' on *Top of the Pops*. Behind him, DJ Maximum wears the Sports Banger 'England' T-shirt.

We did the creative for Skepta when he was on *Top of the Pops* on Christmas Day in 2016. This was five days after the nationwide postal strikes and his outfit was a shout-out to the workers.

A Helly Hansen Workwear ensemble with customized 'SHUT/DOWN' mittens made for Skepta.

THE KNOCKING SHOP

Above: MIND THE GAP. If you visit London, this is where
you will find Sports Banger.
Opposite: A spread from Jonny Banger's *Diary of a Bootlegger*,
published by Rough Trade Books in 2019.

Bro your boxers helped at Leeds fest fam, I got sniffer dogged and stripped searched but they found nothing. Thanks to you I made a raise, avoided getting locked up & now I can get all my uni essentials and live a decent uni life

Keep doing what you're doing g and and much respect

We would very much like to feature the following image in the book, in a chapter that discussed the NHS, comparing it to other countries' health systems
-
NHS swoosh poster pasted onto Macmilian poster, reading Cancer is the Loneliest Place

Hey! I'm seeing rapid amount of school kids wearing Slazenger trainers here in Edinburgh. Banger fever is spreading! Fuck Nike

...send you
604 followers 552 posts

CONSERVATIVES ARE TARGETING EVERYONE

The Law Society Excellence Awards 2018

Ravi Naik, Irvine Thanvi Natas Solicitors
WINNER
Human Rights Lawyer of the Year

ravinaikn16 Incredibly proud to be named the Law Society Human Rights Lawyer of the Year! As styled by @sportsbanger

NURSE: SIR, YOU'VE BEEN IN A COMA SINCE 2013

PATIENT: HAS MY SPORTS BANGER T SHIRT ARRIVED YET

greygardens_ldn @jaydavis7 congratulations on starting @goldsmithsuol wearing@SPORTSBANGER studying politics you made it! Now go change the world!

kid_drama_cmrx
21:14
7:54 pm
Had one of your slazenger Banger sweatshirts on and the security at Brussels airport said it was the 4th one he's seen today and asked me about it

Jonny Banger @BangerJonny · 6m
if u told 14 year old me I'd have 3 pages in DJ Mag. I was obsessed with this magazine. It's quite good interview. Go buy a copy for old time sake

Jack Morgan @MackJorgan · 42s
Replying to @BangerJonny
If you told me a 24 year old me would have a sports t shirt by the time I turned 27 that would be quite good. Send me my t shirt for old time sake

---

Hi Jon,

I've asked our set design team for different sized presents, so should be all good.

We are looking into what we call a snow roller rather than a blower as discussed last night I think a snow blower will be too noisy. A snow roller drops snow rather than blows snow. I'll update you about this as soon as we hear from our SFX man.

Do you really want a confetti burst as well as snow though Jon?

I would suggest one or the other. If the snow roller doesn't happen then a white confetti burst would be cool but personally I wouldn't have both.

I will also ask about powdered snow for the top of the post box and around and come back to you.

In terms of a sleigh, again I will ask our design team if we can get one but sorry can I ask Jon that you pick up the cost of this please? (costs approx. £600 plus transport).

The postbox, bags are costing us about £225 plus £160 transport and this doesn't include the trolley yet (ps. - do you still want a trolley?). I don't have any pennies left for a sleigh as well I'm afraid.

Also, just to update you I had a chat with our Compliance advisers. There is an issue with us having Royal Mail bags so I have asked for some plain sacks and we can still have Royal Mail bags but need to disguise them so that the logo is not blatantly on display and on camera.

Whilst we are talking about Compliance - do you know what Skepta's outfit will be? Have you sourced it yet? Please can we also make sure please that it doesn't have Royal Mail or any other company logo on it? Just a nice neutral, no-logo outfit would be great - thanks.

Last thing Jon, here's a picture of the TOTP Neon sign that I mentioned to you last night that might be another option to put in front of DJ decks if we all like? Have a look let me know your thoughts, just an option, no agenda.

Thanks

Series Producer – Top of the Pops Christmas & New Year
BBC Music Television

From: [mailto...]
Sent: 01 December 2016 13:15
To:
Cc:
Subject: Re: Skepta - Top of the Pops

Thank you

...can we get the snow machine and the confetti burst... Also loads different sized presents as discussed

Can we have a load of powdered snow to coat on top of postbox and around it please?

Also any chance of a sleigh? Not 100% that we'll use it but good to have the option

Thanks

Jon

Sent from my iPhone

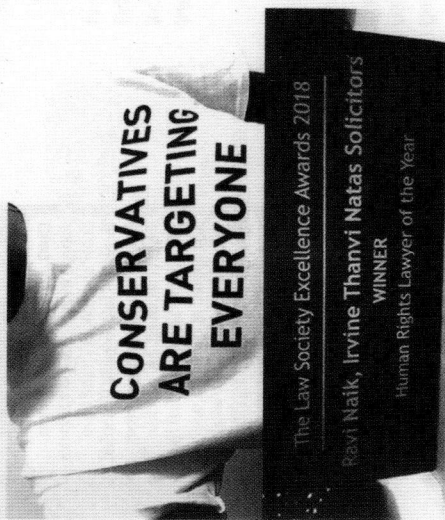

From:
Sent: 01 December 2016 16:25
To:
Subject: Re: Skepta - Top of the Pops

Hi

Thanks yep lets get the snow roller. We'll forget about the sleigh.

Can we get the post trolley, then we can affix his stamp logo ID to that

We just put presents in front of DJ or leave black

The outfit will be debranded

Thanks

Jon

Sent from my iPhone

Moments UK @UKMoments · 8m
Everyone's talking about @Skepta on Top of the Pops. #totp

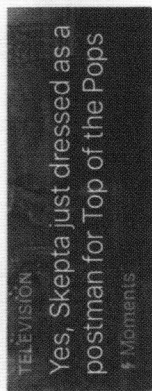

TELEVISION
Yes, Skepta just dressed as a postman for Top of the Pops
Moments

Luis De Jorge Retweeted
SKEPTA @Skepta · 4d
Shouts out to my stylist @BangerJonny #TOTP

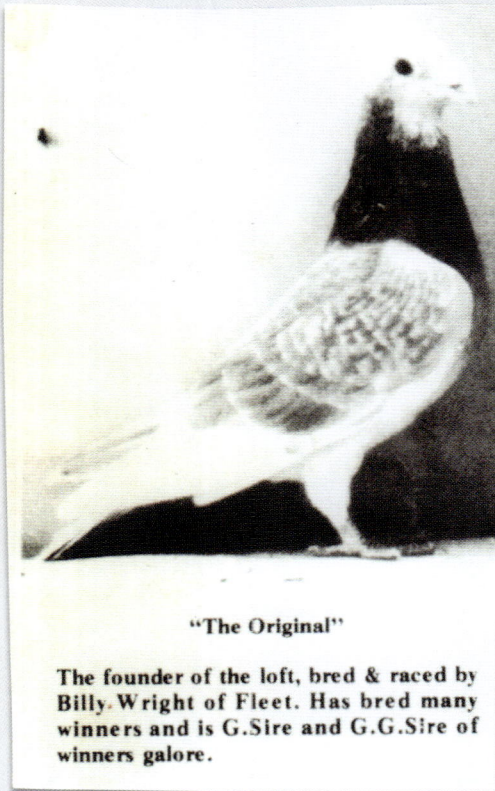

"The Original"

The founder of the loft, bred & raced by Billy Wright of Fleet. Has bred many winners and is G.Sire and G.G.Sire of winners galore.

NATIONAL PIGEON SERVICE

W. C. WRIGHT.

is a Member of the NATIONAL PIGEON SERVICE

Number _NPS/7858._

Signed _J. Selly-Flow_

Secretary

Member's Signature

W.C.Wright

A.M. FORM 1528B.
(3517) Wt. 27453-2295 10,000 9/39 T.S. 700

This is to Certify

FIRST PRIZE

won by

Mr. _W. Wright_

in the _Crookham & Dist R.P.C_ Club/Fed:

Race Point _Bergerac_

Miles _448_ yds _241_ Birds Competing _38_

Ring _NU71N73783_ Colour _Red chq_

Sex _cock_ Vel: _561·1_

Date of Race _15 - 7 - 72_

Signed _H Haircut_

J. Fry. Pres.

P Soane Sec.

SUPPLIED BY: S. & A. PIGEON SUPPLIES 138 CAPE HILL, SMETHWICK, WORCESTERSHIRE

82   THE KNOCKING SHOP

Above, left: THE ORIGINAL. This legendary pigeon was owned by Jonny's grandad Billy Wright.
Above, right: Billy's National Pigeon Service membership. The birds were used by the Royal Air Force and army during the war.

Below: Jonny's grandad's first-prize pigeon flew 448 miles from Bergerac, France to Fleet in the UK.
Opposite: Hand-painted Altern 8 mask gifted to Sports Banger by DJ and producer Mark Archer.

UNDER THE COUNTER

Klose One, Faze Miyake, Smash Hits and Benton in the DJ booth/
kitchen at the Paranoid London show, held at the Seven Sisters
Road studio in 2020.

SLAZENGER BANGER

I've been a fan of Slazenger for years; it's working-class gear and as far removed from hype as you can get. It's got proper history, founded in 1881 by three Manchester brothers. One of them, Ralph, was the Sheriff of London for a year. Slazenger introduced the optic yellow tennis ball to Wimbledon in 1986. The following year, acid house hit the UK. The collab came out of nowhere and felt like a kickback against the exclusive streetwear that makes kids queue for the latest drops. The collection came with a price tag for everyone, not the few.

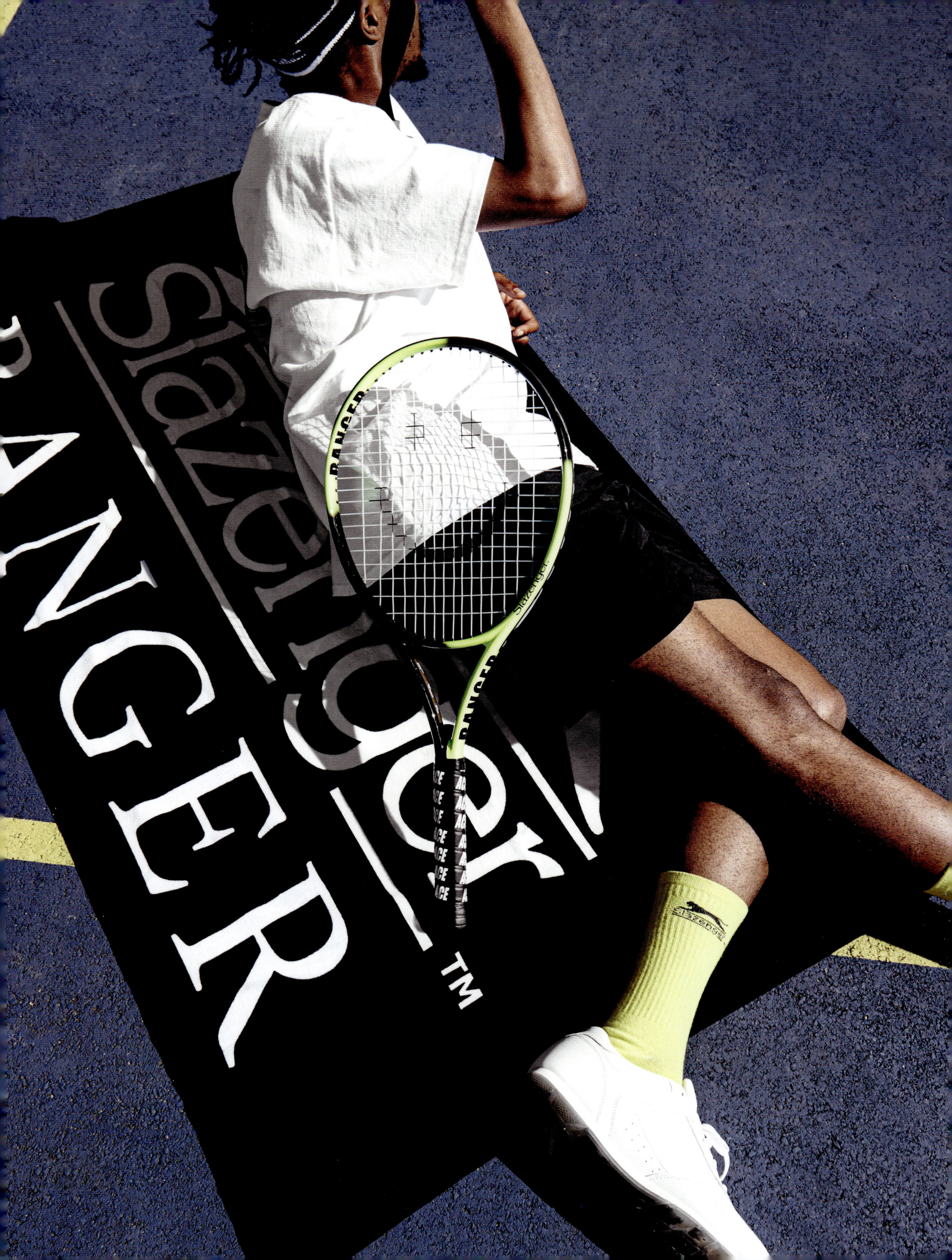
Slazenger
ANGER™
RANGER
ACE

THE KNOCKING SHOP

Previous, left above: Slazenger Banger tennis ball trainers and hot-pink socks.
Previous, left below: A sweatband and beach towel from the collection.
Previous, right: A Slazenger Banger ensemble, including the 'ACID' racket.

Designers Megan Paran-Rutterford and Meme Gold, musician and MC Chunky (interviewed on page 110), friend of Banger Nicole-adaeze Benton, and skipper Marcus Bulley model the Slazenger Banger collection on the estuary in Southampton in 2018. Photographer Ollie Grove described it as 'The most unorthodox shoot I've ever done.'

91   SLAZENGER BANGER

Opposite: BAGGAGE HANDLER. Meme Gold models
Slazenger Banger on Seven Sisters Road.
Above: Jon up a ladder at Wimbledon.
Below: A Slazenger Banger tennis ball.

THE KNOCKING SHOP

Jonny in Slazenger Banger on his way to the Wimbledon men's finals.

SLAZENGER BANGER

A repurposed Slazenger Banger towel-turned poncho modelled by Chunky.

CERTIFIED
Banger

From DJ to promoter to bootleg clothing icon, Jonny Banger is using his Sports Banger brand and new HERAS label to enact positive change and revive the community-focussed, rebellious attitude of rave…

Words: **ANNA WALL** Pic: **MAT PLAYFORD**

BANGER

TEED models Sports Banger

Opposite: The Slazenger Banger 'Piano Tracksuit' in a feature for *DJ Magazine*, 2018.
Above: WELCOME TO BANGTAZIA. Silver skirt raver at Mega Rave 4.

The Criminal Justice and Public Order Act of 1994 clamped down on illegal raves. I've got nothing but respect for free parties, the crews, and the community. Everyone working together to do something they want to do. The raves run on people power – a party for the people by the people. On my first adventure with the Odyssey Soundsystem crew, I ended up sitting in a car on top of a pair of bolt cutters at the front of the convoy. Getting thrown in a van with a bunch of mates and ending up in the countryside watching the sunrise is magic.

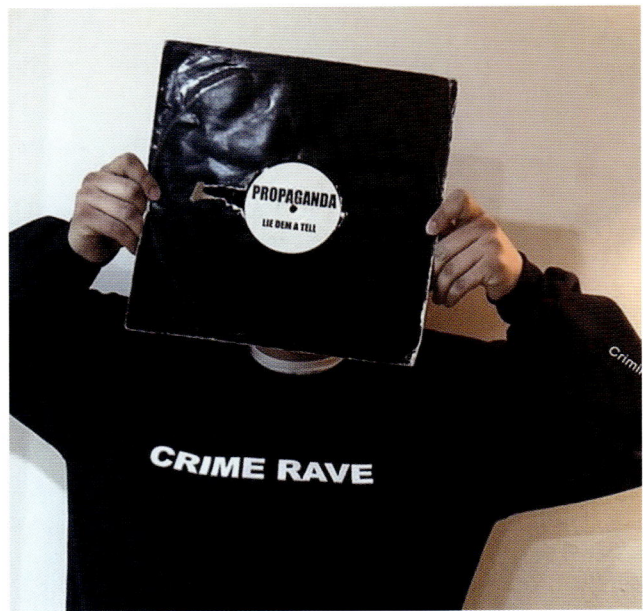

This is an Odyssey Soundsystem member wearing the 'Crime Rave' jumper. The record is by the Norfolk-based free party crew Brains Kan. In 2004 their rave got raided by a riot squad. The hard trance track, 'Propaganda', which they wrote about the experience, is a free party anthem.

Previous, left: A bolt-cut padlock from the Odyssey Soundsystem 10th birthday free party in Cambridge, 2018.
Previous, right: Inside/Outside a Norfolk barn during a Halloween free party with the Odyssey and Equality sound system crews.
Above, centre: Some of the crew at a Norfolk free party, 2019.
Below: Mid-rave debrief in the van.

FREE PARTY IS NOT A CRIME   An illegal warehouse rave in Corby, New Year's Eve, 2019.

Above: Over 100 police arrived to break up the Unity23 free party in Thetford Forest, Norfolk.
Opposite: Front page of ~~the~~ 31 August 2020.

Police attempt to break up a suspected rave in Thetford Forest, Norfolk, where up to 500 people had gathered. It came after officers gained new powers to fine organisers of illegal gatherings up to £10,000, with attendees liable for a £100 fine, in a crackdown on those breaching Covid-19 restrictions. The first of the fines were issued at the weekend. *Page 6*

---

s
noke
y,
old

warn of potential
om Covid

Adam Marshall, director-general of the British Chambers of Commerce, warned: "Raising the tax on business and entrepreneurs they have a chance to recover create serious issues for the tra- ry of the UK's overall recovery.

could slow investment, it could risk taking among entrepreneurs rowth businesses.

verybody in business understands public finances have to be repaired o it too early and you risk choking rowth at the crucial moment."

ccording to the Treasury's own mates, raising corporation tax to per cent would raise £17billion per r, while capital gains tax increases uld generate another £1.05 billion.

utting pension tax relief to 20 per t would raise £11 billion, the Insti- le for Fiscal Studies has calculated. ile a 2 per cent online sales tax uld bring in £2billion and a 1 per nt increase in fuel duty £295 million.

Tory MPs are nervous about any in- ease in corporation tax, in particular, cause increasing it to 24 per cent uld parrot Labour's tax policy.

Stephen Barclay, the Chief Secretary the Treasury, refused to rule out ses and insisted such issues were a atter for the Budget.

Some experts warned that such a move would be seen as a "sea change" tax policy and send a signal that the K was "closed for business".

Chris Sanger, head of UK tax policy at accountants EY, said: "The UK has been on a long journey to reduce its corporation rate, which is seen by many businesses as an indicator of how competitive a country wants to be.

"The UK has prided itself on having the lowest corporate tax rate of any G20 country. The Saudis have a rate of 20 per cent so it will stop them claim- ing that and be seen as a sea change in tax policy."

Matthew Lesh, head of research at the Adam Smith Institute, called on the

Continued on Page 4

Head teachers 'refusing to fully reopen schools'

By Tony Diver

HUNDREDS of head teachers will defy government orders and block their pupils' return to the classroom this week, a union has said.

A survey by the National Association of Head Teachers shows more than 700 schools, or 3 per cent of the total num- ber, will phase students back or use "transition periods" to reopen.

The Prime Minister has said all schools should be fully reopened from the start of September, following heavy disruption to the summer term amid the coronavirus pandemic.

Many local authority areas are due to return to school tomorrow.

But some head teachers still have concerns about fully reopening, de- spite guidance on student "bubbles" and measures to promote frequent handwashing in most schools.

The NAHT said the schools postpon- ing their reopening represented a "tiny percentage" and any delays were in- tended to "alleviate pupils' anxieties about the return". The survey came as research by *TES* magazine suggested that nine in 10 teachers have concerns about social distancing.

Its poll of nearly 6,000 school staff in England found that 86 per cent thought minimising contact between pupils was not possible, while two thirds feared guidance to avoid busy corri- dors, entrances and exits was unrealis- tic. The survey also found that more than a quarter of staff may not comply with the test-and-trace programme should their school have an outbreak.

More than a third felt that the Gov- ernment's approach to coronavirus safety in schools would not work and left them "at risk", the poll showed.

Teaching unions have already warned the Government that safety measures will not be enough to protect pupils and staff, and want ministers to introduce rules on face coverings in schools in areas under local lockdown.

Paul Whiteman, general secretary of the NAHT, urged parents to send their children back to school despite the concerns. "Please do not let the very public political difficulties and argu- ments cloud your confidence in schools," he said.

"With co-operation and understand- ing between home and school we can achieve the very best return possible despite the political noise."

A government spokesman said: "Get- ting all children back into their class- rooms full-time in September is a national priority because it is the best place for their education, development and wellbeing."

Reports: Page 5
Molly Kingsley: Page 14
Editorial Comment: Page 15

---

chief warned to replace licence fee in funding battle

playing field" by awarding broadcast- ing licences to commercial rivals. The media regulator Ofcom has already granted a licence to a new channel named GB News promising coverage "distinctly different from the out-of- touch incumbents".

Meanwhile, Mr Davie will be chal- lenged to replace the licence fee with a new funding model or face a battle when the BBC charter is renewed in 2027, Whitehall sources said.

It is understood that Mr Davie will make no mention of the licence fee during his first speech as director-gen-

new funding model. One senior White- hall source said: "The decriminalisa- tion of the licence fee is a done deal. It will be done sooner rather than later.

"But it may be the least of the BBC's worries. There is a real interest in level- ling the playing field with more compe- tition."

One minister said: "There is real op- timism that the BBC will come up with a palatable alternative to the licence fee themselves, Tim Davie seems open to the idea of a subscription model."

The BBC Licence Fee (Civil Penalty) Bill is due for its second reading in Par- liament in November. A senior govern- ment source said: "One in 12

'The decriminalisation of the licence fee is a done deal. But it may be the least of the BBC's worries'

magistrates' court cases are for non- payment of TV licences and there is a disproportionate amount of women who are penalised.

"A lot of them are vulnerable over- 75-year-old widows. Do we really want to see people like that being brought before the courts?

"The BBC is living in a fantasy world if they think the status quo is viable."

It is understood that Robert Buckland, the Justice Secretary, has told col- leagues that prisons should be for "dangerous" people, not pensioners who have failed to pay fines.

BBC insiders said the corporation ex- pected the Government to decriminal- ise the charge. In his speech, Mr Davie will outline plans to offer better "value for money" to licence fee-payers by producing programming that "better reflects the British public".

Mr Davie is concerned, a senior source said, that the BBC produces too much content designed to appeal to a Left-wing London-centric audience. "There's nothing wrong with metro-

politan programmes, but we do make too many of them," one BBC source said.

Mr Davie will also launch a crack- down on BBC presenters who air their political views on social media after re- peated accusations of bias and clamp- down on presenters making thousands of pounds on the side by hosting corpo- rate events or moonlighting.

A BBC spokesman said: "The licence fee is the way of funding the BBC un at least 2027 and our focus is on provi ing the best possible value to the pub who pay for us."

Editorial Comment: Page 15

BUSINESS

Warning over £2.1bn

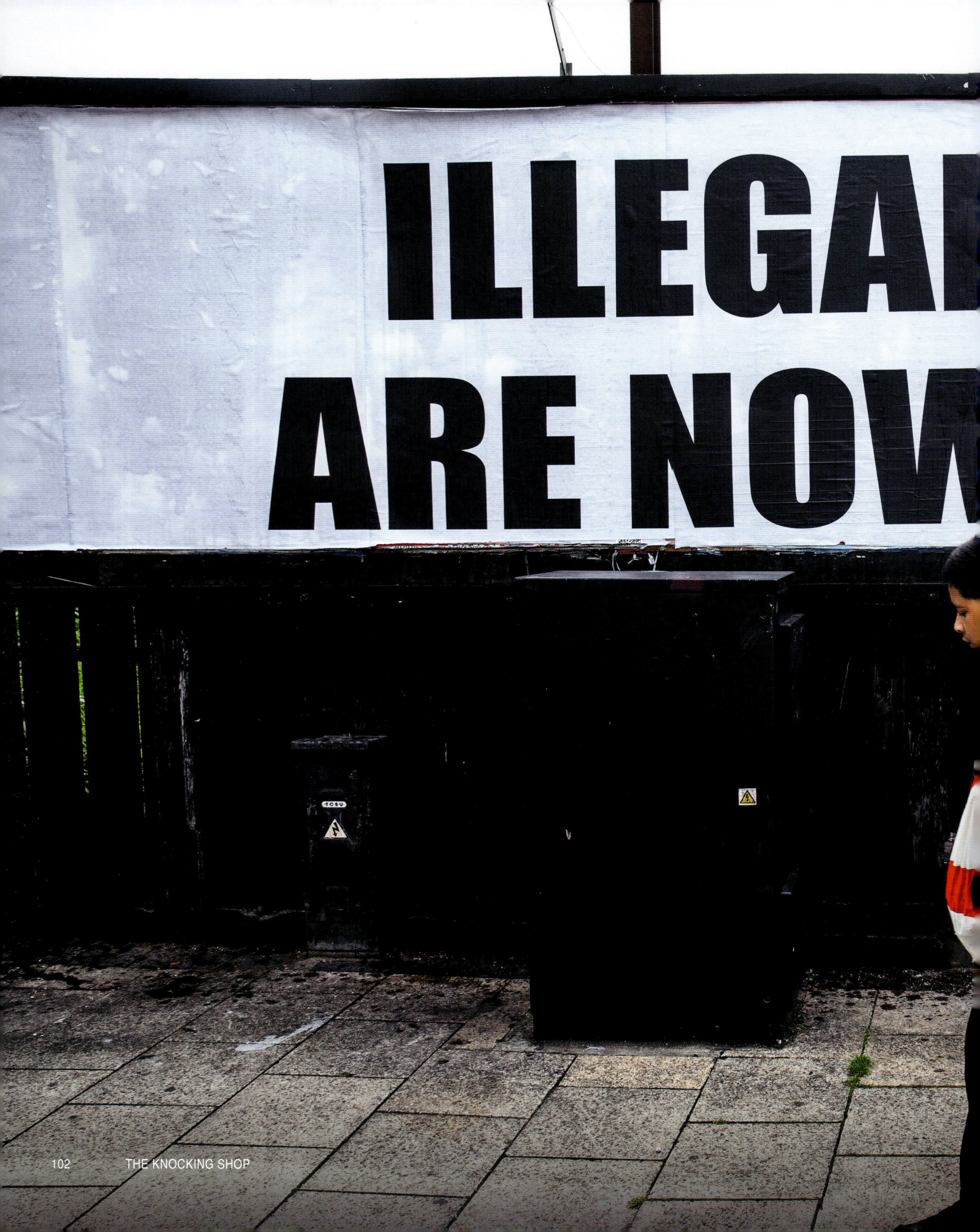
ILLEGAL
ARE NOW
TCSU

RAVES ILLEGAL

WHITE HORSE ROA
LONDON BOROUGH OF TOWER HAMLETS

FREE PARTY IS NOT A CRIME

In 2021, Sports Banger released a series of billboards across the UK in response to the introduction of new police powers to punish illegal rave organizers.

THE KNOCKING SHOP

ON THE HIGH SEAS OF TOTTENHAM. [ ] (interviewed on page 106) raises the flag for the 'People Deserve Beauty' fashion show.

Anonymous Fri May 15 23:50:06 2015
w2c the t shirt on the right

ⓕⓘⓜⓓ !ZxCHLOeFEI Sat May 16 03:53:38 2015 No.9850364

>>OP

that shirt is so fuckin british

fookin chav m8

No Subject
Today at 15:40

Jonny
I thought i'd share my story after recently ordering a NHS tee.
As with many of your customers I have bought the tee with substantial respect and gratitude to the NHS.
With an underlying heart condition since birth the role of the NHS in my life cannot be understated.
After a cardiac arrest (think similar to Fabrice Muamba) at 17 I was required a pacemaker, a operation which in America could cost up to £80,000 , a figure which my
family undoubtedly would not have been able to afford. I'm now and 22 and my pacemaker is still doing its thing. Its safe to say without the NHS I would not be here today.

Big respect for what you're doing.

Customer note:

buying this for my 17 year old who impaled himself climbing over railings in Finsbury Park
Friday night! The Fire brigade, paramedics, air ambulance, and NHS at Royal London Hospital saved him and stitched him back together he is extremely grateful!!! Keep up the good work and we will get a hoodie if you get them in again!!!

← **Tweet** 🔍 ✎

Sktchr
@eruchiness 🐦+

What does jonny banger even do?

26/04/2014 00:50

[Sports Banger] your work is shit

the boss via Big Cartel   Add to contacts 02/12/2014
To: jonsportswright@hotmail.com ⌄

From: the boss ▨▨▨▨▨▨▨▨om)

its all upside-down so sorry but no

Sent from your contact form at http://www.sportsbanger.co
Please report spam to Big Cartel support.

sportsbanger ⋯

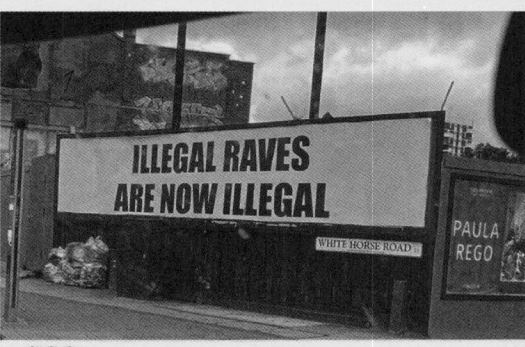

ILLEGAL RAVES ARE NOW ILLEGAL

Liked by **biglordbunnyrabbit** and **others**

gideon_dj_official Fuck the new police powers. Fuck Boris and Priti.
dave_swindells It can't be a coincidence that the poster is on White Horse Road, the location of so many raves (before and after they were illegalised!) 💀

From: ▨▨▨▨▨▨▨▨uk>
Sent: ▨▨▨▨▨▨
To: jo▨▨▨
Subje▨▨▨

Hi Jonny,

We've not met, but I've bought a few things from your site in the past.

You posted up my picture of me in the NHS tick tshirt in A/E on Christmas Day. I can see how passionate you are about health services through your posts and the testimonials you've been posting. Thought I'd share with you the brilliant responses that the tshirt got when I wore it that day as an A&E doctor. Loads asked where I'd got it from and loads shared stories of their gratitude to the health service through experiences, similar to what you're receiving in your inbox it would seem. I wish I'd written them down really. All amazing insights & made me proud of our system, none of which I'd have heard if I wasn't wearing your tshirt I guess.

Lets get out of ur comfort ones.

LONDON24
LONDON FOR LONDONERS

HOME | NEWS | SPORT | ENTERTAINMENT | CHRIS
Business | Crime | Court | Politics | Health | Olympics / Paralympics | Educati

'Team Nigella' graffiti in Stoke Newington removed by council

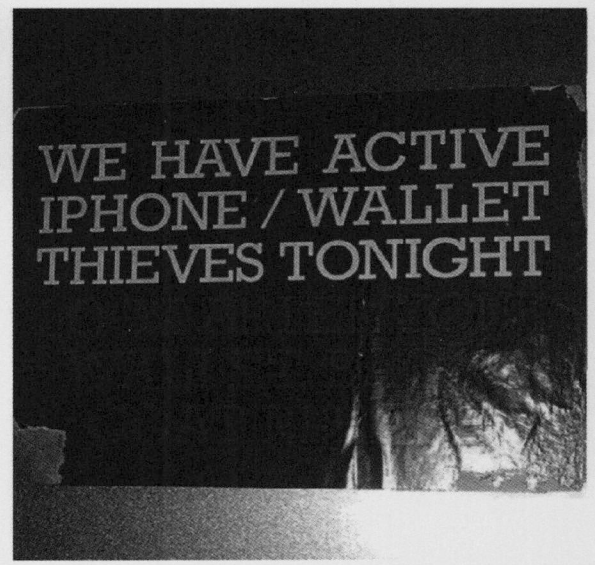

WE HAVE ACTIVE IPHONE / WALLET THIEVES TONIGHT

From: ▨▨▨▨▨
(Shaun ▨▨▨

Johnny

I'm probably too late in asking this but being an older (62) member of the public I'm not exactly 'down with street culture'.

I am hoping to secure one of the NHS tshirts for a very special person, the surgeon that saved my life. I was involved in a very bad accident and required life saving surgery. I am now fit and healthy and wish to show my gratitude to Mr Franks who I will be forever indebted to. Can you let me know if you have any stock that could be purchased - I would make an assumption that Mr Franks is a Large.

Thankyou for taking the time to read this, I am happy to provide payment and address for postage if one is available.

Keep up the good work.

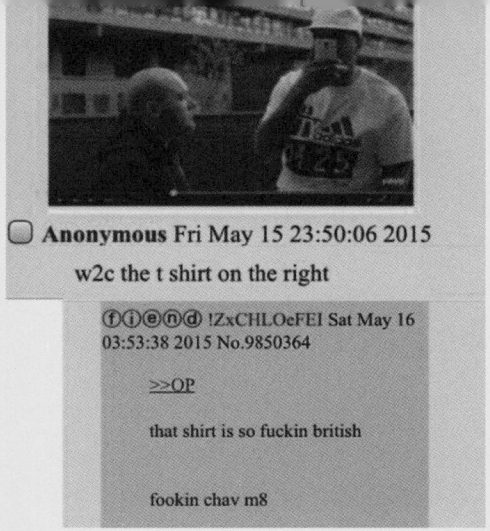

Shaun

The Economist 1843 🔍

The British fashion label dissing the establishment

Member of free party crew Odyssey Soundsystem ~~[scribble]~~

HOW DID YOU FIRST MEET JON?

So it was 2017, and a load of us were out raving in Barcelona at a squat party a friend had organized. I remember getting a text a few days after the rave about a memorial party for Keith Robinson, a real pioneer of the scene and part of the legendary Desert Storm sound system. There were some other proper crews on the text: Acme, IRD and Everyone Sounds. I remember clocking Jon in the rave and thinking, swear that's the geezer who makes the T-shirts. We ended up chatting in some room waffling on and I showed him some pics of our rig. I'd only just moved to London at the time and didn't really know anyone, so meeting Jon was a blessing.

WHAT IS IT YOU DO?

We run a free party sound system. I joined in around 2008, a few of the older lads in the area took me to a few parties and my mind was blown. We set about saving some dough for some cheap amps, subs and tops – it was a pretty decent rig, tbf. We did, however, lose the lot a year later at a UK Tek in Wales. I got arrested twice that day, but that's probably a story for another time, haha. I will add: I'd never been nicked before that. How's your luck!

Anyway, after losing the rig, we ended up back trying to build some money to buy another. It wasn't long and we had a proper rave stack built. Twelve 1850 subs and six Turbosound TMS2s. We took it everywhere – the Turbosound tops all lined up were just iconic. Even farmers recognized it if we were rinsing the same area, haha. We had that for a few years. We then upgraded to a new system, which we still own to this day: ASS MX900 tops with USBs, which are mid-bass subs, and Invaders, which drop to 30 Hz, so it was a well-rounded system. It done a two-stretch after a big UK Tek in Lincolnshire (that hit national news). A phrase shouted about then and still used to this day is 'Protect the generator'. It was a bit emotional at the time [when it was seized], but it all lives on, which is jokes. Nowadays we are running a full EM Acoustics system: Quakes and X3s.

We were lucky to learn off proper crews, so we knew the ethos of the free party and how it should be done. We've always tried to carry that on as much as we can and do parties with younger crews to pass down the right way of doing things.

YOU COINED THE PHRASE 'ILLEGAL RAVES ARE NOW ILLEGAL', WHICH SPORTS BANGER TURNED INTO A SERIES OF BILLBOARDS. WHERE DID THAT COME FROM?

Well, they've always been illegal, but when the country was locked down, it was like, oh fuck, they really are illegal now. We've done so many and got away with them. Occasionally, there would be more of a police presence, sometimes ending worse than it needed to. Some UK counties got hit so hard with raves they introduced zero-tolerance rules. You'd have to either have a real vendetta against that police force or really not want your system anymore, haha, as it was pretty much guaranteed to get seized. Some counties were pretty tolerant as long as you didn't take the piss. There was an understanding between both parties – police and ravers – and you could work with them to make sure the parties ended on good terms. When we went into lockdown, the ten-grand fines came in, and it was like, shit, is this really the end of it?

WHAT IS SO SPECIAL ABOUT FREE PARTIES?

The main thing has to be the music, the people and the feeling of being free! You have people of all ages, all walks of life. It's a safe space. Everyone together.

When I first started, it was a hell of a buzz going out with a massive squad every weekend. We'd all ring the party line Saturday night and convoy down to meet-up points and you'd start seeing cars likely heading the same place as you. Usually a banged-out Corsa with the bumper hanging off, haha. The mystery was what kind of location would the party be at? Forest, barn, warehouse – you just never knew. One of the first parties I went to was on New Year's Eve 2008/9 in a lottery-funded leisure centre that had shut down. The sound system was in a basketball stadium with tiered seating. They had a mental laser writing all sorts on the walls all night. There was a fully stocked gym, rock climbing walls, you name it, it was there. People discovered the roller skates and were whizzing round the dance floor all night. Hats off to Storm and AZ1 on that one, will probably never be topped!

You make friends with people from all over the country, some I can say are now my best friends. I even met my girlfriend at a party we done, and seven years later have a little boy together.

Shout out a few crews who influenced, helped or done it with us over the years: EQUALITY, STORM, AZ1, ONE UNITY, BRAINS KAN, DISRUPTION, CHEMICALLY DRIVEN, HYBRID, KOALITION. And more recently: STAGE 3, DIGITAL DISTURBANCE and B12.

UNITY 23

FUCK·YOUR·RULES

THE WORLD IS OURS TO SHARE

Sumitra Upham

Curator and head of public programmes
at the Crafts Council, London

I HEAR YOU CONVINCED JON TO PARTICIPATE IN A PANEL DISCUSSION AT THE DESIGN MUSEUM.

Well, the museum ran this annual exhibition called 'Beazley Designs of the Year' that showcased progressive and innovative designs that have impacted the year globally. I was putting together a public programme of discussions and events to run alongside the show, and one of them was about fashion and activism. Being a mate of Jon's I was aware of the impact and significance of Sports Banger's 'NHS' T-shirt, and I thought the talk would be a great springboard for him to discuss it. I knew Jon hadn't spoken publicly about that particular project – or Sports Banger more widely – before, and I wanted to use the T-shirt as an example of the impact design can have on social change as well as health and well-being. I also felt like it would be a good platform for the T-shirt to be acknowledged as a great piece of design in a way perhaps it hadn't been before.

HOW DID HE GET ON?

I mean, he was bricking it beforehand. I met him in Holland Park, and he was sat on a bench, kind of gathering his thoughts before the talk. Holland Park is famous for having the most ridiculous dogs owned by the rich people who live there. So he was just sitting there, feeding the pigeons and looking at the scene in front of him, kind of hyperventilating. Obviously, I was a bit nervous for him, but I knew he'd be great, and in the end, he got a standing ovation. He spoke so earnestly and honestly about that project. He talked about his relationship to the NHS, his mum, and what that T-shirt meant to him personally, not knowing the impact it would have. I think it was a bit of a transformative moment for him, for all of us, really – just to see Jon expose himself in that way. And as a result, I think it's done wonders for him in the sense that parts of the cultural sector have opened their doors to him.

HOW DO YOU THINK INSTITUTIONS TYPICALLY VIEW SPORTS BANGER'S WORK?

I think cultural institutions are showing an interest in Jon's work now because they see the power in what he does. They see his art and designs as progressive, but I think they also see him as a vehicle for connecting with different types of communities. He provides a way of inclusively talking about really, really important issues through cultural outputs, whether that be T-shirts, parties, fashion shows, or raves. He tackles these complex, urgent political issues in a playful, warm and accessible way, and that's why institutions love him. That's why young people love him. That's why we all love him.

SPORTS BANGER REALLY SEEMS TO RESONATE WITH PEOPLE ON A PERSONAL LEVEL.

People are really invested in Sports Banger. They want to support Sports Banger and support Jon. I think that's a massive part of the engagement. If we take that talk, for example, nobody had heard anybody speak like that in an institution before, or at least in that institution. And Jon's got such a loyal following, particularly among young people. You could really see it in the room that day. I would say something like 70% of the crowd in that 200-person auditorium were there for Jon. Having him on stage does a lot for those types of spaces because it means that his posse are going to follow, and they're going to step inside the Design Museum and sit in an auditorium and listen to a panel discussion, which might be a first for many people. So having Jon and the brand represented in those spaces brings in different types of people who have otherwise felt excluded, and that's a really beautiful thing.

HOW DO YOU SEE SPORTS BANGER RELATING TO THE WORLDS OF ART AND DESIGN?

It crosses all of those disciplines: he has a social-cultural practice, he activates spaces, he curates cultural activities and produces visual outputs to address pressing political issues that are not being addressed by the government. If that's not art, what is?

What I really love about Sports Banger is that he hates labels, doesn't he? Which is really funny because he runs one himself! But that resistance towards defining the brand, rejecting the idea of marketable identity, leaves a bit of uncertainty around what Sports Banger actually is. In a way, the mystique and elusiveness of Sports Banger feel very akin to experimental art practices and collectives.

WHAT'S IT BEEN LIKE FOR YOU TO WITNESS THE EVOLUTION OF SPORTS BANGER?

It's been amazing to see Jon welcomed by the cultural sector, while also maintaining trust and relevance in his own community. For the art world to consider him an 'artist' and accept him as a serious practitioner and thinker that can be put on a stage with other interesting minds is amazing, and long overdue. It's very admirable that he can remain relevant in all of those different worlds, from raving to fashion to contemporary art to the community work he does, and working with kids. He's a very unique soul, and it takes a really special kind of someone to be able to be loved and revered within all of those different contexts. It's probably only something that Jonny Banger, aka Jon Wright, could do.

Chunky

Musician, MC and DJ, Manchester

DID YOU KNOW ABOUT SPORTS BANGER BEFORE YOU
MET JONNY, OR DID YOU MEET JONNY FIRST?

There was no Sports Banger when I met Jonny. He
was Jonny Banger, with everything he'd accomplished up until
that point. Jonny's done a lot that people don't even fuckin'
know about, you know? Like, this guy is potentially one of the
people who shaped how UK rap works. Arguably. I would argue
for it, you know? We were doing this Swamp Records/School
Records thing on Brick Lane. Jonny was somehow managing
to do that pretty much every Sunday. Heads like Klose One
would be there and our good mate, rest his soul, Aset [Jan
Francis]. Just a big crew, a big ATG contingency.

This was around the time I'd freshly moved to
London. So we were doing the Swamp shows on Rinse, which
later became Norwood Soul Patrol. We were just playing
records on Rinse, you know? This led to playing records on
Brick Lane; it wasn't even an MC thing. Loefah was bringing
a lot of people together, Jan as well. Jonny didn't really want
to get on the mic back then. He'd get on the mic for raffles
and that, but he wasn't really MCing. I was like, 'Jonny, fuckin'
touch mic.' I'm not the catalyst, but I definitely helped with
that. But yeah … so then Jonny's getting on flyers and shit, you
know, and it's like, we're doing the Swamp raves, and Jonny's
one of the main MCs. We're doing stuff in Croatia, Outlook
Festival. It's sick. Loefah and Jonny were talking about T-shirt
ideas and all this kind of stuff, and then bits and bobs start
popping up, like the 'Upside-Down Reebok' T-shirt. Jonny's
bullying the brands and getting all those fuckin' cease and
desist letters and shit.

It's playful, but at the same time, there's a point to
everything he does. There's a conversation he's having – if you
choose to have it back, then it's with you. Jonny's a people
person anyway; he's got these relationships from all the
different roles he's had. So different people are supporting
him, and things are moving, you know …. Somehow, some way,
he's ended up with this Slazenger thing. I'm like, 'You're gonna
have to get models now!' – you know what I'm saying? Next
thing I know, we're on a fuckin' speedboat in Southampton,
with Jonny's logos stuck on the front. We've got a guy who
looks like he's from *Miami Vice* driving the boat in a fuckin'
yellow Slazenger bathrobe with a pair of sunglasses and his hair
blowing in the fuckin' wind. All of a sudden, we're like fuckin'
models, and we're fuckin' popping up in *Vogue* wearing all this
fuckin' stuff. Next thing, we go on another little shoot with
Ollie Grove, who's another crew member. I mean, we do them
shots, and then it's fuckin' *Vogue Italia!* I'm wearing a T-shirt
and shorts, a pair of trainers, some pink Sports Banger fuckin'
socks. I'm thinking, 'Errr, what?!' I mean, like, my face is in
some high fashion shit, wearing some everyday normal guy
business. I think it's just beautiful to see it in my world. And
it's inspiring to me.

TELL US ABOUT THE FASHION SHOWS. BECAUSE
THERE'S THIS THING ABOUT YOU TAKING PEOPLE'S
PHONES FROM THE FRONT ROW …

It's like, you've got a whole bunch of high performers.
When you put them together, and everyone is invested in
accomplishing the mission, we all support each other to secure
the bag, you know? There isn't anybody incompetent. Maybe
just me – I might be stoned. Or I've got another wrong train
and showed up 40 minutes later than I was supposed to.

The running of the shows, it's not just Jonny,
obviously. Meme did a little bit of directing on the first one.
Manu, she's done quite a lot, Celeste, Klose One on the music
– there's a team, and they keep it moving. That time it was me
and Black Josh. Jonny had come up to Manchester and basically
found all these fake baby Moncler jackets and shit. And he
fashioned these outfits out of them. There's a stigma around
the kind of people who wear these kinds of clothes. So before
we went out, Jonny was saying to us, 'phone thieves', as a cue
to go nick them. I think Black Ops was playing – it was mad
hyped. So when we walk out there, I start grabbing phones off
people because everyone's filming, they're not watching, and
that ruins the vibe a bit. People are genuinely scared, but then
they kind of check themselves, like, 'There's loads of witnesses;
it's a fashion show.' Jonny gave us the space to be able to do that.

HOW'S IT FEEL FOR YOU TO BE DOING STUFF LIKE THIS? CATWALK SHOWS, *VOGUE ITALIA* …

It feels crazy. In Manchester, we don't have tube trains, so, like, after school, we'd just run on the bus, like bum rush it to avoid paying. Five or six of us all at once. It feels a bit like that. It feels like we're doing naughty things. It's like, 'Look how far we've got. Do you think the driver's gonna stop the bus?'. But then also, it feels proper natural. As a crew – or even Jonny, as an individual – I don't feel like we're occupying space where we don't belong. It's just really showing people that this don't have to be this thing you've been presented with – all these impossible expectations that you need to try and meet.

WHY DO YOU THINK SPORTS BANGER HAS ACHIEVED WHAT IT HAS SO FAR?

It's just really honest. I mean, it's very, very honest. It's a real reflection of Jonny, who is, like, a buzz to be around, a fun person – someone who has a good time and knows not to take himself too seriously. But at the same time, he's got a really big heart; he cares about these issues. He's like, 'This is what I care about, so there it is.' It resonates because people care about the same shit: people care about their families, their relatives, whose eating and who's not eating. When lockdown came, you know, I know Jonny weren't planning to do no big food run or whatever, but as soon as it came, he naturally was like, 'Yeah, obviously.' Not everyone's like that. And I think a lot of people deal with the roughness of it all by withdrawing, and I'm sure that sometimes happens with Jonny too. But ultimately, he just channels that energy into another thing.

I think what people are into is the realness. I mean, there's nothing else. Catch Jonny in the summer, and he's wearing his Ralphies and his Reebok classics. That's what he loves. That's what he's into. I mean, his granddad was a pigeon fancier. So he's into pigeons. He made a pigeon tracksuit – you know what I mean? He's not like, 'What do the kids want?' He's like, 'Yo, I know about pigeons. Check this pigeon tracksuit.' And that's it. It's not about selling you something – it's just to celebrate something or nod to something, whether that's an issue or, you know, something that he thinks is amazing.

People just like honesty, especially if honesty is a fun thing. Ultimately, whoever you are, you resonate with truth. It's gonna sound proper corny nineties hip-hop type shit, but Jonny Banger is the truth. You can quote me on that. Banger is the truth!

BANGER TAKES YOU INTO VOGUE ITALIA

111

NRG!
SOLIDARITY WITH STRIKING WORKERS
GIZ A FIVER
NHS
HACKNEY HARDCORE
FUCK BORIS
MAISON DE BANG BANG
not bad for a woma
Slazenger BANGER
WORLD PARTY
'LET'S RAVE TOGETHER AS A FAMILY'
CRIME RAVE
GOLF SALE
YES
SLAZENGER BANGER

Previous, right: Where's my T-shirt? Photos sent in from the people.
Above: Boxes of stock and customer orders packed and
ready for posting.
Opposite: Scan of an original Sports Banger logo T-shirt.

Sports BANGER

1.

3.

4.

5.

6.

7.

8.

9.

10.

11.

THE T–SHIRTS

1. FREE TULISA, 2013
2. Logo, 2013
3. PHONE THIEVES, 2013
4. If it's Nice, 2013
5. Classic, 2013
6. Sportsbanger.com, 2013
7. TEAM NIGELLA, 2013
8. Zed Bias, 2013
9. Smile & Wave, 2014
10. Sports Smiley, 2014
11. Artwork, 2014
    (front and back)

12.

13.

'92

14.

15.

16.

17.

18.

19.

20.

21.

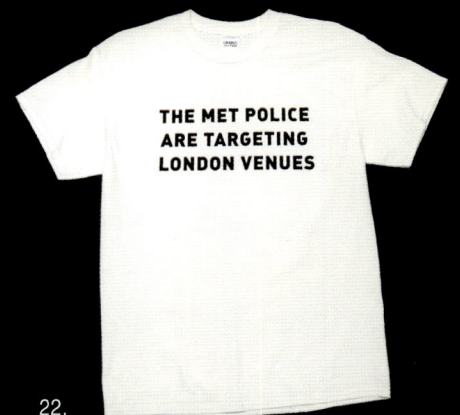

22.

THE T-SHIRTS

12. Lifestyles Hotline, 2014
13. Mr.Shuffle, 2014
14. ZOMBY, 2014
15. Golf Sale, 2014
16. Wimbledon, 2014
17. Reebok Air, 2014

18. Mr.Freeze, 2014
    (front and back)
19. Sports Logo, 2014
20. ALIF, 2014
21. Ultra, 2014
22. Save Fabric, 2014

23.

24.

25.

26.

27.

28.

29.

30.

31.

32.

FAZE MIYAKE

B Y

FAZE MIYAKE

33.

34.

118   THE T-SHIRTS

23. Sports Bear, 2015
24. Eclipse, 2015
25. England, 2015
26. Big Apple, 2015
27. BRUM, 2015
28. Queen of Croydon, 2015

29. Loefah Vandross, 2015
30. Under the Counter, 2015
31. More Classic Lovers, 2015
32. Nice and Safe, 2015
33. Faze Miyake, 2015
34. Reebok Ice, 2015

36.

36. YES PEACE, 2015 *(front and back)*
The graphic on this T-shirt is from an image of the soul singer
Luther Vandross wearing a peace sign T-shirt with a raised
clenched fist. There can never be too much peace. This is the
peace sign we use through all our work, straight off Luther's
chest. When Saint Laurent dropped 'Yves', we dropped the
'YES' T-shirt – same YSL font, peace on the back. Yes to peace.

37.

38.

39.

40.

41.

42.

43.

44.

45.

46.

THE T-SHIRTS

37. Hackney Hardcore, 2016
38. Deptford Market, 2016
39. EBIZA, 2016
40. You're a Keeper, 2016
   (front and back)
41. Pirate Radio, 2016

42. ICE Records, 2016
   (front and back)
43. Jimbo in Ibiza, 2016
44. Goldie, 2016
45. Prince, 2016
46. Make Croydon Bait Again, 2016

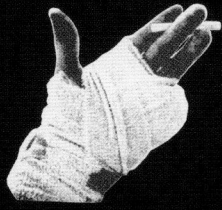

47.

48.

47. JOSH, 2016
I read about a raver called Josh who accidentally yanked off his little finger trying to pull a fire alarm off the ceiling at a rave in an old Royal Mail sorting office in Croydon. Apparently, he wrapped his T-shirt around his bloody hand and carried on dancing until his mate took him to the paramedics. As the raver recounted to one newspaper: 'I said [to the paramedic] is there any chance you can bandage it up and I can just rave on?' He was like, 'Nah, you're going to hospital mate.'

48. RUNNER, 2016
This design is based on a marathon T-shirt. We put the Adidas Equipment logo next to the Autobahn graphic because it reminded me of Kraftwerk's album cover. It's a homage to the M25/London Orbital Motorway, which paved a path for convoys of ravers to travel to the free parties in the rolling hills of the English countryside. A road to rave.

49.

50.

49. MUD, 2017
My favourite Reebok Classics are the ones caked in authentic Norfolk rave mud. Big up Equality and Odyssey Soundsystem for one hell of a free party. One of the best raves I've ever been to. I think I nearly cried, I was so deliriously happy. I put my trainers straight on the shelf when I got home. Took a pic. Made this T-shirt.

50. BAD GIRLS, 2018
I was at a rave and the DJ Josey Rebelle (probably my favourite DJ in the world) said she wanted the classic London tourist T-shirt but with a Tottenham twist.

51.

52.

53.

54.

55.

56.

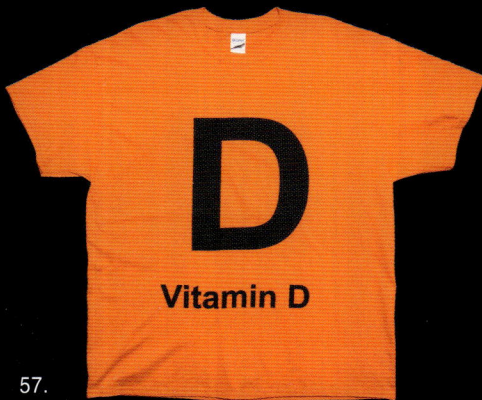

57.

58.

59.

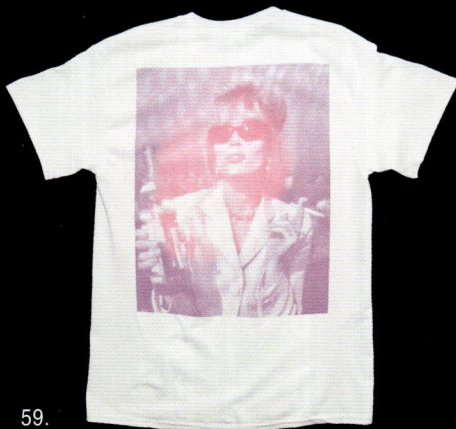

59.

60.

61.

THE T-SHIRTS

51. HERAS, 2016
52. Sock Bally 313, 2016
53. Fabio, 2017
54. Love Doves, 2017
55. Sid The Snail, 2017
56. Dance Maniacs, 2017

57. Vitamin D, 2017
58. Spot, 2017
    (front and back)
59. Pat on The Back, 2017
60. Top Buzz, 2017
61. World Party, 2017

62.

63.

64.

65.

66.

67.

68.

69.

70.

71.

THE T-SHIRTS

62. Happy Hardcore, 2017
(front and back)
63. Everyone, 2017
64. Hak Baker, 2018
65. Clancy, 2018
(front and back)

66. Crime Rave, 2018
67. Optimo Espacio, 2018
68. Three Lions, 2018
69. Ralph Slazenger, 2018
70. World is Yours, 2018
71. Spice, 2018

72.

72. EU RALPH, 2015 *(front and back)*
The mounted policeman on this T-shirt is cut from a photo taken at the Battle of Orgreave in 1984. The original shows an officer taking a swipe at a protester (Lesley Boulton, a member of Women Against Pit Closures) with his truncheon. The police later claimed the image was doctored. The photo of Margaret Thatcher is a 1987 press pic of her walking through wasteland on the site of a demolished steel foundry. A 'Ralph Lauren' T-shirt with a photomontage of Thatcher getting clattered round the head is arguably an upgrade.

73.

74.

73. RAVING SHOES, 2015
This T-shirt is based on the 1992 Shut Up and Dance track 'Raving I'm Raving' with the lyrics 'Put on my raving shoes and I boarded a plane'. In our version, we wear Reebok Classics and board trains to go raving, so we used the National Rail logo.

74. PAT ON THE BACK, 2017
At Snowbombing festival in Austria, a bunch of us had to DJ after Pat Sharp from 'Fun House' (without the twins or the mullet). Backstage, we made up a game where you had to name a famous Pat you'd like to pat on the back. Pat Butcher aka our patron saint Pam St Clement from 'EastEnders' was the clear winner, so we made this colour-changing T-shirt in her honour.

not bad for a woman

fuck off

75.

76.

77.

78.

79.

MAISON
DE
BANG BANG

80.

HOUSE
OF
BANG BANG

81.

82.

83.

THE T-SHIRTS

75. Not Bad for a Woman, 2019
      (front and back)
76. ELLE, 2019
77. MEGA RAVE / FUCK BORIS,
      2019 (front and back)
78. Bangtazia, 2019

79. Chino the Demidog, 2019
80. Maison de Bang Bang, 2019
      (front and back)
81. Paranoid London, 2020
82. Giz a Fiver, 2020
83. Pirate, 2020

84.

85.

86.

87.

88.

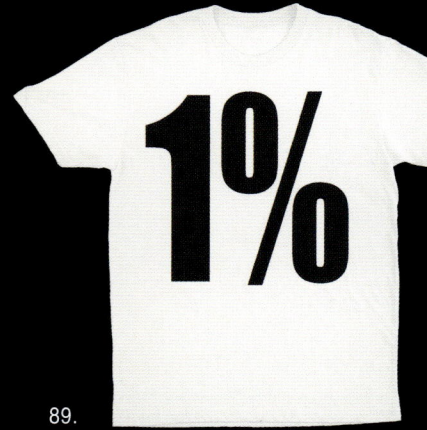
89.

90.

91.

92.

93.

94.

95.

THE T-SHIRTS

84. Exhibition T-shirt, 2020
85. Twisted, 2020
86. Britannia, 2020
87. Tommy Hilfiger, 2020
88. Margiela Bang, 2021
89. Pay Rise, 2021

90. Annihilate, 2021
91. Absolut Banger, 2021
92. Jonny Jeans, 2021
93. Maison Brass, 2021
94. HERAS Ghost, 2021
95. HERAS Records, 2021

96.

97.

96. MCQUEEN, 2019
My mate Lisa got me the Alexander McQueen book for my birthday. I love this photo so much, I bootlegged it upside down. The photographer Gary Wallis got in touch and said you can't do that. I emailed back, explained myself a bit, and he said, 'Don't worry about it. Keep it up.' We met up, and he gave me a tour of Central Saint Martins – mad place. Thanks Gary.

97. DOBERMAN, 2020
We bootlegged this R&S Records logo (because we're dog people, not horse people) to make a T-shirt for the 'Doberman' EP by Scottish producer Neil Landstrumm (interviewed on page 300), the first record we released under HERAS.

98.

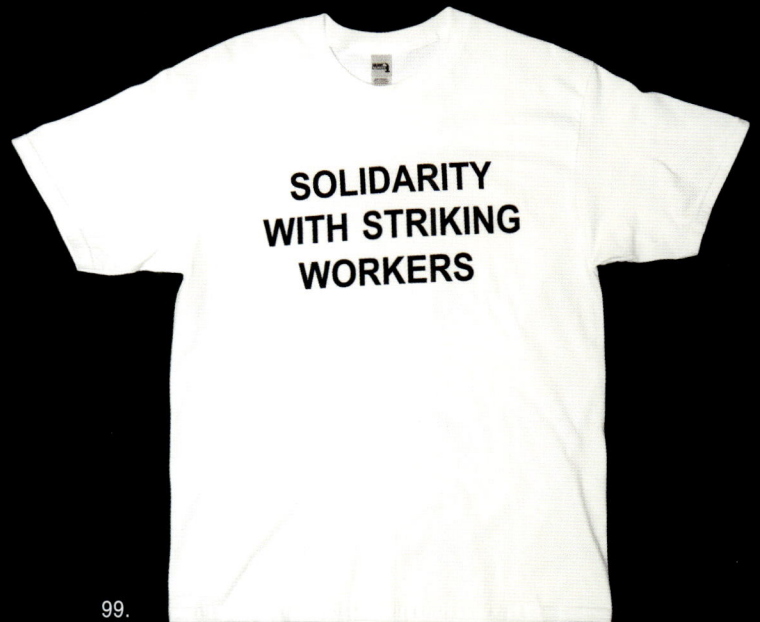

99.

98. BOTA, 2022
Eliza Rose is the baddest DJ and east London queen. When we first started chatting, I was loving her mixes and she posted me a book she'd just finished reading. Giving someone an old book is like giving them a record from your collection. It's proper. We made this T-shirt when 'B.O.T.A. (Baddest Of Them All)', Eliza's single with Interplanetary Criminal hit number one in the UK charts.

99. SOLIDARITY WITH STRIKING WORKERS, 2022
This T-shirt was free for any workers on strike. A load of them came with £5 Greggs vouchers so you could buy tea for your local picket. By the time this book is published, the Tories will have pushed an anti-strike bill through Parliament. Defend the right to strike. Join a union and kick the Tories back to hell.

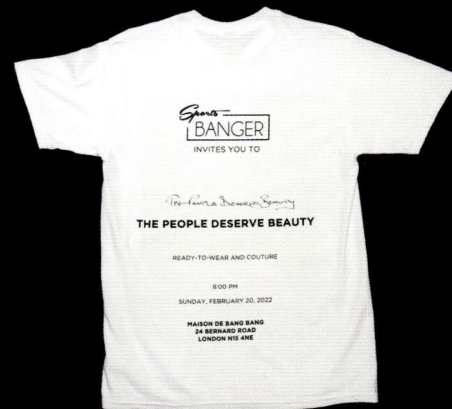

100.

101.

102.

103.

104.

105.

106.

107.

108.

109.

100. Powered by, 2022
101. NRG!, 2022
102. Rod Again, 2022
103. Bastards, 2022
104. Max Banger, 2022
     (front and back)

105. Banger Smiley, 2022
106. TPDB, 2022
     (front and back)
107. Archives, 2023
108. Riot, 2023
109. Designer, 2023

NOT FOR SALE

NOT FOR SALE

NOT FOR SALE

Scan of 'Not For Sale' patches cut out from Banger T-shirts.

NOT FOR SALE

VL
LA
BOO

VA

VA

TLEG

KNOCKING DOWN THE WALL
by Jonny Banger

I'd looked at this wall in the studio for years and knew it had to come down. So we took it out along with another wall and stuck in a back door. With the two walls down, there was suddenly a straight line from the back of the studio to the front, and all I could see was a runway. London Fashion Week was two weeks away, so I thought: fuck it, we're doing it. At the same time, we'd just built a sound system. We were gonna buy something off the shelf, but Matt Harriman said, 'Look at the money we'd spend – let's just build one.' The sound was amazing. I'd never been to a fashion show, never even watched one, but we had a sound system and a straight line. Half the job was done.

The night before the show, the toilet blocked and the studio flooded. We scooped all the shitty water up with dustpans and were up till five in the morning, wiring and soldering all the lights for the runway ourselves. The show was a complete trip, and my brain must have rewired because after that night, I stopped biting my nails, which was a lifelong habit.

Fashion shows are some next-level buzz. Putting one on is essentially the same as organizing a rave, but you make the clothes, dress the models, handle hair and make-up, figure out music, lighting, casting, cameras, food, invites, shoe sizes, call times … it's shit loads of work for a 30-minute party. And even by DIY standards, it costs a lot. You're throwing money in the bin, but it's so much fun. That's why we fully ramped it up for our second show, 'Pop Culture is Trash', which we put on six months later. For that one, we had 57 looks, 18 bass bins, one *Vogue* journalist, zero buyers, and about 200 people watching and willing us on. The atmosphere at these things is just mad. Five of our models thought it was a good idea to do a load of mushrooms before walking to calm their nerves. Never do that.

It's such a diverse and spectacular bunch of people who come together to make a Banger show happen, and we're all friends. I think it could only really happen in London. We made these proper big shiny bomber jackets with metal nameplates bolted on and BANGER embroidered across the back. When one of our star models, Eloise, was walking down the runway, she surprised us all by suddenly taking hers off and slinging it across the floor. We watched from the sides as she got on her hands and knees, crawled the length of the runway, then got up, did a flying high kick towards the photographer, turned around, picked up the jacket and threw it into the crowd. I asked her where the fuck did that come from? She smiled and said, 'Dunno bruvs'.

That was the end of summer, 2019. When Covid happened, a lot changed, but we kept working, and I employed my housemates – who were now out of work – to pack T-shirts. What we got done over that time is something I'm still really proud of. We didn't do anything that radically different from what we were doing before – just joined the dots and channelled T-shirt sales into action. I called up my friend Meriel, who was about to open her restaurant, Club Mexicana, when Covid hit. She knew loads of out-of-work people from the industry and pulled together a huge network of independent street food sellers who otherwise wouldn't have been able to keep their businesses going. Together, we ended up coordinating daily deliveries of healthy food across London – supplying fresh meals and juices to staff at intensive care and mental health units, a hospice, and an HIV centre. Our friend Susie worked in public health and hooked us up with a point of contact at every hospital, giving us shift times and staff numbers. After a teacher at a local primary school reached out following the government's free school meal fiasco, we also set up a food bank for kids and families at the school. T-shirt sales paid for everything.

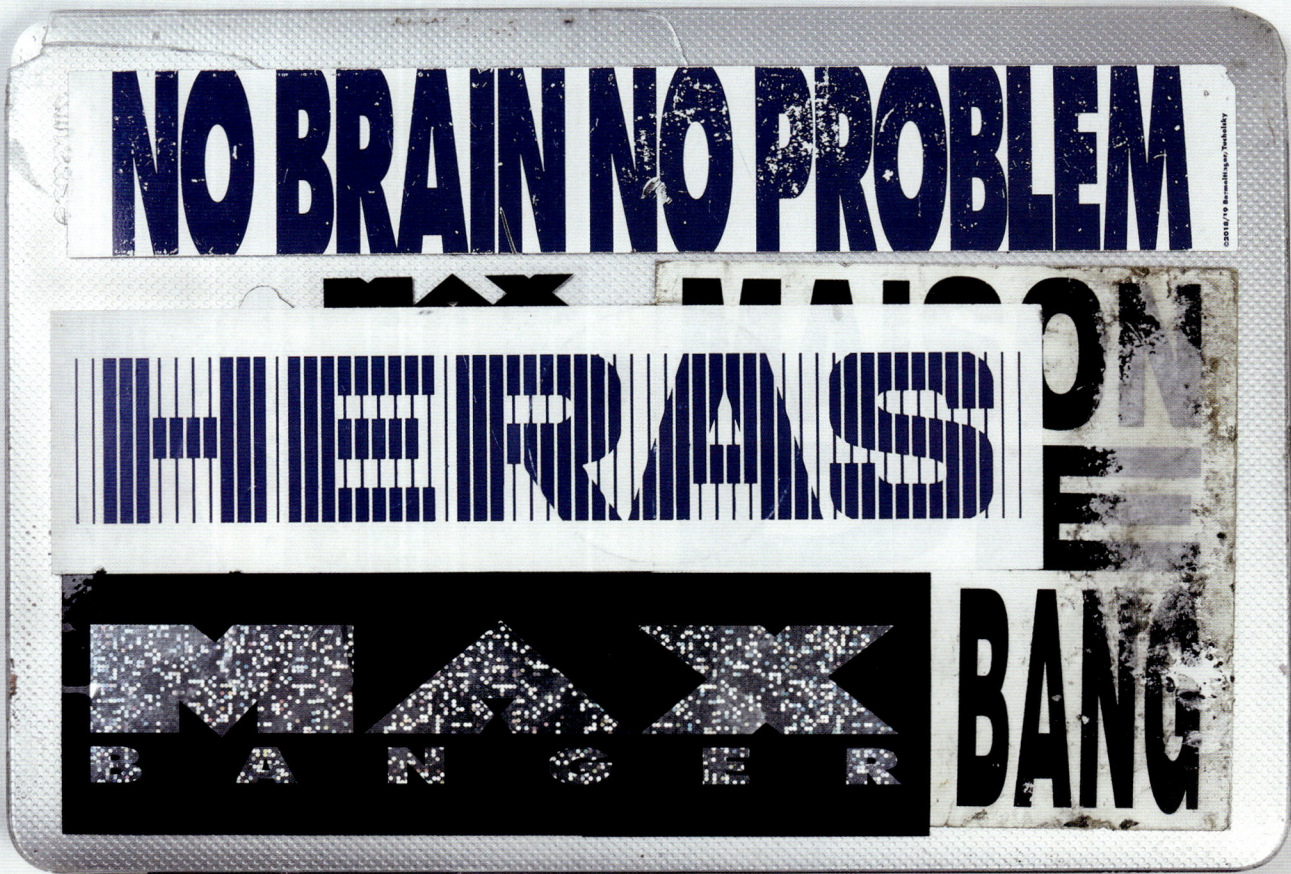

NO BRAIN NO PROBLEM

HERAS

MAISON

ONE

MAX
DANGER

BANG

NEAS

NULL
+VOID

DEVON
ANALOGUE

#DaliDuchamp

L. A.
R.MUTT
1917

私の薬物チームには
MY DRUG TEAM HAS A
激しい問題があります
RAVE PROBLEM.

NEIGHBOURHOOD

134   VIVA LA BOOTLEG

Previous, left: Mega Rave 7 at Fabric, London.
Above: Jonny's battered laptops.
Opposite: The poster atelier at 'My First Fashion Show', 2019.

SPORTS BANGER.COM

I know where you live

Above: A photocopied mailout included with Sports Banger orders.
Opposite: Olu the Banger shop dog with sack loads of T-shirt orders.

VIVA LA BOOTLEG

The magnificent David Hoyle in 'Solidarity with Striking Workers'
T-shirt for a performance at Volksbühne Berlin, 2023.

I was buzzing when we got commissioned to make two outfits for 2 Chainz and only had 24 hours to do it. He went from wearing the most expensivest shit in the US to the cheapest shit in the UK.

KNOCKING DOWN THE WALL

Above: 2 Chainz performing at Lovebox Festival wearing an improvised Slazenger Banger ensemble, 2019.
Overleaf: Sports Banger's bootlegged billboard at Seven Sisters station, 2019.

The 'Best Fu
Brand of the
isn't even a

Awards 2017

Which?

Banking Brand of the Year

Nationwide Building Society. Head Office: Nationwide House, Pipers Way, Swindon, Wiltshire, SN38 1NW.

POTOKRANS.79

prime

324102
king
ear'
bank. Again.
Awards 2018
Which?
king Brand of the Year
BANGER
SPORTS BANGER.COM

We held our first show in our studio on Seven Sisters Road. We put it all together in a couple of weeks with limited resources and fuck all money. Our shows happen away from the official London Fashion Week schedule. We drag people down to our level, invite a bunch of mates round, and call it Off London Fashion Week.

VIVA LA BOOTLEG

Previous, left: A still from BTS footage shot by the back door of the studio.
Previous, right: A still from a video of the show shot by an overhead 360-degree camera, featuring Novelist, Skream and Meme Gold premiering repurposed Banger looks on the runway.
Above: Models Maëva Berthelot and Emanuelle Soum in the runway make-up look.

MY FIRST FASHION SHOW   Chunky and Meme Gold backstage before walking the runway.

Looks from 'My First Fashion Show'. The tightly packed runway was flanked by boxes of stock, and the air was thick with smoke.

We had a bunch of stock left over from the Slazenger collab, which I thought could be turned into a collection. Inflatable lilos became trench coats and towels became tracksuits. Off-the-shelf stuff got overprinted, a dressing gown was cut into a bomber jacket, tube socks became balaclavas, and unused 'bags for life' got sewn into a giant hazmat suit.

Our neighbour Luis from Tottenham Textiles opened my eyes to how clothes were actually made. Seeing the process really inspired me and took us from strictly using T-shirts as the medium for our message to a more DIY approach to making clothes. Holly Harris, a pattern cutter who worked next door, became our shop girl on Saturdays. She's stayed with us and is now head of the atelier at Maison de Bang Bang.

Above: Model line-up on the wall of Tottenham Textiles, next door to the Sports Banger studio.
Opposite: THE HOTTEST TICKET IN TOWN. Invites were sent in poster tubes made to look like giant cigarettes.

FIRST FASHION

WOULD LOVE YOU TO AT

THANKS

Jonny

JONNY BANGER

Above: Tactical vest and bomber made using repurposed Slazenger Banger dressing gowns and 'bags for life' made with Tottenham Textiles.
Opposite: A trench coat made by designer Ancuta Sarca from deconstructed hot-pink inflatable lilos.

DAZED

REVIEW

'London bootlegger Sports Banger threw the vibiest show of fashion week'

Emma Elizabeth Davidson
Dazed, 18 February 2019

Founder Jonny Banger turned the runway into an acid rave at his Tottenham studio.

It's a well-known fact that, when it comes to fashion week, some of the most exciting shows happen way off schedule and far from the beaten track. Proving just that was London bootlegger Sports Banger. Having made his name with his politically charged knock-off tees that remix the Nike Swoosh with the NHS logo and blast the UK's Tory government at every available chance, founder Jonny Banger threw his first-ever fashion show this weekend.

Taking place out at Banger's studio in Seven Sisters, the DIY event turned the runway into an acid rave as models vogued and posed their way through the smoke-filled, sweaty space, and the audience (which included artist Jeremy Deller and Jaime Winstone) shouted enthusiastically from the benches. At one point, Deller climbed onto one to get a better look and danced so hard it felt like it was definitely going to split in half.

'It's all just a bunch of my friends, on the runway and off, really,' Banger explained afterwards as everyone poured out into the tiny yard for post-show drinks. 'I'd wanted to do a fashion show for ages, and it was a bit of an excuse to throw a party. I found out it was London Fashion Week this weekend and was just like, fuck it, I'm doing it!'

Having worked closely with Tottenham Textiles workshop and its young apprentices to create it, the collection itself was made up of repurposed pieces from his core collection, as well as reworked pieces from the recent Slazenger Banger collab that didn't sell: 'I had a load of leftover lilos from the Slazenger line, because who puts a lilo in their suitcase when they're going on holiday? No one – so I made tracksuits and MA-1 bombers out of them. It only really all came together on Wednesday, to be honest – it's been mad. I didn't realize how much work went into [shows].' Each of the vinyl pieces was designed in collaboration with London-based Romanian designer Ancuta Sarca, who Banger met when she came to one of his Mega Raves.

Other looks included sweatshirts and hoodies, an oversized shirt and trouser set covered in dogs which channelled the '90s Moschino and Iceberg looks beloved by the UK garage scene, and two-piece trackies featuring piano strips down the arms and legs, as worn by the full cast as they took their final lap of the delivery box-lined catwalk. With the Sports Banger logo plastered over pretty much everything, looks were finished with bucket hats, scarves, balaclavas, and sports towels, as well as a series of matching dog-sized pieces which were modelled by Chino the staffie (yes, everyone went nuts).

It wasn't just Chino making a cameo, though: also on the line-up were long-time fans of the label (and friends) such as London MC Novelist, Manchester-based designer Meme Gold, and legendary DJ and producer Skream – not that you'd know it, given he was hidden inside a huge yellow hazmat and carrying a massive Mitsubishi in his arms.

Jonny might have explained later that he doesn't take fashion that seriously ('It's all a bit bollocks isn't it, really?'), but the night and the collection itself genuinely felt like a pretty major moment for the label. Having grown the brand from an off-the-cuff T-shirt calling for the release of Tulisa to what it stands at now – with a pretty high-profile collab, appearances in a series of high fashion editorials in magazines including *Vogue Paris*, and as of this weekend, a fashion show under its belt – the designer has established a massive following in just a few short years and proved himself a definite one to watch on the underground fashion scene.

At a time when the UK's future is so wildly uncertain and the creative industries are struggling as a consequence, and major fashion labels continue to mine the depths of youth culture for commercial gain, seeing such a diverse group of people come together to throw a DIY rave runway show with such wild energy and authenticity – particularly at a time when London nightlife is in such a state of emergency – made it clear that exciting things are still bubbling away under the surface. You just need to know where to look.

DJ and producer Skream flew back from a gig early to model the hazmat suit – the closing look for Sports Banger's debut fashion show. If you look closely, you can see him really struggling in there.

VIVA LA BOOTLEG

OH, IT'S YOU AGAIN was a billboard for Oatly, the oat milk brand. We pasted this up at 11pm on the 31 Jan 2020, right when the UK legally left the EU. It was quite an effort, it's fucking massive. The billboard ran the whole weekend, greeting everyone who left Dalston Junction tube station. Oatly ended up sending us weekly deliveries for the primary school food bank we set up, and Buildhollywood gave us 55 free billboards across the UK to do whatever we wanted.

WELCOME. Commuters at Dalston Junction station passing the explicit Banger billboard.

Reebok Classics with £5 notes in the soles are a part of British folklore.
We released the Slazenger Banger Classic at £29.99. We never usually ask
for permission so I was surprized when we got an OK from the Bank of England
to print sample notes on the soles. We wangled the factory to do us a load
of (illegal) pairs with real money in. If you've got a pair you're stepping
on royalty and you're quids in.

It's only ever been Reeboks for Jonny Banger, the Tottenham-based multidisciplinary designer and raver whose sharp slogans and reappropriated logos are renowned for reading the pulse of the nation. Since purchasing his first pair of blue and yellow ripples as a teenager - a rite of passage for any Colchester kid - Jonny has collected Reebok Classics. There's just one pair that's always been out of reach, one step ahead. We took the Victoria line to Seven Sisters Road on a quest to uncover the truth behind the mysterious Reebok 'Five Pound' Ice Soles.

I wouldn't say I'm into trainers but I am into Reeboks. I'm from Colchester and they were the go-to trainer as a kid - they used to be cheap and hard wearing, the perfect trainer for raving because they come up nice when you throw them in the washing machine.

I remember first hearing about the Reeboks with the fivers in the bottom in the playground at school when I was about thirteen. There was a lad in the year above whose dad played for Colchester United and he would wear a green ice ripple and red ice ripple together but no one had ice soles with fivers in, I've never seen them. I heard about them in the playground but a lot of shit gets chatted at school.

I've got friends who say they had a pair, that swear they know someone who did; my mate once told me that their cousin cut the ice sole open, took the fiver out and used it at the shops, but I don't believe that for a minute.

After years of swapping stories and cross referencing mates' testimonies, there were more questions than answers. I spoke to someone from Reebok who was adamant that they were a legitimate JD SMU release, but they didn't have any records or photos to prove it. After that, someone from JD told me they were manufactured but were never actually released because of some legal issue.

A few years back, my friend Jackson sent me a page from his cousin Oliver Payne's exhibition in 2005. He referenced the same rumour by cutting open some ice soles, putting fivers in the bottom and then displaying them on the photocopier. If you hit the button, you got a photocopy of the five pound ice soles.

"I first heard about them after overhearing some kids talking about them on a bus in Kingston," says Oliver. "Then I went down to the Clapham Junction JD where a guy told us that the prototypes did exist but could never be put into production due to some business about destroying tender and the image of the queen."

Gary Warnett is the only person I've ever seen reference the trainers in writing - he wrote something on Crooked Tongues and I couldn't believe he knew about the old wives' tale too. We never met but he was the first person to ever write about Sports Banger. I had so many questions for him - RIP.

I somehow ended up speaking to official trainer don Mubi Ali who reckons:

"The five pound Reeboks existed 100%. They were released in tiny numbers - maybe one hundred pairs - to only a handful of JD Sports in 95-96. I think I saw them in the Croydon one. I've been trying to find images and people with them for ages, but no luck. There's absolutely no record of them in the Reebok archives. All I know is that I 100% remember holding them in my hands."

Fivers make the world go round - if you've got a fiver in your pocket, you'll probably be alright. They've always found a way into my work; years ago I got a laminate machine and laminated loads of fivers then sold them for £5 on the domain reeboklondon.com (which I bought for a fiver) - it was a loss leader because of postage. Everyone can relate to fivers, they come and go.

When I collaborated with Slazenger I got to make the Slazenger Banger Classic and put fivers in the ice soles. There's fifty pairs out there with real money in. The rest are black and white printed. I still can't believe I got the ok from The Bank of England to step on the Queen's face. That was my direct interpretation of the rumour, myth, whatever you want to call it. I don't think I'll ever really get to the bottom of it. I won't be satisfied until I have a pair in my hands. Ideally in a size eight.

SEARCHING FOR THE £5 ICE SOLES

WRITTEN BY JONNY BANGER
INTRODUCTION BY SARA MERKENSCHLAGER
SHOT BY JOE CRUZ

CLASSICS NEVER DIE

Previous, left: An original 1990s Reebok Classic shoebox.
Previous, right: An original advert for Reebok Classic Ice soles.
Opposite: A piece written by Jonny in *LAW* magazine, issue 10, 2021.
Above: An archive pair of the 'Slazenger Banger Classics' with real
£5 notes in the soles.

VIVA LA BOOTLEG

CLASSICS NEVER DIE

THE WORLD'S RAREST TRAINERS (?). Sports Banger released 20 pairs of the 'Slazenger Banger Classics' in black with real £10 notes in the soles. One pair was made using £50 notes, which had to be folded to fit.

OOH AHH SHANGRI-LA. Sports Banger was invited by the Shangri-La crew to open Glastonbury 2022. Hosted by MCs Chunky and Jonny Banger, Mega Rave 5 featured Tasha, Mella Dee, Klose One, Smash Hits, Yung Singh, Temujin and Warner.

On the day that Boris Johnson became prime minister, a dozen activist groups came together to organize a Fck Govt, Fck Boris protest march to Downing Street (coincidentally, exactly 25 years after the major Kill the Bill demonstration against the Criminal Justice and Public Order Act 1994).

Get ready to hack the system!
Hack the planet!
(Get inside?)
Hackers unite!
Hackers unite!
Hack the planet!
Now hack the planet!
Now hack the system!
Get ready to hack the system!
Get ready to hack the planet!
Hack the planet!
Get ready
Acid Burn
Crash Override

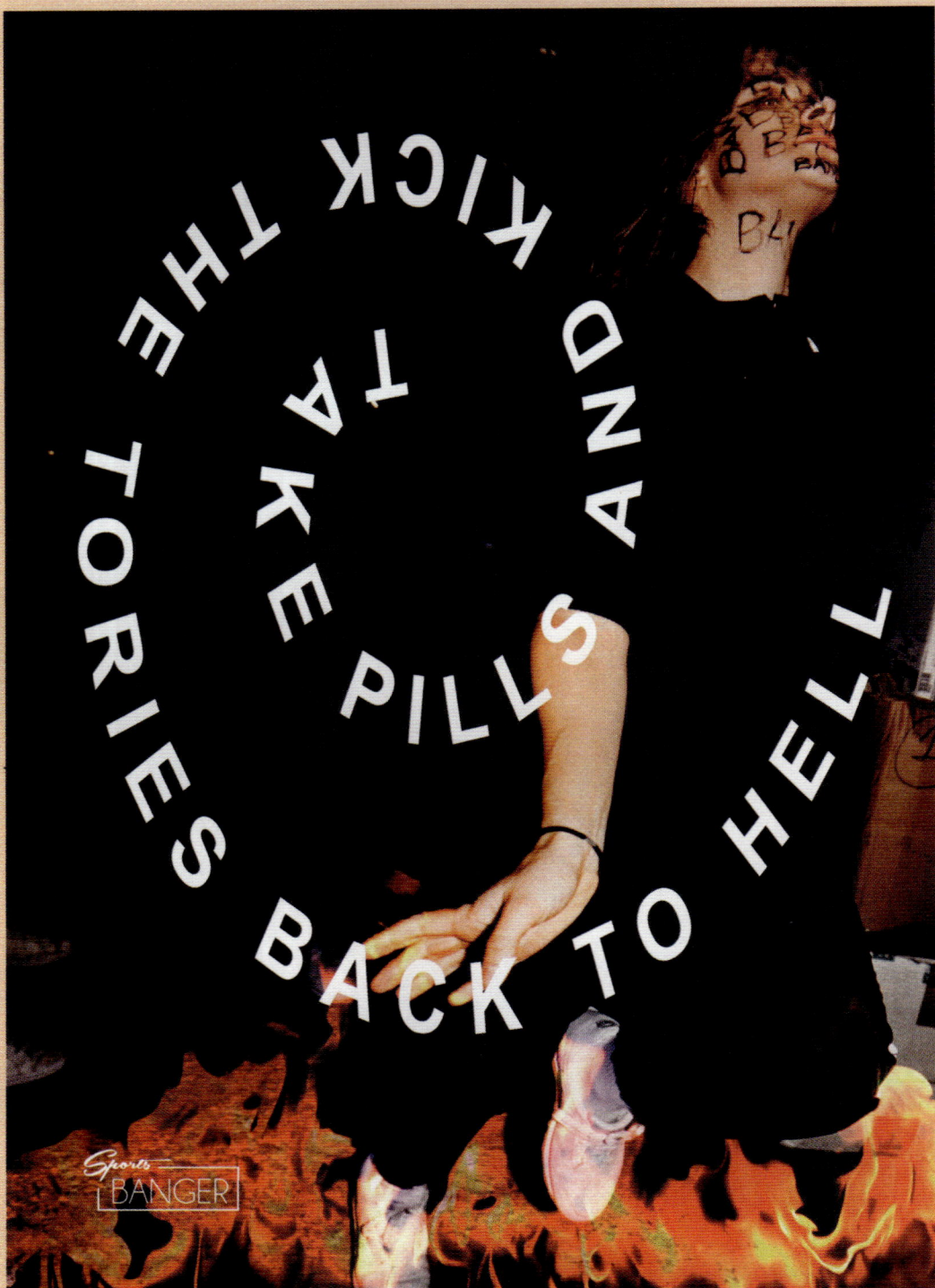

'TAKE PILLS AND KICK THE TORIES BACK TO HELL'
JONNY BANGER

WHO LIES BEHIND THE UNION BASHERS?

FLEET STREET

civil liberties
civil libertie0
civil liberti0f
civil libertOf
civil liberOffi
civil libeOffic
civil libOffici
civil liOfficia
civil lOfficial
civil Officials
civiOfficial S
civOfficial Se
ciOfficial Sec
cOfficial Secr
Official Secre

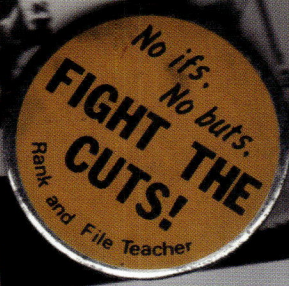

BOOKS ARE WEAPONS

Britannia waives the rules

STOP THIS WARMONGER! THATCHER OUT!

The Thatcher Bag is full of tricks

MERRY CHRISTMAS FROM ONE OF THE 3·1 MILLION UNEMPLOYED

* This figure is liable to be increased without prior warning.

Daily Mail
LABOUR'S DIRTY DOZEN

MAGGIE'S THE ONE

SHE'S DONE IT!

EXPRESS
PRIME MINISTER MAGGIE

The Sun
The first day of the rest of our lives

VOTE TORY THIS TIME

EXPRESS
DON'T FORGET LAST WINTER

No ifs, No buts, FIGHT THE CUTS! Rank and File Teacher

10

Opposite: TAKE PILLS AND KICK THE TORIES BACK TO HELL.
A Sports Banger poster in *Tissue* magazine, 2019.
Above: Patrick Matthews, a photographer who Jonny met on
Instagram, donated political ephemera to the studio from his
late mum's personal collection.

Woman told her 'F*** Boris' T-shirt is illegal by police

Police

Police apologise to woman told to cover up anti-Boris Johnson T-shirt

You can now get Sports Banger's 'Fuck Boris' t-shirt in Animal Crossing

Label

Well, that's what they say in the fashion business, anyway.

A woman wearing the 'FUCK BORIS' T-shirt was stopped by police after a BLM march in central London and told to cover up under the Section 5 Public Order Act. The march was the most inspirational I've ever been to. Handmade signs on scraps of cardboard were everywhere, made by the young people of London. The police kettled the kids at the end of the march, held them in groups, demanded details and wouldn't let them get the last train home. The white middle-class woman wearing the T-shirt got an apology from the Met police, the Black kids didn't.

Clockwise from top left: Headlines from national news websites; bootlegged T-shirts at a London protest; friend of Sports Banger, Mandeep, wears a '*FUCK BORIS*' T-shirt at Notting Hill Carnival, 2019; the T-shirt was briefly made available by a fan using the online social simulation game *Animal Crossing* (it was quickly removed for breaching community guidelines).

THANKYOU SO MUCH! I'm Olivia's friend who reached out to see if she knew anyone who had hi viz for us. You are a star!! A visible legal observer presence makes a huge difference.

🧡

Pleasure

Legal for the people
🧡

Knew my hoard of hi viz would come in useful one day
🧡

Hahaha either an emergency rave or this

I fucking hate this T-shirt.

Before we made it, we were in the lead-up to doing our first-ever takeover at Glastonbury in 2019, and we had hundreds of Mega Rave T-shirts ready to go. The Conservatives were in the process of voting in their new leader after Theresa May fucked it. Boris Johnson is an arsehole and a liar, and we all knew he was going to be the next prime minister. The vibe in the UK was fuck that guy. Right before Glastonbury, we sent the Mega Rave T-shirts back to the printers to have 'FUCK BORIS' printed on the back. Keep the rave close to your heart and turn your back on Boris. We threw about 300 T-shirts into the crowd at the rave.

There was a huge demand for these T-shirts as soon as Boris became PM. We didn't want to sell them (having hundreds of Boris T-shirts lying around your studio is not a vibe), so we gave away the file to anyone who wanted it, and people printed their own.

Shortly after he came into power, we went to a protest march in central London. It was organized by a load of young people, and we gave the last of the tees away. Next thing, I see someone selling 'FUCK BORIS' T-shirts – dangling them off a long pole in the middle of the march. I went up to the car running the sales, and the guy casually leaned out the window with his stash of 'FUCK BORIS' tees behind him and said, 'alright, Jonny'. I laughed, like, what the fuck are you doing? I said make your own, but this is taking the piss. He assured me that he was donating all the cash to charity.

Above left: Sports Banger printed hi-vis vests with the words 'Legal Observer' and donated them to grass roots activist legal support group Green & Black Cross.
Above centre: An Instagram message asking for help with an upcoming protest.
Below: A couple sport the original 'FUCK BORIS' T-shirts at the Fck Govt, Fck Boris protest.

VIVA LA BOOTLEG

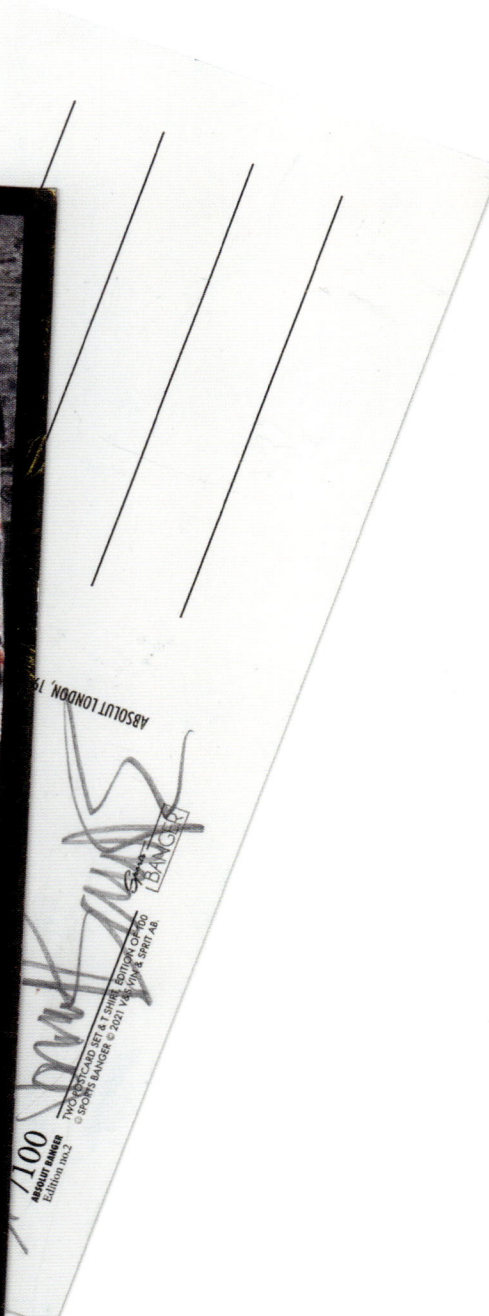

Above: A promotional postcard by Absolut Vodka, 1996. The campaign used iconic images from major cities around the world.
Below: Sports Banger's bootleg postcard from 2021 featuring the disgraced Prime Minister, Boris Johnson.
Opposite, above: Make your own anarchist sock balaclava.
Opposite, below: A Sports Banger poster from 2017.

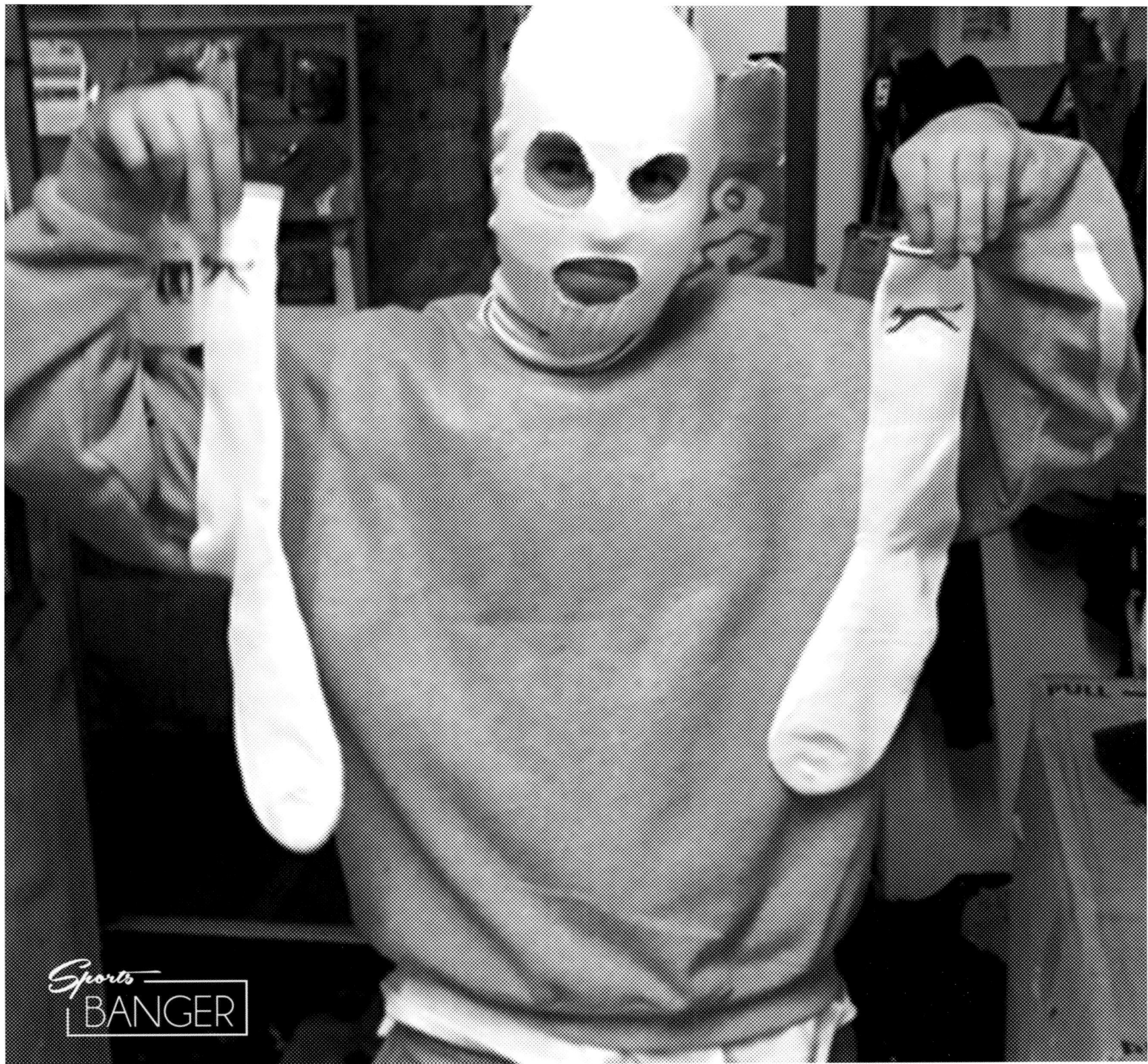

Sports BANGER

SNATCH SQUAD
1. Snatch Squad Ready

2. Line opens, squad goes through, takes prisoner, and returns through line.

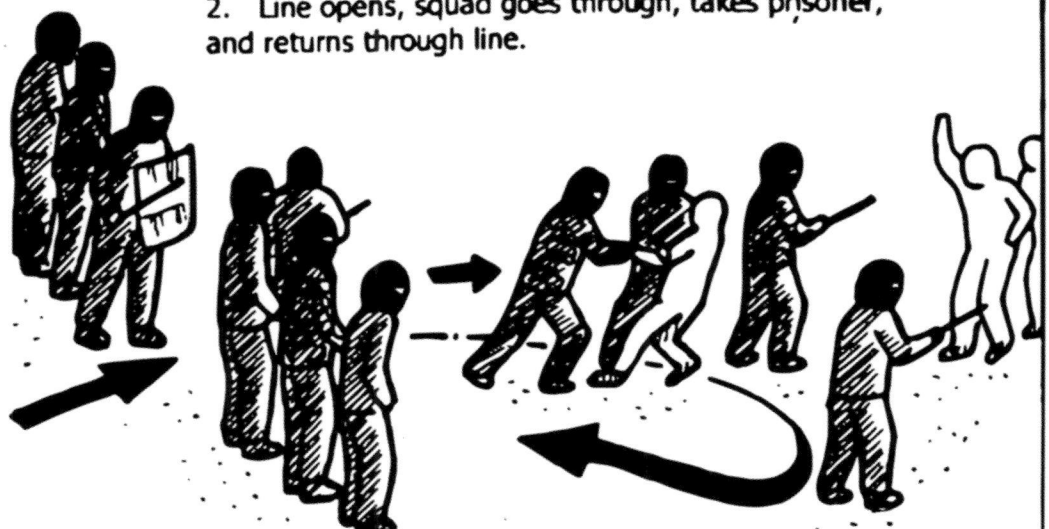

Celebrated fashion designer, Jonny Banger created one of the most powerful pieces in the show. Three shrouded figures wearing Union Jack cowls. His fashion house and label *Sports Banger* has become a launch pad for broader statement-making. He has made incalculable moves to level up London, from giving out free school meals to championing the NHS. When asked what his take is on the importance of Pigeon Park and artists having a message, Jonny closes things up: "My piece is called The Three Stooges. I've had the flags for about five years. I put these together to comment on the country, you know, pretty fucking bleak, hang your head in shame, past, present and future. The Holy Trinity. There are a million things I could say about it. As an artist, for me, if it doesn't do anything or doesn't say anything, and if it's not for anyone, then what's the point really? I want my work to either make people smile or piss people off. All the emotions! If you've got a platform and can say something, then do. I think a lot of people have got platforms, and they can say something but they don't. Being a raver, there's a duty of care. It doesn't stop when you're not in a rave. Bring it into your day-to-day, and I feel that's what Pigeon Park is doing as well." ʜ

UK Civil Service ✓
@UKCivilService

Arrogant and offensive.

Can you imagine having to work with these truth twisters?

5:53 PM · May 24, 2020 · Twitter for iPhone

11.7K Retweets   **16.3K** Likes

Cabinet Office ✓
@cabinetofficeuk

An unauthorised tweet was posted on a government channel this evening. The post has been removed and we are investigating the matter.

6:47 PM · May 24, 2020 · Twitter Web App

4.2K Retweets   **16K** Likes

A civil servant tweeted 'Arrogant and offensive' from the UK Civil Service account right after Boris Johnson gave a press briefing defending Dominic Cummings. The twat drove all the way from London to Durham in the middle of lockdown. An hour later, the Cabinet Office posted: 'An unauthorized tweet was posted on a government channel this evening. The post has been removed and we are investigating the matter.' We put the 'Twisted' T-shirt out and the next day got a friendly message from the legend who wrote it.

After all the clapping and praise that NHS workers received during the pandemic, the government proposed a 1% pay rise following a pay dispute. The offer was seen as a disgrace and a real kick in the face. We made this T-shirt in response and gave it away for free to any NHS worker who wanted one. Nurses wore them under their scrubs to work as a quiet fuck you.

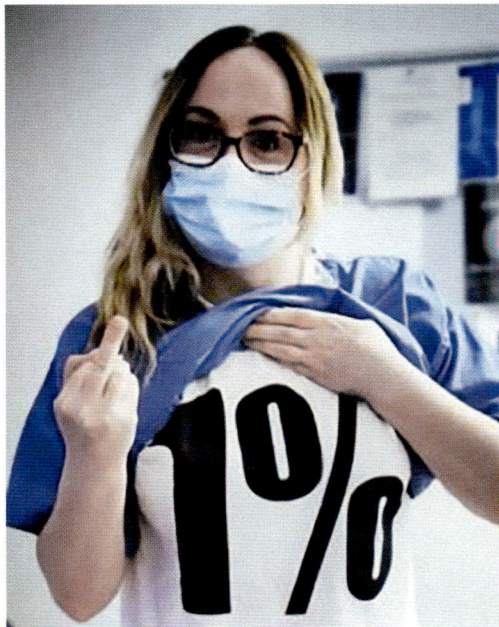

Opposite: Huck magazine piece featuring Jonny's sculpture, 'The Three Stooges', part of the 2022 group show 'Pigeon Park 2'. The show opened in London the week the Queen died.
Clockwise from top left: The infamous rogue tweet from the Civil Service Twitter account and the follow-up tweet from the Cabinet Office; John John, a rigging technician from Scotland, wears the Sports Banger 'Twisted' T-shirt; an NHS nurse in a '1%' T-shirt.

Our second show was a tear-down of popular culture. We had a pissed-off town crier, unpaid nurses, sexy bunnies, a cross-dressing judge, vindicated celebrities, young phone thieves, a homage to Thierry Mugler and a tribute to Keith Flint from The Prodigy. Using classic Banger T-shirts as our reference points, FREE TULISA became a knock-off Chanel twin-set, and the headline T-shirts became gallows-style billboards. There were so many crazily layered stabs at stupidity and hypocrisy in our society, you'd do well to unpick them all.

174

Previous, left: Jonny walks with youth worker Big Lew down the runway in a pre-show rehearsal for 'Pop Culture is Trash'.
Previous, right: Ballroom dancer Karteer captured backstage by artist Joe Cruz.

Clockwise from top left: 'YOU'RE ALL FUCKING RESPONSIBLE, ALL OF YA!' Dressed as the Banger 'town crier', photographer Gavin Watson (known for his documentary photographs of early British skins, punks and rave culture) opens 'Pop Culture is Trash'; ~~contemplates~~ contemplates how he got roped into walking the Sports Banger runway again; Kash Doll in her first look waits backstage.

POP CULTURE IS TRASH

Model Ami Benton (interviewed on page 298) with HERAS fence
face mask and body cage.

VIVA LA BOOTLEG

POP CULTURE IS TRASH

Above: Every runway look from 'Pop Culture is Trash'. The show was both a takedown and a celebration of everything in the Sports Banger universe.
Overleaf, left and right: Captured by artist Joe Cruz: An 'English Muffin' printed bathing suit completes one of the many Nigella Lawson tribute looks on the runway, and an NHS print on a velour cropped top.

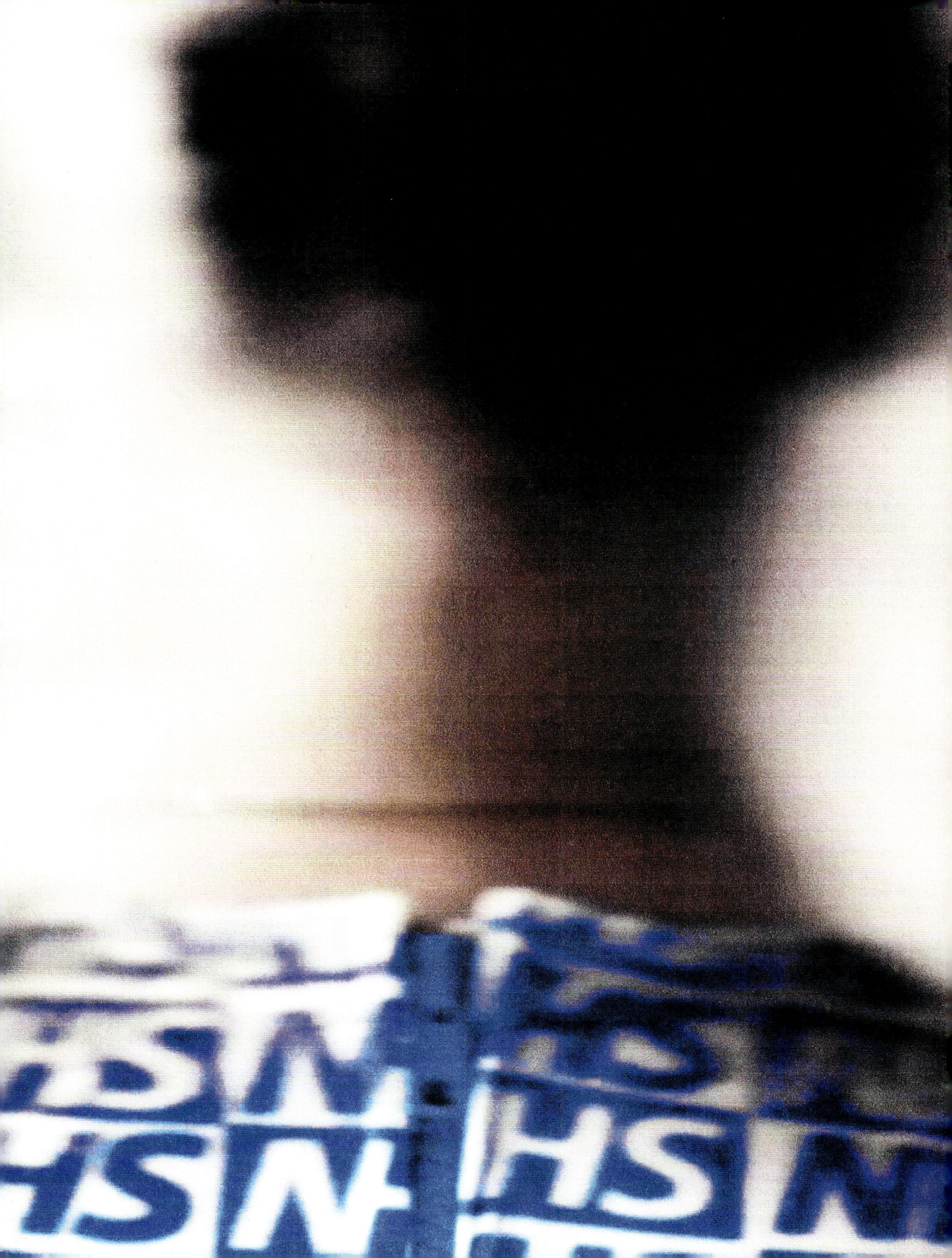

Above: Made by Tottenham Textiles, a gilet constructed from hundreds of mini gilets.
Opposite: Rapper Black Josh snatches phones from the front row. His outfit was made using bootlegged Moncler children's puffer jackets bought from a counterfeit dealer in Manchester.

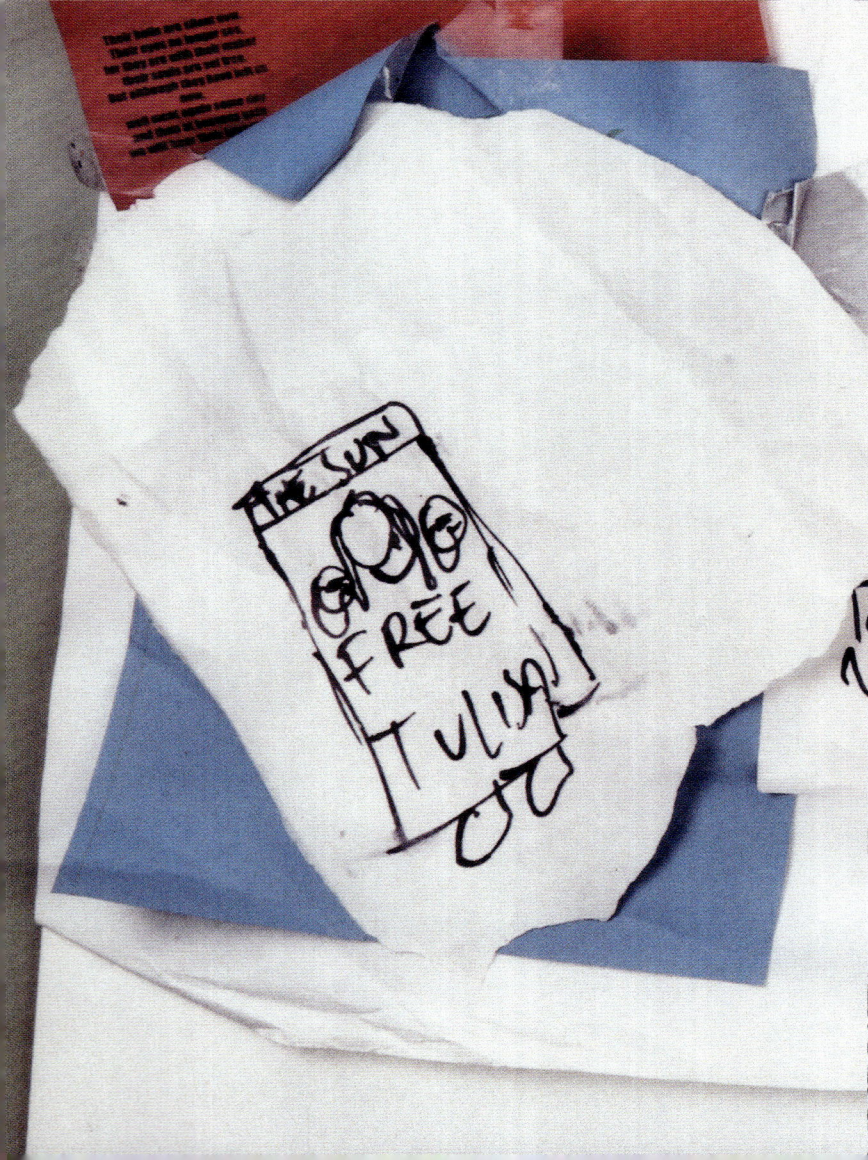

Opposite, clockwise from top left: A sketchbook page with skirt suit references; Eloise Smyth in the 'FREE' skirt suit with photographer Will Robson-Scott; a gallows reference image; the original sketch for Banger's tabloid newspaper sandwich board gallows.
Above: A Chanel-inspired fuchsia skirt suit with appliquéd 'FREE' patches and silk lining.

VIVA LA BOOTLEG

Above: A Banger corset made from studio scraps by designer
Max Allen (interviewed on page 232).
Opposite: Emanuelle Soum on the runway in the full Sports Banger
x Max Allen look.

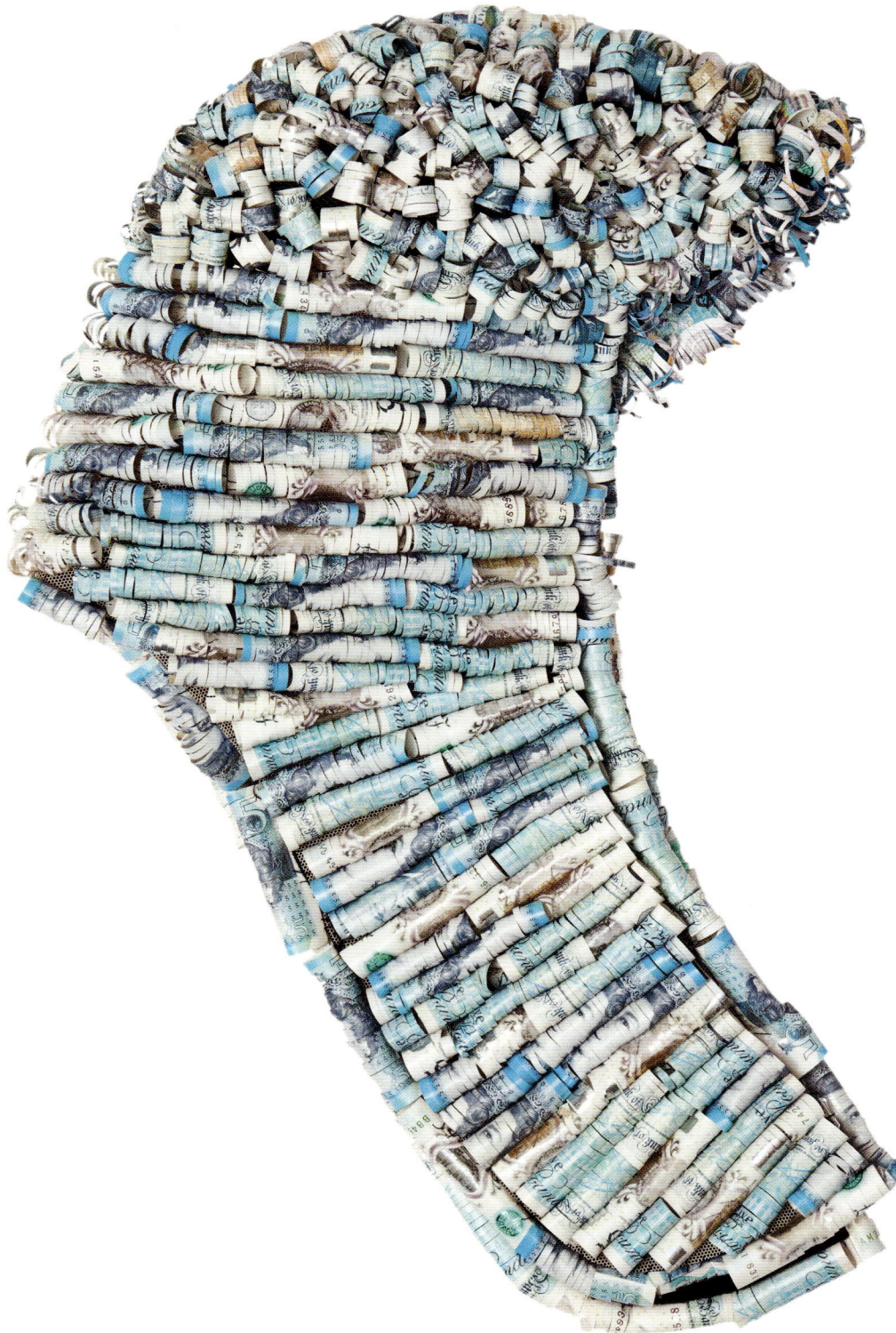

VIVA LA BOOTLEG

Above: A judge's wig made entirely from £5 notes by designer Fred Butler.
Opposite, clockwise from top left: Drag performer Diane Chorley walks
the runway as 'the judge'; the 'Queen of Croydon' Kate Moss silk shirt
and the 'GIZ A FIVER' velour skirt worn by Chorley; the cover image from
a 1974 issue of *Mole Express*, a Mancunian underground publication first
released in 1970; the cut and rolled £5 notes used to make the judge's wig.

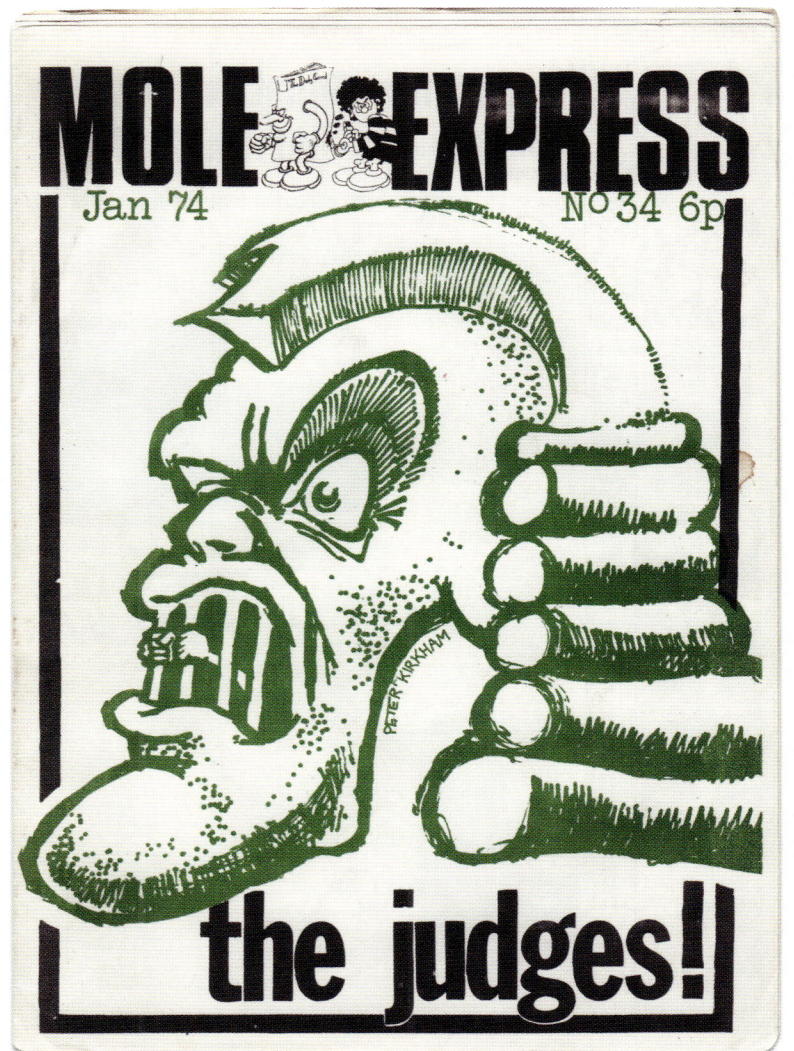

MOLE EXPRESS

Jan '74   No 34 6p

the judges!

Shinny2piece
trackSuit
have any record of
ment of Health
Department
of Health &
Social Care
Hi Jonny,
We've not met, but I've bought a few things from your site in the past.
Wearing my NHS tee on way to work I got an 'oi oi Sportsbanger!', shouted at me from two girls driving a white van, and then a copper saying nice tee mate
I also have another order. You got any Largies left?
These trade marks
3-LOOK
5-LOOK
Team
Nigela
2piece
Nigel
phone thieves
Heras
corset
Heras
dufflebag
Umberella's
Golf Sale
Gloves
Towel
Swimwear
Sexy
Wiggly
① Scrubs
② repeat pattern
BODY SNATCH - JUST 4 U LONDON
CHUNKY
?
STEVE.
CHUNKY
colonial revolution
KARTER MUGLER
NAGATO MUGLER
CHACHOU MUGLER
Vogues
BBBagdress

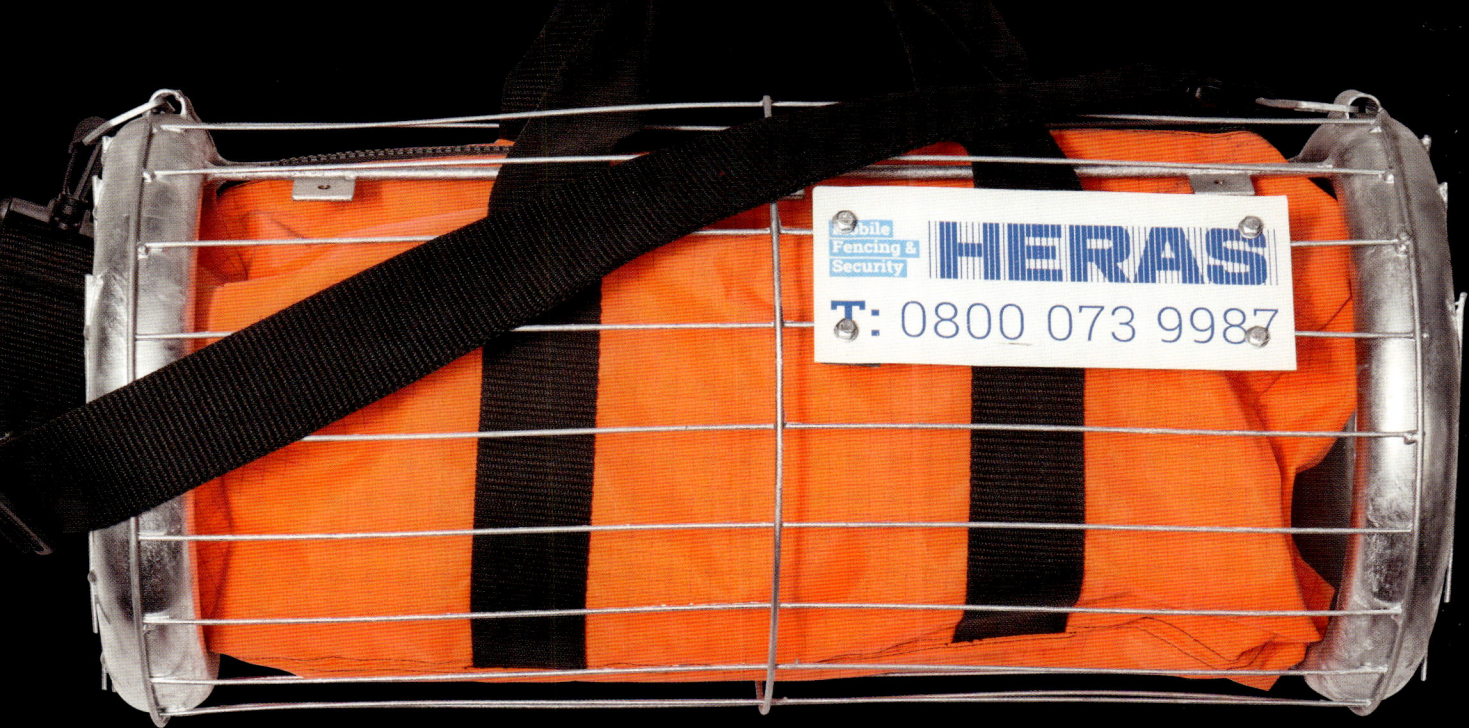

Opposite: Details from the original show plans and casting boards.
Inset, top left: Sports Banger's nurse's scrubs, printed with
letters from doctors and nurses alongside legal warnings from the
Department of Health & Social Care. *Inset, centre:* Artist Celine
Celeesi strikes a pose at fittings for the full NHS look.
Above: Duffle bags made by metal worker Jack Hanson using cut,
rolled and welded HERAS fence panels.

'It was a super fun evening that made me feel young at heart, especially the dancers from London and Paris!'

— Irene Bridges (aka Jonny's nan), 97 years young.

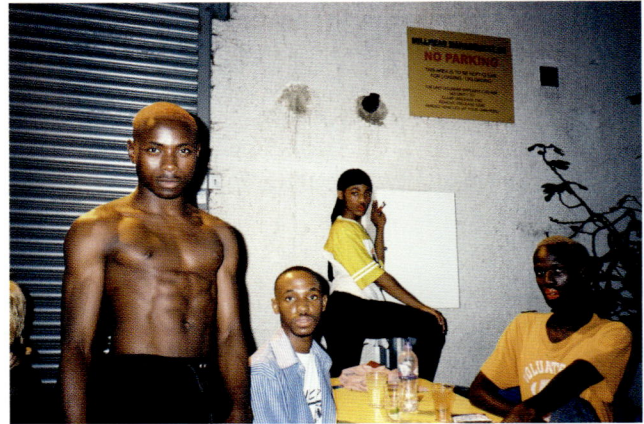

Above: Jonny and his nan Irene at the 'Pop Culture is Trash' runway show. Rolls-Royce kindly organized a driver and a Phantom *(opposite)* to take her home afterwards.
Below, left: A trashy ballroom nod to Thierry Mugler with bin-lid hats and shiny bin bag bolero's on the runway.
Below, right: Performers Taboo, Slim, Seryah and Webster outside the venue.

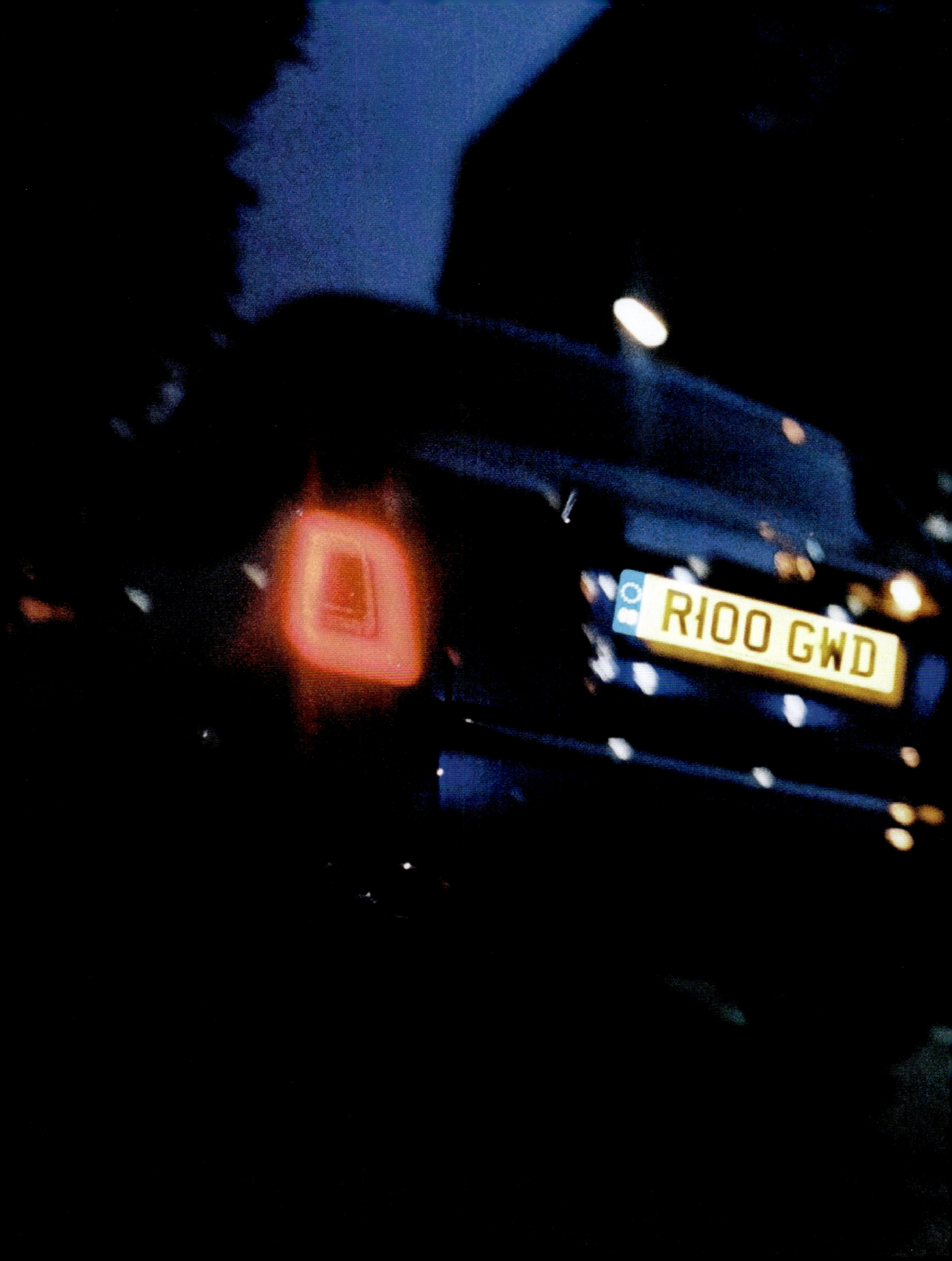
R100 GWD

VOGUE

REVIEW

Sports Banger:
Spring 2020 Ready-to-Wear'

Luke Leitch
Vogue, 17 September 2019

When a model blinded by the mask of his hot-pink recycled-pool-toy hazmat suit veers off the runway and hits your laptop with a wheel-wide replica ecstasy pill, well then that's quite an unusual fashion show. The same applies when the photographer Gavin Watson – of Skins and Raving '89 – opens it dressed as a town crier decrying modern culture in the sweariest of terms, or when the comedian Diane Chorley struts past in a top printed with Kate Moss as the queen and a judge's wig made of five-pound notes created by sometime Gaga and Björk collaborator Fred Butler. It is also surprising when the models snatch iPhones from the front row while wearing outfits made from reassembled child-size Moncler jackets and tiny, doll-size leather trousers and jackets. And as for the voguing section ...

This was the second show from Sports Banger, a fast-growing guerilla collective effort whose hub is the Tottenham-based bootlegger Jonny Banger. Held in a very North London industrial unit late on Sunday night, it collided politics, music, hedonism, humour, and fashion to uproarious effect. The product was a show that felt akin to, say, going to Blitz, the Wag, Kinky Gerlinky, Taboo, or Soul II Soul way back when, or maybe spitting and snarling with the punks in the '70s, or losing your sweet mind at Shoom in '88 or Castlemorton in '92: Something was happening here.

The early part of the show used a big bloke wearing billboards to signal four past themes in Banger's guise of bootleg T-shirt designer. British tabloid targets Tulisa Contostavlos and Nigella Lawson, both past subjects of supportive Banger T-shirts, were two of them: a velour tracksuit printed in tabloid splashes (front-page stories) screaming about Lawson made by Banger's neighbour Luis Tottenham Textiles was especially funny. The Nike Swoosh × NHS design in support of British health-service workers featured a dress worn by Natalie Amoatin, who was cured of sickle cell disease at age 14 by pioneering NHS treatment. A Tottenham-based NHS midwife, who kept her mask on for anonymity, wore scrubs printed with legal letters that Banger received complaining of copyright infringement as well as letters from NHS workers in support. There were also designs casting F-based judgment on Prime Minister Boris Johnson and the policies of his Conservative Party.

After the politics, an interlude: Ballroom scene dancers from Paris and London emerged in trash-bag blouses and trash-can hats (the collection was entitled Pop Culture Is Trash) and did their thing un-be-lievably to the accompaniment of an MC named Taboo, choreographed by Emanuelle Soum, aka Elle Miyake Mugler. Banger said afterwards: 'Often when they do voguing in fashion, it is white females. We wanted to rep what it is; butch black gay men femme.' In between some raucously worn high-camp dresses, some made of pool toys and studio scraps, others referencing Thierry Mugler and Fantazia raves, there was the phone-snatching Moncler section as modelled by rappers Black Josh and Chunky. Banger said the point was to highlight the wave of London 'moped muggings,' in which young kids steal phones to buy designer clothes. The Moncler look, made of counterfeits he'd bought in Manchester, was quite genius.

All through the show, the sound system at the end of the runway was doing its thing. My bench was bouncing. And at the end of it, an audience that had laughed and screamed throughout the show screamed for more. Outside, Banger name-checked the designers – Maria Bracher, Max Allen and Ancuta Sarca – who had helped him build this hilarious and excellent show. He said: 'This has been the work of a lot of people who've come together and had fun. And we're starting to think let's just focus on the fashion, and try and build a team, and do wages and make a fashion house – and use it to smash heads together.'

POP CULTURE IS TRASH   Meme Gold at the end of the runway.

MODERN METAL IS TRASH
by Nathalie Khan

The opening scene of William Klein's film *Who Are You, Polly Maggoo?* (1966) features models walking awkwardly down a runway wearing grotesquely tailored aluminium sheet dresses. Based on the director's personal experience of the fashion industry in Paris and New York, the film satirically mocks the fashion system and sends up fashion's absurdity and excess. Fashion history has shown that such parody rarely has a long-lasting effect, as the film predates Paco Rabanne's now iconic, 'unwearable' metal dresses. Just like Klein's attitude towards fashion is implied through the absurdist costumes in this scene, metal continues to have a subversive status as a material in fashion.

The first time I witnessed a Sports Banger runway show was in 2019, when I attended 'Pop Culture is Trash' with my son Conrad. Having met Jonny at a panel discussion on hype a few years earlier, I was familiar with the way Banger uses bootlegging as a form of agency – appropriating logos to ironically engage with the commodification of streetwear culture. So, I expected some parodic anti-fashion statements, but what I found went beyond mockery. The show was a loud and excessive spectacle celebrating community and collaboration. Grime legend Marcus Nasty and ballroom MC Taboo walked the runway in floor-length black rubber coats, performer Diane Chorley donned a judge's wig made entirely of five-pound notes, and models wore sportswear printed with bold graphics that breached copyright while promoting the NHS. The show also featured another bootlegged brand from outside fashion whose logo Banger appropriated: the metal fencing company, HERAS, whose portable fences hem in crowds at music festivals and raves.

Sports Banger has a very specific way of elevating signs that do not have any association with fashion. With its use of the HERAS brand, Sports Banger goes beyond taking a logo out of context, and turns the material itself into a point of reference. In the lead up to the show, Jonny put a call-out on social media, encouraging people to steal the branded metal plates from HERAS fences and send them into the Banger studio. Over the next few weeks, he received hundreds in the post. He then enlisted the metal artist and maker Jack Hanson to shape the HERAS plates into accessories and garments.

One of the first items Hanson created for Banger was a HERAS duffel bag* – made using actual metal fence posts, rolled and welded into a cage-like cover that holds a fabric bag compartment, with a HERAS metal plate attached to one side. The bags appeared at the 'Pop Culture is Trash' show – simultaneously completing a look and becoming an object as the model spontaneously set it down on the floor and emphatically rolled it down the length of the runway. Seeing it hurtling ahead of the model, heading straight for the audience, made the former fencing appear at once like a toy as well as a kind of weapon. In this moment, the bag no longer seemed like a consumer good, as its materiality seemed to set it free from commodification.

Over time, Sports Banger's use of HERAS's logo and its metal plates has grown beyond any reference to fencing, crowd management, and even the original hard material. Since 'Pop Culture is Trash', HERAS has become a kind of emblem for Sports Banger. It has become the name of Sports Banger's record label, and its metal plates have been used to make or decorate a record box, a corset, earrings and, perhaps most notably, metal roses**, which all appeared in 'The People Deserve Beauty'. HERAS is now so frequently used by Banger that shaping branded metal fence plates into roses makes perfect sense. In fact, appropriating an industrial, mass-produced material that is loosely connected to rave and festival culture and creating something beautiful out of it may be at the core of the Sports Banger ethos.

William Klein's metal dresses in *Who Are You, Polly Maggoo?* were about socio-economic interactions and systems. For Banger, the HERAS metal becomes a post-industrial statement on fashion that breaks with its own material connotations. By turning metal fence plates into roses, the material takes the appearance of something else – it becomes a sign of collaboration.

In a way, I was expecting something far more farcical when I started searching the 'Pop Culture is Trash' show for parody. Those who have seen the shows will agree they contain plenty of spectacle, but none of it is trash.

* Pictured on page 191.
** Pictured on page 256.

Made for our second collab with Slazenger, the pigeon tracksuit is a homage to Birmingham Roller pigeons. They stop flying mid-air and just tumble; it's beautiful to watch. My grandad was a pigeon fancier; he raced pigeons and had a few rollers. I've always been obsessed. It's in my blood.

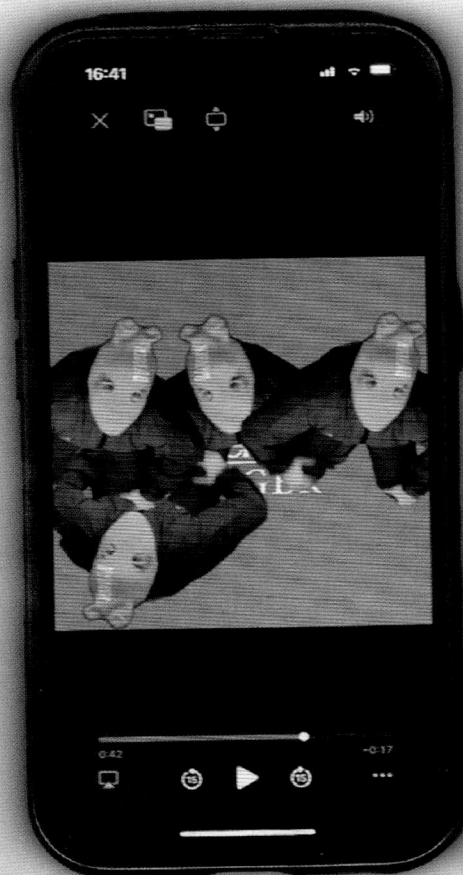

Previous, left: Pigeon tracksuit lovers secure the bag.
Previous, right: Stills from the pigeon tracksuit promo video by artist Leila Ziu, featuring Birmingham Roller pigeons and soundtracked to Birmingham bassline.
Above: An image from a shoot for Slazenger Banger's second collection inspired by the lyric 'I just like to walk with my head in the clouds' from Baby D's 1996 track 'Day Dreaming'.

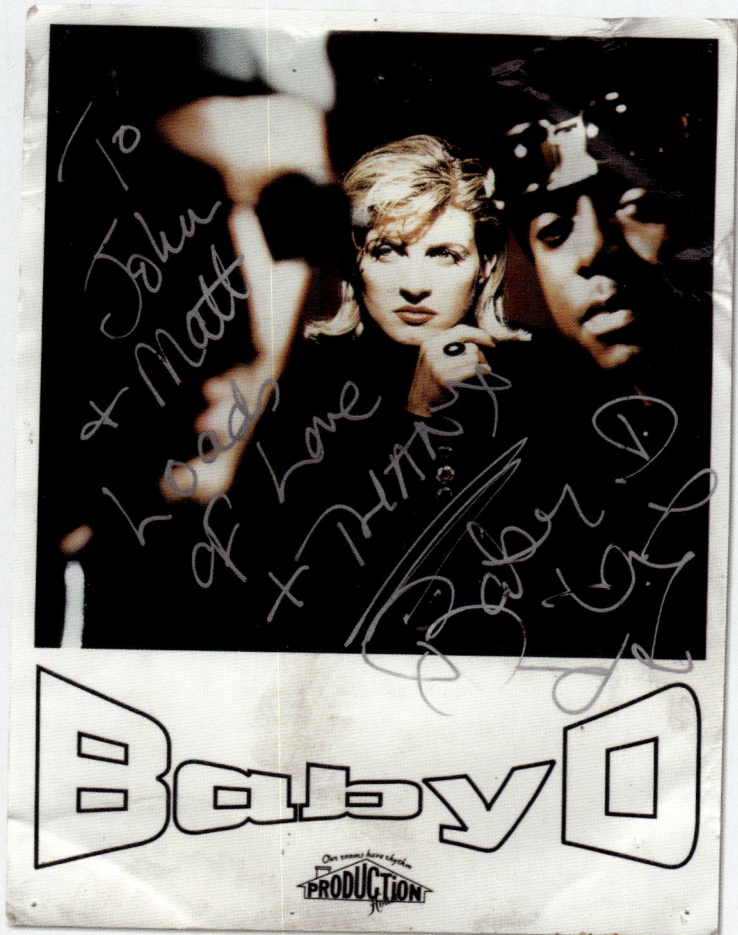

Baby D

To John + Matt Loads of Love + THANX ♥ Baby D

Our sounds have rhythm
PRODUCTION

Adoration of the Pigeon

① PIGEONS MATE FOR LIFE. BOTH PARENTS MAKE MILK AND TAKE TURNS FEEDING THEIR BABIES.

② PIGEONS DO NOT CARRY DISEASES. THIS IS A MONEY MAKING LIE TOLD BY GREEDY EXTERMINATORS.

③ PIGEONS HAVE REMARKABLE HOMING INSTINCTS. THE LOCATION WHERE THE BIRD IS BORN IS WHERE HE WILL SPEND HIS ENTIRE LIFE; SAY HELLO TO YOUR RESIDENT PIGEONS.

④ PIGEONS ARE HIGHLY INTELLIGENT. THEY PASS THE 'MIRROR TEST' ABLE TO RECOGNIZE HIS REFLECTION. IS ONLY ONE OF 6 SPECIES, AND THE ONLY NON-MAMMAL TO DO SO.

⑤ THE REASON YOU DON'T EVER SEE BABY PIGEONS IS BECAUSE UNLIKE MOST BIRDS THAT FLEDGE AT 2/3 WEEKS, PIGEONS FLEDGE AT 2 MONTHS. BY THEN THE BABY IS FULLY FEATHERED AND LOOKS LIKE A GRUMPY OLD MAN WITH BIG BEAKS.

⑥ A FULL GROWN PIGEON HAS ABOUT 10,000 FEATHERS.

⑦ PIGEONS HAVE BEEN KNOWN TO LIVE UP TO 30 YEARS. CITY BIRDS ONYL LIVE UP TO UPTO 2 YEARS BECAUSE THE LACK OF FOOD AND CLEAN WATER.

⑧ BIG CITIES DO NOT PROVIDE BIRD BATHS OR CLEAN WATER FOR THE WILDLIFE. PIGEONS LOVE TO BATHE AND PREEN. THEIR FAVORITE FOOD IS CRUSHED PEANUTS AND HIGH QUALITY BIRDSEED. MY FAVORITE THING TO DO IS SIT ON A PARK BENCH AND FEED THE BIRDS. IT IS FUN TO GET TO KNOW THEM.

⑨ LOOK AT PIGEONS THE SAME WAY THAT YOU WOULD LOOK AT A ROSE OR A BED OF WILD FLOWERS. THEY ARE BEAUTIFUL AND UNIQUE WITH EACH ONE BEING DIFFERENT FROM THE REST. It IS A PRIVILEGE TO HAVE THEM HERE.

MOTHERPIGEONBROOKLYN - INSTAGRAM

MOTHERPIGEONBROOKLYN.COM

How to find Peace

The News, September

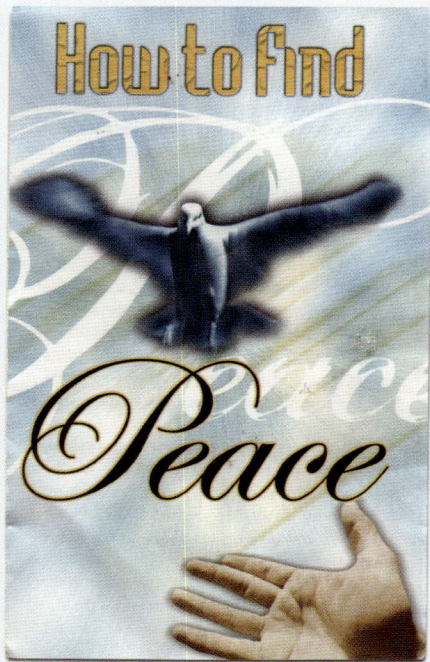

Birds of a feather flock together

RETIRED RAE mechanic Billy Wright has friends all over the country – thanks to the pigeons which live at the bottom of his garden.

For Mr. Wright, of Connaught Road, Fleet, is constantly in touch with many of the hundreds of people who share his special interest.

Mr. Wright has been a pigeon fancier for over 40 years and now boasts a beautiful flock of 30 Belgian birds.

Half the pigeons are kept for breeding and the others are used for racing.

During the racing season, between April and July, Mr. Wright races the birds at least once a week with a local club.

He has many certificates, trophies and medals to prove that his pigeons have a winning streak.

During the war he was a special police constable and a member of the celebrated National Pigeon Service.

The Service men and their birds formed an important communications system, especially well known for their work carrying messages in and out of occupied France.

Mr. Wright's pigeons did not go so far as France in those days, but instead carried messages between the south of England and the Isle of Wight.

He explained: "We had contacts with other pigeon fanciers on the Isle of Wight. We used to exchange half a dozen pigeons each, so that they could be sent back home with messages when required."

Opportunity

Apart from keeping pigeons for his own enjoyment, Mr. Wright is also the man Fleet

people turn to when any lost or "stray" birds are found in the district.

It is his duty to find out who the pigeon belongs to and contact the owner to inform him of his bird's whereabouts.

It is usually just a simple task. Attached to each racing pigeon's leg is a special number.

The number is also listed in a central register held by the Royal Pigeon Racing Association, with the owner's name and address.

Mr. Wright said: "People are always finding lost or exhausted pigeons in their gardens, and they often fly into my own loft.

"Many of them come from

up north and I have had pigeons from Ireland and Scotland which have been found around here.

"The lost birds are usually very young and have not been very used to long distance flying.

"They have often been liberated down south and got

But training is both time consuming and expensive when all the special food, identification tags, time clocks and other equipment is taken into account.

To begin with young birds are taken just a short distance away from their home, but the distance increases with their

age. It can take up to six months before a pigeon is ready for a long flight. During an average journey an adult bird can fly at an amazing speed of 50 mph.

Contact with other pigeon fanciers is made almost every week.

Some of his best adult birds have been liberated in Spain and have flown back to Fleet without any problems.

caught in bad weat...

course my pigeons sometimes as well... another fancier co... say it has been from...

"I have friends... country now, th... pigeons. There se... great communica... just between the fa...

Pigeon fancier Mr. Billy Wright, holding one of his many trophies.

Club. It is said that during the war he used to bring a pigeon to work with him. If required to do overtime, he attached a message to this effect to the pigeon's leg, released it, and let his family know almost as quickly as if he used the telephone.

Clockwise from top left: A signed photograph given to Jonny and Smash Hits after they tore the roof off Isle of Wight Festival, warming up for the legendary dance act; a printout by NYC street performance artist Mother Pigeon, gifted to Jon after a friend hand-delivered the artist a Banger pigeon tracksuit; Jonny Banger's grandad, Billy Wright, pictured in a local paper; a leaflet handed out in Tottenham by a local church group.

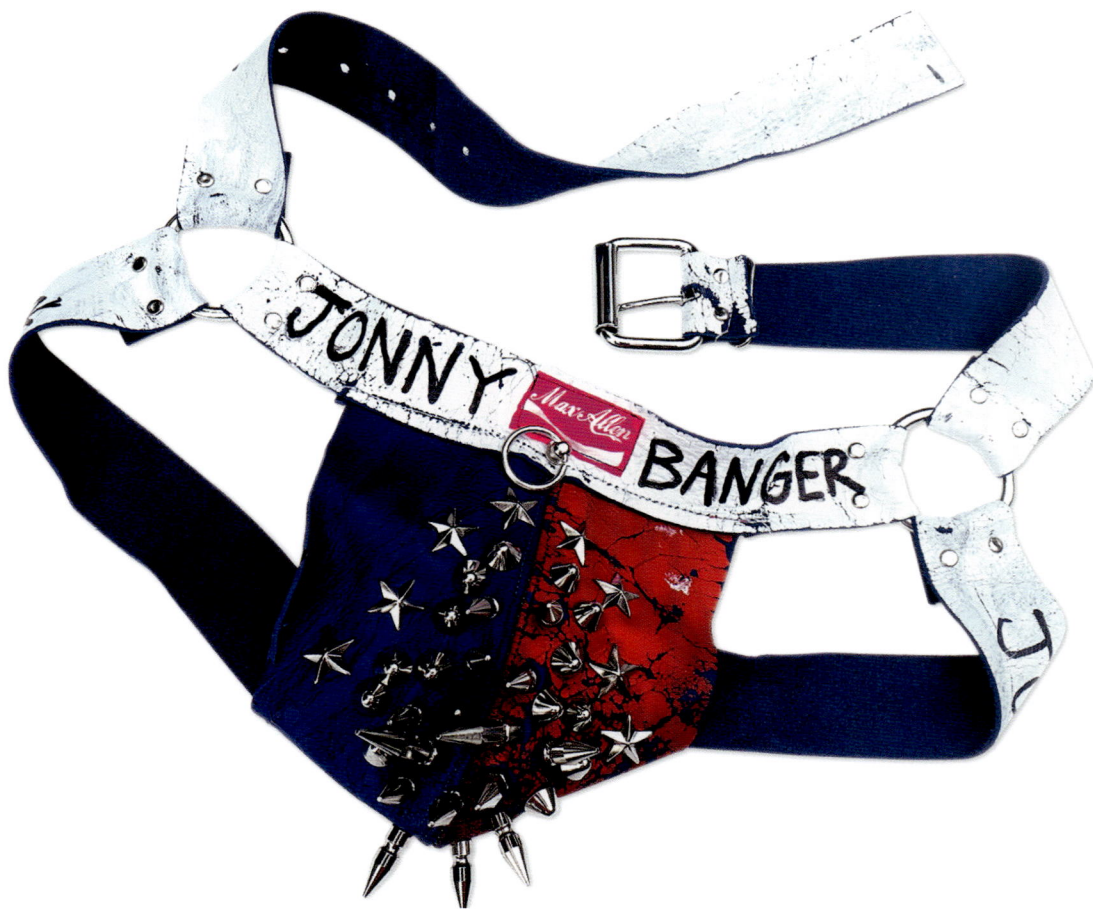

This wasn't a show, it was a party. Anarchic acid house fuckers Paranoid London played live. We built a wardrobe and changed their looks six times. We got sent 50 bottles of Absolut for the show, which was jokes – we only had 50 guests. Everyone got a bottle of vodka in a Banger sock (?) on arrival. We'd heard that Tommy Hilfiger was going to be showing in London for the first time in 20 years, so we did our own unhinged homage, with Josh Caffé in an original 'Fisting Tommy' look by Max Allen. It was mash up. Not long after, Tommy Hilfiger reached out to us for an official collab.

VIVA LA BOOTLEG

Previous, left: A hand-painted, studded jockstrap made for Sports Banger by Max Allen.
Previous, right: Josh Caffé as the 'Fisting Fairy'.
Above: Made by Max Allen, the complete 'Giz a Fiver Fisting Fairy' ensemble: a velour top adorned with found bottle tops, ring pulls, mirrors, beads, sequins and junk; multi-coloured bondage pants; and hazard pattern trouser cuffs.

not bad for a woman

Above: Josh Caffé at Sports Banger's Off London Fashion Week party, held at the 724 Seven Sisters Road studio.
Below: Paranoid London members Dels and Clams in their makeshift wardrobe during the performance.

'I'm inspired by the way Banger translates pop culture into meaningful products and experiences. He makes people think.'
— Tommy Hilfiger

Above: Hand-painted 'Tommy Hilfiger' sensory deprivation mask made by Max Allen.
Opposite: A repurposed biker jacket worn by Clams on the night was adorned with 1,600 stainless steel nuts and a laser-etched branding plate. It weighs a ton.

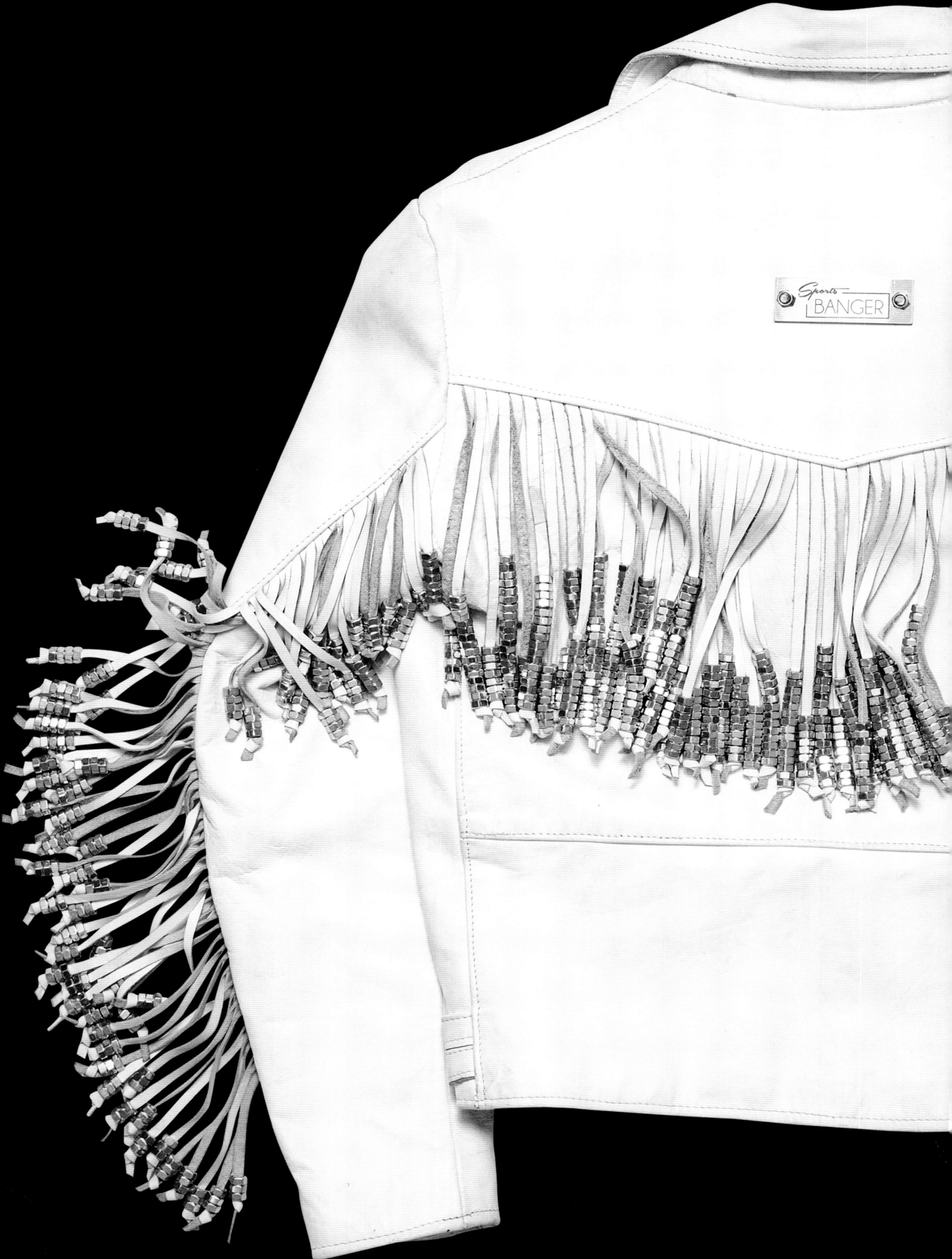

VOGUE

REVIEW

Rave Review:
Sports Banger's Hardcore
Homage to Tommy Hilfiger

Luke Leitch
Vogue, 18 February 2020

On the night that Tommy Hilfiger brought his juggernaut Now show to London's Tate Modern, the ragtag Seven Sisters fashion/rave label Sports Banger threw open the doors of its 50-guest capacity studio – Maison de Bang Bang – and paid homage. About 20 minutes into a show/party that was soundtracked, modelled, and co-hosted by the acid house specialists Paranoid London, the singer Josh Caffé came out in his second look. Created for Banger by Max Allen, it was both a Hilfiger tribute and subversion, a bit of bootleg brilliance, and a piece in which it was hard to see where the spandex ended, and the studded jockstrap began. Caffé's first look, also an Allen arrangement, mixed 'Giz a fiver' printed pieces from last season and two sinister wings printed with fixed, wide, paranoid eyes peering through the Venetian blind that acted as this show's backdrop. Banger called the ensemble 'hedonist warlord'.

Elsewhere, Caffé's co-MC Mutando Pintando did his thing, which is to stimulate and enrage via distorted guttural utterance, in his Stetson and a Banger-adapted Western jacket featuring fringing edged with steel nuts. Behind them, Gerardo Delgado and Quinn Whalley, the co-founders of Paranoid London, were playing records and torturing a 303. As the set progressed, they changed through printed velour tracksuits, band label sweats, and a couple of 'found' pieces that included a shopping bag hat and tube sock balaclava. The audience gibbered and danced the whole way through, screaming with every fresh look revealed. Those who suggest that London has 'lost its cool', poor things, should think again: Banger is just one upstart outpost of on-the-fringes brilliance bubbling under in the capital right now.

Josh Caffé performs in Max Allen's twist on Aaliyah's classic
Tommy Jeans outfit, updated with a gimp mask, studded jockstrap,
branded boob tube, leather cap, hand-painted denim chaps and
riding whip.

T-shirts don't change the world but sometimes they're a good start.
You need action and coordination. As soon as the pandemic hit, we partnered
with Club Mexicana to deliver hundreds of daily meals to healthcare workers
across London and set up a food bank at the local primary school. Everyone plays
their part. People adopted the T-shirt as a sign of support for NHS workers
and hung them in their windows across the country.

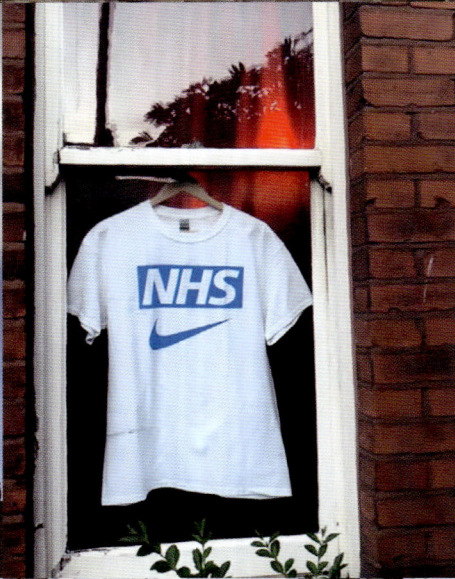

If you can throw a rave, you can organize a food bank.

Previous, left: Mega Aid stickers labelled bottled juices and smoothies.
Previous, right: A London child with a makeshift flag of solidarity.
Opposite: The 'Under the Counter' T-shirt in windows across the UK.
Above: School teacher Shane, Matt Harriman, Hannah Shogs,
Olu the dog and Jeremy Deller at the school food bank.

UK Government

This is a vital update from the
Government about Coronavirus

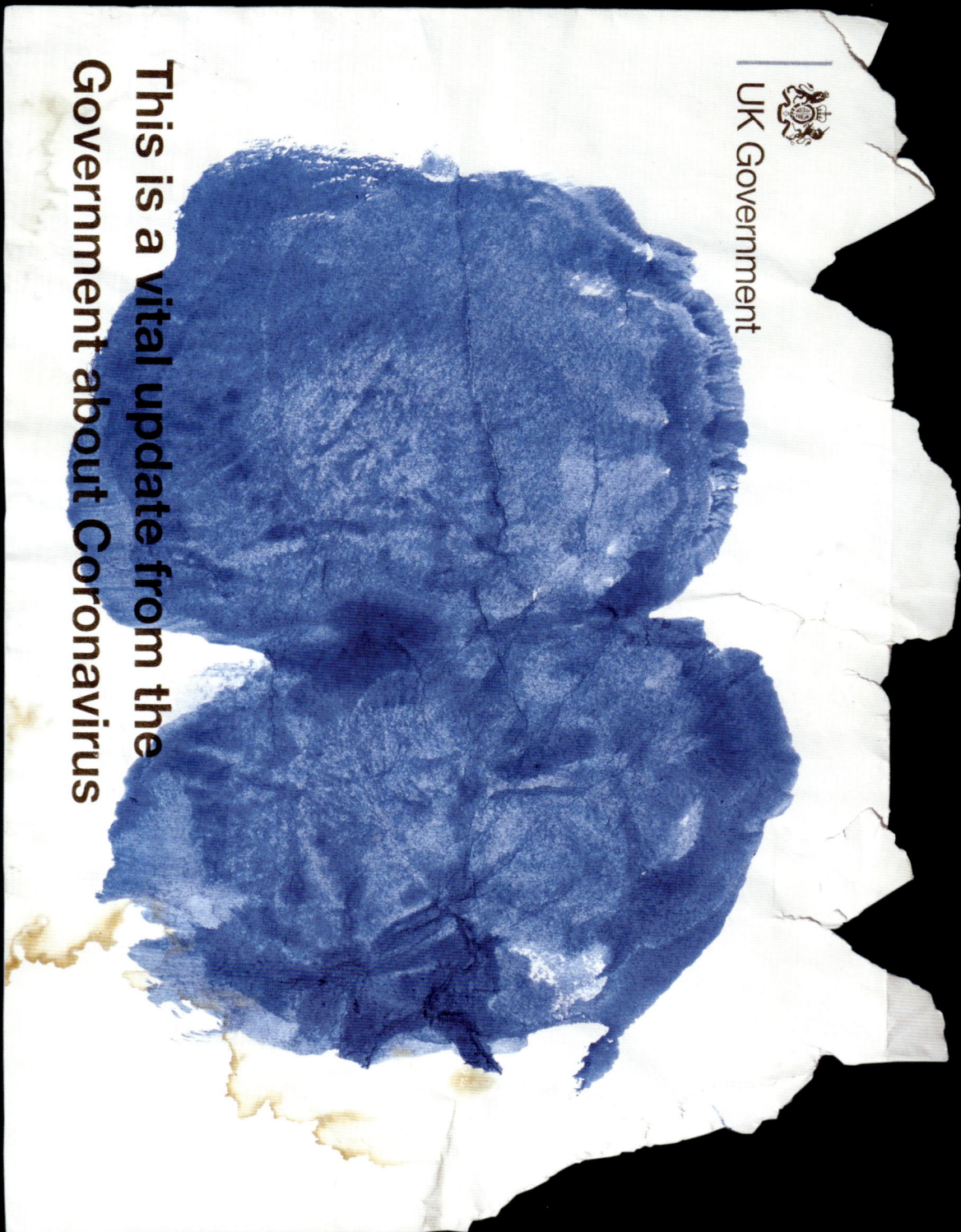

As the country went into lockdown, Boris Johnson wrote a letter intended for every UK household, urging residents to stay at home, protect the NHS and save lives. At this stage of the pandemic, his government had already made a complete mess of things, and everyone was pissed off. In response to the letter, we invited young people under the age of 16 to deface it as a way of expressing their feelings.

10 DOWNING STREET
LONDON SW1A 2AA

THE PRIME MINISTER

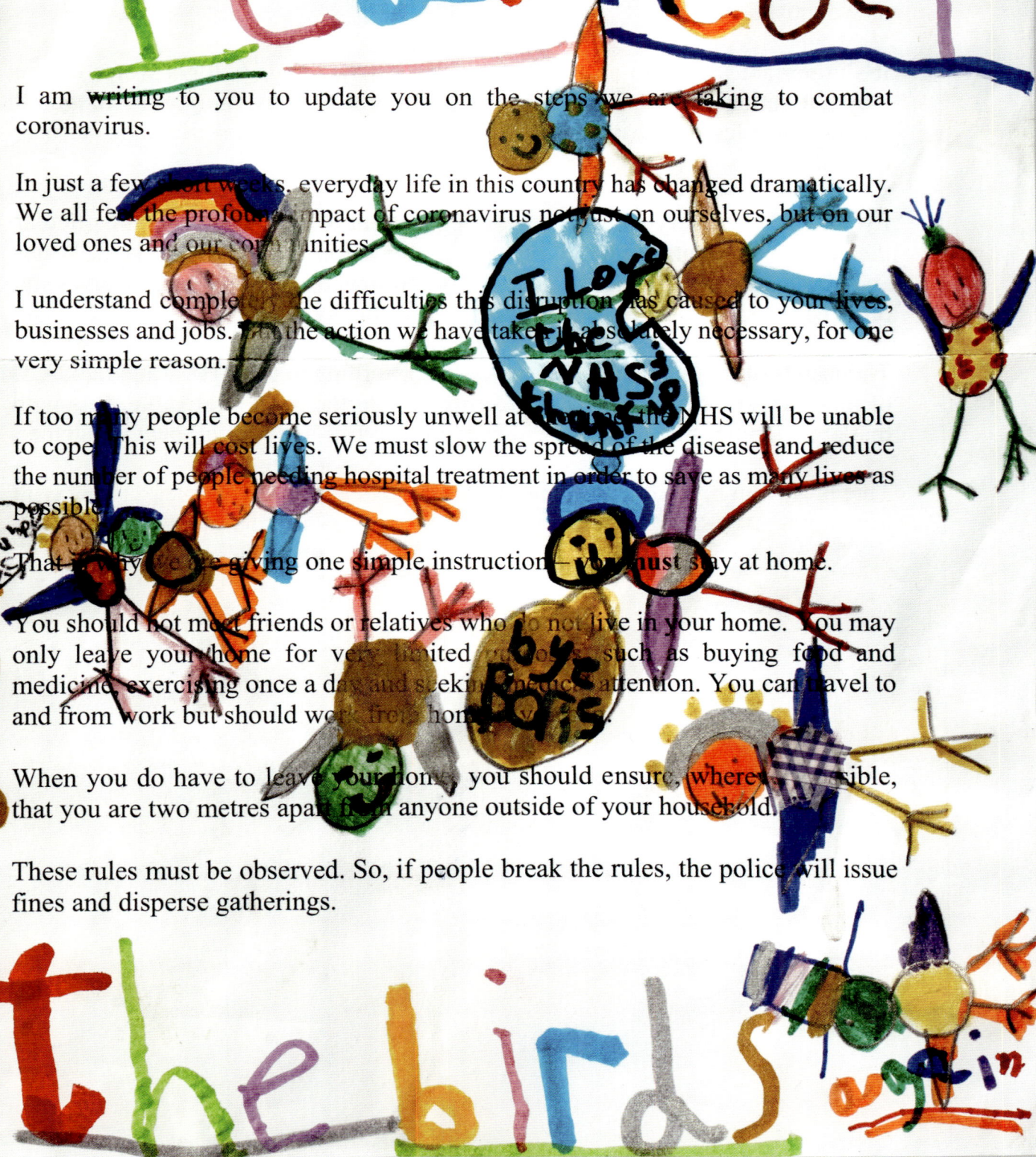

I am writing to you to update you on the steps we are taking to combat coronavirus.

In just a few short weeks, everyday life in this country has changed dramatically. We all feel the profound impact of coronavirus not just on ourselves, but on our loved ones and our communities.

I understand completely the difficulties this disruption has caused to your lives, businesses and jobs. But the action we have taken is absolutely necessary, for one very simple reason.

If too many people become seriously unwell at one time, the NHS will be unable to cope. This will cost lives. We must slow the spread of the disease, and reduce the number of people needing hospital treatment in order to save as many lives as possible.

That is why we are giving one simple instruction – you must stay at home.

You should not meet friends or relatives who do not live in your home. You may only leave your home for very limited purposes, such as buying food and medicine, exercising once a day and seeking medical attention. You can travel to and from work but should work from home.

When you do have to leave your home, you should ensure, where possible, that you are two metres apart from anyone outside of your household.

These rules must be observed. So, if people break the rules, the police will issue fines and disperse gatherings.

V&A

REVIEW

'Pandemic Objects:
Government Letter'

Meneesha Kellay
V&A Blog, 15 May 2020

Sports Banger No.10 Downing Street Letters Competition

If you're reading this in the UK, you're one of the 30 million households that received a letter from the Prime Minister about the coronavirus crisis. Maybe you read it feeling strangely connected to others across the country, knowing they have read the same words, or perhaps having seen its content reported elsewhere, it went straight in the recycling. Some of you may have responded to London-based fashion label Sports Banger's straightforward call on social media, 'if you've received a letter, design a poster'. The rules were simple: you must be under 16 years old, draw straight onto the letter itself and 'no digital'.

The tools for the competition – pencils, pens, crayons – are deliberately ubiquitous and re-appropriation of the letter is in true bootlegging style of fashion designer Sports Banger. The label is known for its subversion and appropriation of branding through an interrogation of British pop culture, class and politics. The defaced letters-cum-posters came flooding in, from toddlers as young as 17 months to teenagers. In total, 203 posters were submitted; the entries ranged from sweet and heartwarming to wonderfully puerile and acerbic. Many posters illustrated messages of love and support for the NHS or advice such as 'wash your hands'. One colourful submission by a seven-year-old featured drawings of birds with smiling faces (not beaks) and the text 'I can hear the birds'. Some feature the familiar rainbow that can be seen in windows of residential streets across the country. Others responded directly to the author of the letter and were more critical of the government's approach, with calls to 'fund the NHS' and 'we need more PPE'.

In ordinary times a government letter is a one-way communication. This intervention subverts that notion through questioning its motive, turning it into a medium of dialogue, criticism and, in some cases, protest. 'Little anarchists spreading joy' is how Jonny Banger, the designer behind the label, describes the response to his competition, 'I couldn't be happier using my platform to give the kids a voice.' Rather than the letter being a top-down mechanism, its function has been transformed through this intervention into a tool for debate and discussion. Jonny Banger has received proud messages from parents whose children submitted designs saying they 'discussed the welfare state, NHS and taxes [...] and the task formed part of their home schooling. This has been one task they all managed to enjoy.'

Amidst this global pandemic, where we are infinitely connected and receive minute-by-minute live updates on the status of the crisis, it felt oddly analogue to receive post from 10 Downing Street. Government transmissions are often how we record important moments in history; we may look back on this letter as the turning point when the government caught up with the national mood on the pandemic. Perhaps this modest yet poignant response to the government's actions from the youngest in society is one way we will record their voice in the extreme circumstances of enforced home schooling and restricted time outdoors.

The idea for the competition came to Jonny Banger when someone, on receiving their NHS T-shirt the same day as receiving the Prime Minister's letter, posted, 'one of these is going in the bin'. The NHS × Nike bootleg T-shirt was originally designed in 2015 in support of the junior doctors strike; the re-issue raised £100,000 in three drops of the T-shirt, each selling out within an hour.

All sales of the NHS × Nike bootleg (T-shirts are £21.99) go towards providing healthy food and fresh juices round the clock to ICU teams at five hospitals across London.

Support for the NHS has united the country during this crisis; our love for the NHS is a force that has galvanized everyone during lockdown. For Jonny Banger, 'being a bootlegger means do what you want. Start where you are, use what you got, do what you can.' In many ways, the perfect mantra for getting through this strange time.

217   BANGER PIRATES & THE COVID LETTERS

Previous, left: Bum print artwork on government envelope by four-year-old Kit from Bristol.
Previous, right: Submission from Lacey, aged seven from London.
Above: Sports Banger pirates with their artworks and certificates.
Below, left: Each artist received a bootlegged Blue Peter pirate badge.
Below, right: Every under-16s art competition should have a PO Box.

FUCK CORONA

Fuck Boris

JOHNSON IS A PICKLE

Cock a doodle didn't

THANK U NHS

BIGGEST IDIOT

We will get through this!

Me and my mum Love the NHS They keep Me Well

Is a wally!!

I ♥ NHS

OR

GET DOWN THE TOILET

NHS Stop Stealing from us Boris!

Covid-19 disease we will fight this

keep saving

CORONA VIRUS!

IS A TWAT!! BORIS OUT!!

BANGER BANG

DOWN

FUND THE NHS

Sports BANG

THE PRIME MINISTER

I am writing to you to update you on the steps we are taking to combat coronavirus.

In just a few short weeks, everyday life in this country has changed dramatically. We all feel the profound impact of coronavirus not just on ourselves, but on our loved ones and our communities.

I understand completely the difficulties this disruption has caused to your lives, businesses and jobs. But the action we have taken is absolutely necessary, for one very simple reason.

If too many people become seriously unwell at one time, the NHS will be unable to cope. This will cost lives. We must slow the spread of the disease, and reduce the number of people needing hospital treatment in order to save as many lives as possible.

That is why we are giving one simple instruction – you must stay at home.

You should not meet friends or relatives who do not live in your home. You may only leave your home for very limited purposes, such as buying food and medicine, exercising once a day and seeking medical attention. You can travel to and from work but should work from home if you can.

When you do have to leave your home, you should ensure, wherever possible, that you are two metres apart from anyone outside of your household.

These rules must be observed. So, if people break the rules, the police will issue fines and disperse gatherings.

10 DOWNING STREET
LONDON SW1A 2AA

HOME

Johnson

Love you Glasgow

10 DOWNING STREET
LONDON SW1A 2AA

PRIME MINISTER

Ou

NH

writing to you to update you on the steps we are taking
virus.

a few short weeks, everyday life in this country has changed dra
feel the profound impact of coronavirus not just on ourselves, b
ones and our communities.

rstand completely the difficulties this disruption has caused to y
sses and jobs. But the action we have taken is absolutely necessar
mple reason.

many people become seriously unwell at one time, the NHS will b
e. This will cost lives. We must slow the spread of the disease, an
nber of people needing hospital treatment in order to save as many

why we are giving one simple instruction — you must stay at hom

RICH !!!

ould not meet friends or relatives who do not live in your home. You may
ave your home for very limited purposes, such as buying food and
cising once a day and seeking medical attention. You can travel to
k but should work from home if you can.

to leave your home, you should ensure, wherever possible,
tres apart from anyone outside of your household

Must be observed. So, if people break the rules, the police will issue
perse gatherings.

THE PRIME MINISTER

10 DOWNING STREET
LONDON SW1A 2AA

I am writing to you to update you on the steps we are taking to combat
coronavirus.

In just a few short weeks, everyday life in this country has changed dramatically.
We all feel the profound impact of coronavirus not just on ourselves, but on our
loved ones and our communities.

I understand completely the difficulties this disruption has caused to your lives,
businesses and jobs. But the action we have taken is absolutely necessary, for one
very simple reason.

If too many people become seriously unwell at one time, the NHS will be unable
to cope. This will cost lives. We must slow the spread of the disease, and reduce
the number of people needing hospital treatment in order to save as many lives as
possible.

That is why we are giving one simple instruction — you must stay at home.

You should not meet friends or relatives who do not live in your home. You may
only leave your home for very limited purposes, such as buying food and
medicine, exercising once a day and seeking medical attention. You can travel to
and from work but should work from home if you can.

When you do have to leave your home, you should ensure, wherever possible,
that you are two metres apart from anyone outside of your household.

These rules must be observed. So, if people break the rules, the police will issue
fines and disperse gatherings.

10 DOWNING STREET
LONDON SW1A 2AA

MINISTER

ssh!

FUCK

Boris Johnson

fuck

I would draw
big man Boris but
that would be Haram
THE PRIME MINISTER

10 DOWNING STREET
LONDON SW1A 2AA

stay home

boris

poop horse

no more

THE PRIME MINISTER

10 DOWNING STREET
LONDON SW1A 2AA

'The Covid Letters' exhibition was great. Jeremy Deller was a trustee at the Foundling Museum, so invited us to show the works there and helped us curate it all. Due to lockdowns, it opened, closed, opened, closed – I think we managed to keep it open for a total of ten days. It was amazing for all the kids to see their work hanging on the walls of a museum alongside works by William Hogarth, the grandfather of the political cartoon. The atmosphere was brilliant. Strangers were talking to each other and the place was full of good energy, hope and laughs.

Previous pages: A selection of the 267 defaced government letters sent in to Sports Banger from kids around the country. All artworks were also featured in a book about the project, *The Covid Letters*, published by Sports Banger in late 2020.
Above: Jeremy Deller, Dom Ridler and Jonny in the Picture Gallery at the Foundling Museum.
Opposite: Artists' open day at the Foundling Museum, held on Halloween 2020.

"Boris Johnson is a pickle", "Get your friends to pay taxes", "We want PPE!" When British designer and bootleg king Jonny Banger invited kids to repurpose letters about Covid-19 issued by the Prime Minister's office, the messages that came back ran from the uplifting to the unrepeatable.

Designing the posters with their children, parents discussed the NHS and the Government's response to the pandemic: the kids, in return, made their feelings clear.

The "Government Letter" posters have attracted the attention of the V&A and later this year a selection of the 203 posters submitted will be exhibited as "pandemic objects". You know some pretty sweary kids, I tell Banger (not his real name), judging by the entries I've seen. He prefers the positive designs. They have, he says, "brought joy to my life".

Eloquent cultural artefacts they may be, but the posters are just one part of a much bigger story.

Three months ago, a sweaty, extravagantly dressed crowd piled into a workshop behind Tottenham Textiles on Seven Sisters Road. The small space pulsed to a set from Paranoid London, who did double duty as DJs and models. Sports Banger's contribution to London Fashion Week was not so much a catwalk show as a party pegged to a few outrageous garments, among them giant angels' wings printed with Peeping Tom eyeballs, and a faux Tommy Hilfiger gimp mask.

Within a month, Banger had turned his considerable energies and network to a new mission: feeding healthcare workers and local families, using funds from T-shirts and hoodie sales. He resurrected a T-shirt design he'd made during the 2015 junior doctors' strike: the NHS logo atop a Nike swoosh. Nike were fine with the T-shirts but Banger received persistent legal emails from the Government's identity protection team asking him not to use the NHS logo. Today the T-shirts carry such clout that they even appear in the video game *Animal Crossing*.

The NHS is part of Banger's heritage. His mum and gran had both been nurses. As a teenager he witnessed the care his mum received when she got leukaemia. She died when he was 15. You could say that he has found an alternative family within the underground music scene.

The poster competition came about after a friend received their NHS T-shirt in the same postal drop as the PM's letter. "They said, 'One of these is going in the bin'. So I thought, 'There must be something better we can do with that'." Twenty minutes later he announced the competition on Instagram, offering T-shirts and pirate badges in return.

Banger's enterprises seem to come together with the lightest of guiding touches. "All I ever do is get people to do what they do anyway – I'm just joining the dots," he says. It's an MO born from years of parties and festivals – organising quickly on a small budget, in less than ideal circumstances – and it's left him well suited for crisis situations. It turns out you bank a lot of good will if you spend years throwing great parties. "I've helped a lot of people out. So a lot of people owe me favours."

Sports Banger started as a rave label disseminating messages with attitude – about the ill treatment of women by the British tabloids, the police crackdown on nightclubs, or the political ascendance of a certain tousle-haired Tory. Later it became something closer to a fashion house, albeit an unconventional one, with its own eccentric and very British iconography. Its high street collaboration with Slazenger included plastic "Slazenger Banger" prosecco glasses, a lilo, and T-shirts reading, "Giz a Fiver".

Somewhat on a whim last year Banger started staging catwalk shows alongside London Fashion Week, but has no aspirations to be the next Burberry. "I'm not seduced by shiny things. I just want to a build a fashion house based on action, community and friends," he says. "I don't own my own house, but I've got a judges' wig made out of fivers." (The wig was made for his show last autumn by accessories designer Fred Butler.)

Just before lockdown, Banger had

❝ I want to build a fashion house based on community

Fashion maverick Jonny Banger's latest project for the V&A involves children giving their responses to the PM's pandemic letters, he tells **Hettie Judah**

Jonny Banger with some of his fashion designs (right); a child carrying one of his NHS/Nike T-shirts (left)

Jonny Banger (left); one of the 'Government Letter' posters (inset), and a Sports Banger design

The weekend's television

EMILY BAKER

An exhilarating race through time and tricks of memory

» **Homecoming** Amazon Prime Video, available now ★★★★★
» **Citizens of Boomtown** BBC2, Saturday, 9.20pm ★★★☆☆

The first series of **Homecoming**, the excellent drama about a controversial private programme treating soldiers with PTSD, was nominated for multiple Golden Globes on its release in 2018, and featured Julia Roberts in her first starring TV role. Those wary that a second series might suffer since she left have nothing to worry about: Janelle Monáe, musician and star of *Moonlight*, is entrancing, and more than capable of picking up where the Oscar-winning legend left off.

Monáe plays Jackie, a woman who wakes up in a rowing boat in the middle of a lake with no idea who she is or how she got there. The only thing she does know is that she has done something terrible. Over the first two episodes, we follow Jackie as she attempts to uncover her identity, a quest that leads her to the doors of wellness company Geist. After that, we're thrust back in time to uncover exactly how – and why – she has found herself in such an unnerving position.

If you have watched the first series, alarm bells will be ringing here, as Geist is the same company responsible for the Homecoming programme designed to remove the memories of war veterans without them knowing. When word gets out, a race to cover up the scandal engulfs the story.

The series' strength is in how it plays with the concept of memory and timelines, but it would be nothing without the exceptional acting of its cast. The difference in Monáe's character before and after the time jump speaks to her ability switch guises, while outstanding performances from Chris Cooper, Stephan James and Joan Cusack build on an already transfixing story. It's fast-paced, breathtaking and delightfully intellectual TV.

If you choose to create a 90-minute music documentary,

you'd better find a decent subject – one with a little mystique or a tragic story. Unfortunately, **Citizens of Boomtown** director Billy McGrath chose The Boomtown Rats, an Irish band whose history is so well publicised and a little clichéd that it really doesn't warrant such a magnifying glass.

As the story is told almost entirely through archive footage and photographs, the extent of the research needed to create this film was impressive, but there's only so much these physical memoirs can tell us. Music's power is in how it makes you feel and the influence it has on the world. But despite the number of journalists telling us theirs did change the world, this documentary felt oddly emotionless. And with the addition of film student-style scenes of the band walking through a tunnel behind a figure wearing a gas mask and pulling a board laden with rocks (me neither) promoting their latest album, the whole project felt rather self-congratulating.

However, it wasn't a total waste of time. As a potted history of Ireland's recent past it was fascinating, charting the tensions between a young population and the old guard of church and state. Live Aid, too, was an inevitable but vital event and one that warrants Geldof another pat on the back.

The band themselves – Sir Bob Geldof, Johnnie Fingers, Pete Briquette, Simon Crowe, Gerry Cott and Garry Roberts – rarely appeared on screen, despite narrating their own tale. At times it felt as though they were reading from a pre-approved script, devised to eradicate any apparent cracks in the band's foundations. More insightful were their fans – Sinéad O'Connor, Bono and Sting – who were more than willing to make up for the Rats' lacklustre enthusiasm.

Twitter: @emilyrbakes

Stephan James (Walter) and Janelle Monáe (Jackie) in 'Homecoming' AMAZON

---

straight to them," Banger says. If they don't need food it's redirected somewhere else. Managing supply and demand is important: he says a lot of well meaning people have been dumping food at A&E departments, creating extra work for over-stretched staff.

Has he turned into a saint overnight? Hardly. He still enjoys needling people. When asked on Instagram where the T-shirt money was going, Banger gleefully responded "fast girls" (Mega Aid's speedy delivery team is led by female volunteers). He seems delighted that *Vogue* pulled an article on the NHS T-shirts after Condé Nast's lawyers raised concerns about celebrating a self-confessed bootlegger in their bible to expensive brands.

He is quick to make a public spectacle of idiocy, such as when *Harper's Bazaar* featured his NHS T-shirt, then noted that it was temporarily out of stock and directed readers instead to a knock-off on Etsy. *Harper's* apologised and made a donation to Mega Aid.

While he has been shifting smoothies, and using his platform to share skills and information, Banger has been disappointed by the silence of other figures from the British music scene "Where are these voices within this period?" he despairs: "Kids look up to them, and it's like they've been missing for two months. They shout politics in one breath, and now go quiet in the biggest time of one generation's lives?"

That packed party in February now seems a world away – it's going to be a while before Banger is back in the real world. While he waits, he has started a record label – named Heras after the fencing brand (he describes both fences and music as "obnoxious, industrial, ravey, metallic"). Beyond that? "I don't know how it's going to pan out. Whatever it is, we'll give it a good go. I'm not going anywhere," he says.

I believe him: he's pretty adaptable.

For more information, visit: sportsbanger.com and vam.ac.uk/ blog/projects/pandemic-objects-government-letter

---

I've helped a lot of people out. So a lot of people owe me favours

The food distribution service has been dubbed Mega Aid: a nod to the Mega Raves he used to throw.

Behind the irreverence, what Mega Aid has achieved is impressive, and it's been done with care and integrity. People are paid for their work, food is largely purchased not donated, and goes only where it's needed. "We have a point of contact for the ICU units and then deliver

---

a DJ wearing one of his old -shirts. It seemed a good mo-o print more, "but I wanted it to some actual action". n conversations with nurse and public health workers th the help of Meriel Armit-o runs the vegan street food 'lub Mexicana, he put togeth-work to provide healthy food ces exactly where and when eeded.

er and his team have raised 100,000 and are delivering als a day to health workers ice and community treat-entres, as well as hospital le was also contacted by a acher who had been field-ful calls from parents un-feed children usually on free meals. So they set up a food o, distributing to 150 fami-first week, and set to grow.

Jon Wright

SPORTS BANGER

Thank you for your incredible efforts in making a difference in our community during the coronavirus pandemic.

Sheila Peacock

Councillor Sheila Peacock
Mayor of Haringey (2019–2020)

September 2020

HARINGEY
HERO

Haringey
LONDON

Previous pages: Pages from *The i* newspaper, featuring a piece about 'The Covid Letters' project written by Hettie Judah. *Above:* A certificate awarded to Jonny by Haringey Council for his work in the local community.

Steff Yotka, *Vogue* fashion news and emerging platforms editor

Over a month of fashion shows in New York, London, Milan, and Paris, I saw so much—and so much to love—from Rick Owens's bubbles to Dries Van Noten's incredible Lacroix collab. But for the first time, I also saw something I'd never seen before: An actually fun fashion show. In London's Tottenham Hale, Jonny Banger put on a fashion-show-party-rave for his

Hi Jon
This is your grandmother Esme who was a founder member of the NHS in 1948 having qualified as a SRN in 1939. For many years she was night sister at Fleet Hospital and a lifetime volunteer with the British Red Cross. Esme had always wanted to visit Japan but sadly never did and the nearest she got to going on a plane was at the Farnborough Airshow in 1952 when she treated the injured and dying after a plane crashed into the crowd. A remarkable woman who would be so proud of her grandson.
DAD xx

Hey Jonny
Random offer of help - I work at Mishcon de Reya lawyers in the art team and a am big fan of yours.
If you need a hand with all the legals do get in touch
). I want to introduce you to my partner   in IP department who heads up the fashion and retail sector and is best placed to help - if you need.
Best wishes,

sportsbanger is just blue inc for people who think they are too cool to shop in blue inc (but they are not)
07/06/2017, 12:26

@HackneyAbbott @hackneycouncil why would this be allowed opposite dalston dalston train station where I was stood waiting for a bus this morning with my 9 year old daughter? @StokeyUpdates

FUCK YOU

Replying to @StokeyUpdates   and 2 others

There was a Oatly ad that read "oh it's you again" or something to that effect. It must have been vandalised

Stokey Updates @StokeyUpdates · 9h
Replying to   nd 2 others
Quite an effort

bazaaruk

Hi, we sincerely apologise for the oversight and have removed the product from our gallery. We in no way condone plagiarism and are putting steps in place to make sure this doesn't happen again. We are big fans of Sport's Banger's original design and fully support your fundraising efforts - we'd like to make this up to you in any way we can and to feature the T-shirt once it's back in stock.

No probs. Apology accepted. I'll remove post. It was just very stupid.. Would you like to donate £500 to the food bank we are setting up at a local school? Thanks Jon

Thank you for accepting the apology and removing the post. We'd be delighted to donate - please do let us know details, we'd love to know more about the project. And please do let us know if you release any new

Best party ive ever been to in my life. youve set a new benchmark for raving that wont be beaten mush. Keep em comin i wanna again! One love mr BANGER! Oi oi! ♨️📊🦯

Hey man, my son just got accepted in to his primary school and he is so hyped now coz he actually thinks he's going the Banger Fleet Pirate School, check the logo out 😂😂

Leigh

This had made his whole school transition so easy 😂😂 🏴
🏴 Thank U

ES news
Evening Standard @standardnews 5m
Four hundred pirate radio stations shut down in London in just two years
bit.ly/1NBuq2n

🔁 13   ⭐ 4

"From the enquiries we've carried out, this problem doesn't exist in New York or Rome or Paris - it's a London phenomenon."

RE: RECORDS
To
Good mornin
Your records have now been made available for release at King's Lynn Police station. You will need to attend during opening hours and bring a form of identification with you. If asked you can give them property reference
The Public Office opening hours are;
 • Mon – Wed: 9am – 5pm
 • Thurs – Sat: 9am - 6pm
 • Sun: Closed
Please be aware for future reference that property seized at illegal raves is often disposed of and not returned to any owner.
Thank you

THE SPIRIT OF POLICING

Caro Howell

Director of the Foundling Museum, London

CAN YOU TELL US ABOUT THE HISTORY OF THE MUSEUM AND THE WORK THAT IT DOES?

The Foundling Museum's mission is to transform lives through creative action. We tell the story of the Foundling Hospital, which was founded in 1739 as a home for children whose mothers couldn't keep or care for them. As well as being the UK's first children's charity, the artist William Hogarth made it the UK's first public art gallery by donating works of art and persuading other artists to do the same. Handel conducted benefit concerts of Messiah in the chapel, and later, Charles Dickens became a supporter too. They showed how art can improve lives and promote social change. Today, we use our art and objects to keep our history alive and relevant, particularly for young people who feel a personal connection to our story. Working with artists, writers and musicians, we run training and mentorship programmes for care-experienced young people. We also run workshops to support disadvantaged children in their early years and work in hospitals with children in transplant and psychiatric wards.

HOW DID 'THE COVID LETTERS' FIND ITS HOME AT THE FOUNDLING MUSEUM?

In my experience, it's artists who solve unsolvable problems, and Covid was a monster. In the first lockdown, with the museum closed and our exhibition programme in tatters, I rang the artist Jeremy Deller, who was one of our trustees, to talk through the challenge facing the museum. We had no income, no idea when we'd reopen and almost no staff, as everyone was furloughed. However, we needed an exhibition that could be put together in weeks, not years, that would tempt people back, that felt relevant and in the spirit of the museum, and, most importantly, was joyful. Jeremy started to tell me about a project he'd been following on Instagram, and the more he spoke about it, the more I realized we'd found the perfect solution.

DID YOU FEEL THERE WAS ANY RISK IN TAKING ON THE EXHIBITION, CONSIDERING ITS SUBJECT MATTER?

There will always be people who prefer children to be seen and not heard, or only heard if they say the right thing politely, but that's not us! To me, the exhibition was a no-brainer. With its story of childcare and creativity, the museum was the perfect platform for children to use their art to speak about a situation that was affecting them profoundly but over which they had no control.

WHAT ARE THE FOUNDLING FELLOWS AND WHAT IS THEIR ROLE?

The Fellows are remarkable creative people – visual artists, musicians, writers and activists – who in different ways work to make the world a better place. Fellows join the life of the museum and create a project that brings our core story to life, and projects have ranged from murals and sound installations, to novels and a museum take-over. We feel hugely honoured to have Jon as one of our Foundling Fellows. He once said: 'You have to start where you are, use what you've got and do what you can.' William Hogarth couldn't have put it any better.

YOUR HANDWRITING WAS USED ON THE INVITES FOR 'THE PEOPLE DESERVE BEAUTY'. WHAT DID YOU MAKE OF THE SHOW?

The show was exhilarating, inspiring, and summed up everything that Sports Banger is about for me: genuine inclusivity, serious mischief-making, radical action and joy. I wasn't at all surprised that the gods decided to get in on the action, contributing torrential rain and gale-force winds, although had I known the show was being covered by *Vogue*, I might have re-thought sitting in the front row in my mac and wellies!

Eloise Smyth

Actor, London

SO HOW DID YOU END UP BEING THE SPORTS BANGER MUSE?

Jon and Matt [Harriman] were living in Stokey in a warehouse where Matt had built all of these rooms. I would go back there, and I was all up for causing loads of trouble (in a fun way). After being out really late on a big night out, for some reason, I'd always want to change my clothes – I'm quite a sweaty Betty. I would get there, and I'd be like, 'I need a tracksuit. I need a T-shirt,' and Jon instantly was like, 'Come with me. I've got you.' He was refreshingly enthusiastic, which I really appreciated. With young people in London, there's like a pressure to be nonchalant and uninterested in things and unfazed by things, you know? His level of enthusiasm was rare and kind of like pure and childlike. And that was really refreshing because I was young and I was excited. It was cool to be around someone who was like, 'I'm excited, you're excited – let's be excited!' He would hurry me to his room and be chucking T-shirts at me. I was like, 'Sick, I'm getting free shit,' and I felt like he really wanted me wearing his stuff. That's where it started, I guess.

HOW DO YOU FEEL ABOUT THE TITLE OF 'MUSE'?

It makes me really happy and warms my heart a little bit. Maybe it's to do with my self-worth, but I would never say that about myself. But when you hear people say it, it feels really sweet and nice. It's also lovely to look back and think I've been part of this with Jon from the jump, and I've watched him do something amazing. Like, it does make me quite emotional.

SO IT WAS ALMOST LIKE A LOGICAL PROGRESSION FOR YOU TO WALK THE RUNWAY AT THE FASHION SHOWS.

Yeah, yeah. Jon just felt like my mate or like my brother, and he still does – all that lot do, and it felt very much like family. Also, when you lose someone, with Jan [Francis], when you lose someone from a family and a team, it solidifies what that family is. Of course, I was gonna be asked to do the show, and I would've been sad if I wasn't, you know, it felt like I had to be part of that.

YOU'RE KNOWN FOR BEING ONE OF THE ROWDIEST PEOPLE AT THE SHOWS.

Being part of the Sport Banger shows, I was completely allowed to be myself, all my rough edges and that was really freeing. I didn't have to pretend to be anything that I'm not. In fact, I could celebrate all of my quirks and foibles, you know?

DO YOU HAVE ANY ANECDOTES ABOUT WHAT GOES ON BACKSTAGE? ARE THERE ANY MEMORIES THAT STAND OUT?

I mean, there's loads. The first show was like this beautiful chaos, and I think what makes it so brilliant is that Jon really lets everyone be themselves. There's no like, 'Stand over there in that line, and be quiet and do it in an orderly fashion.' It's all done in a completely *disorderly* fashion. But that's what makes it so great.

There was a moment when I got my make-up done for the first show and Jon's chain-smoking fags and drinking beer. I was really charged already and quite nervous, which meant I was going at like 100 miles an hour. I had a brief moment with Jon, where any nerves and any weirdness slipped away because of the manner he has with me. He had this big smile, and he'd be like, 'You alright?' And I'd be like, 'Yeah. You alright?' It's that little jovial, brotherly sisterly moment. It meant that I was like – this is so jokes and fine and bless, and it's just gonna be great, whatever happens, you know?

Anytime I go to something like that, whether it's a fitting or whatever, there's always a bit of like – oh god, I need to make sure I do a really good job for this. And the minute I get there, and I communicate with Jon, he's like, 'It's great, this is great, you're wicked, it's going to be wicked.' I have always felt really pumped up and supported and celebrated by him. He doesn't want to change anyone – he celebrates everyone. And I think that's made me feel really good about myself, you know? He's a big supporter of everyone. And I think that comes back in turn with how everyone supports him.

WHAT DO YOU THINK MAKES SPORTS BANGER WHAT IT IS?

The big thing about Sports Banger is that it's for everyone, and it's a celebration – for the people, for everyone. It's all-inclusive, you know? And rides against what's unjust about the world in so many ways. I mean, there's not a lot of like breaking chains and breaking kind of, like, fucking restrictive boring constructs, you know? So yeah, I suppose that's it, I would say.

Jaime Winstone

Actor, London

HOW DID YOU AND JONNY FIRST CROSS PATHS?

Oh, that's a tricky one because we share loads of mutual friends. We were mutual friends of Jan 'Aset' Francis, and I remember seeing and talking to Jon and connecting with him again at Jan's funeral, which was really emotional. Jan brought people together, even in his passing.

I really started paying attention to Jonny's stuff a good few years ago when he was doing the mock-up T-shirts, the proper bootlegged ones. I just really love that spin on taking what would normally be an over-fucking-priced T-shirt and spinning it on its head by making it obviously bootlegged.

I really believe in what Sports Banger are doing – I just love it. It's taking what the street says and giving it a proper platform.

CAN YOU EXPAND ON THAT IDEA?

Fashion is a big gateway to the rest of the world. You look at people like McQueen, who was working class, but just had an eye for culture and politics and managed to express that through art. Fashion can be a way to get a message out – mirror whatever's happening in the streets or going on in politics. And Sports Banger is kind of the only brand that's doing that authentically right now. It feels like Banger is for the people, and it's growing because there's a massive thirst for a cultural voice. I think that's more important now than ever.

IT DEFINITELY FEELS LIKE AN ANTIDOTE TO A LOT OF BULLSHIT.

Yeah, it does, and it's growing because there's a big hunger for it, you know. It appeals to everyone, and it's exciting. It's an amazing thing to see something grow authentically and ruffle feathers.

WHAT HAS BEEN YOUR MOST MEMORABLE MOMENT OF BANGER MADNESS?

There was a moment with the 'Chanel' dress that was just so *beyond*. The model was walking down the runway in this epic gown, and she kind of got it caught on her foot. And I jumped out of my seat to help because I just so badly didn't want it to go wrong for her. Also, the sign of the times is, you know, the country's gone to shit, and she's head to toe in this dress made out of Chanel-print toilet seat covers.

THERE ARE PHOTOGRAPHS OF YOU IN THIS BOOK WEARING A TRIBUTE TO BARBARA WINDSOR. HOW WOULD YOU DESCRIBE YOUR INVOLVEMENT WITH SPORTS BANGER?

If I'm honest, I'm a fan. I'm a buyer. I love wearing a T-shirt. I'm a Banger sister. I'm always dropping the name whenever I can, and I'm always talking about Jonny because I know how hard it is when you have to … without blowing smoke up your own arse … you have to generate your own movement sometimes. I guess that's because when you're not from a certain class, and you don't come from wealth, you do have to kick the doors open. It feels like an authentic family, and I'm all about it.

Emanuelle Soum
(aka Elle Miyake Mugler)

Choreographer and performance artist, Paris

HOW DID YOU GET YOURSELF INTO THE MESS OF WORKING WITH SPORTS BANGER?

Oh my god, that's a good first question! The first time I met the Sports Banger team, it immediately felt like being with family. Jon was so fun and genuine. So I think it's his energy and the values of the brand, the way they care for people – it just touched me. Jon knows where his heart is. It's not about being punk just for the sake of being punk. There's no bad ego involved – it's just very alive.

YOU BROUGHT VOGUING INTO THE WORLD OF SPORTS BANGER. CAN YOU TALK ABOUT THE ROLE OF DANCE IN THE SHOWS? AND HOW DID YOUR COLLABORATION WITH JON ACTUALLY COME ABOUT?

Jon and I started chatting online years ago. One day he invited me to walk his first show, the one they did at their old shop. It was the first time I'd met the Sports Banger crew. The make-up artists wrote BANGER all over my face and quickly after, I was on the runway performing while Jon was screaming. Pure joy and energy. Gag!

Jon mentioned he wanted more dancers and performers in the shows. Back then, it was mostly his mates walking the runway. He was very fascinated by the ballroom scene and all the wonderful muses, creatives and artists it unites. He was all about representation way before it became 'trendy' in the fashion world. At that time, in the ballroom community we were really fighting to represent the movement in the fashion world. So when the second show arrived, in late 2019, I asked Jon if the show could feature a moment with queens from both the Paris and London scenes, and he said, 'Yeah, go for it.' Sports Banger and ballroom are both very inclusive. Sports Banger represents the beauty of difference and it's all about the people, as ballroom is.

It was beautiful to see that we could really mix and match the Sports Banger mates and performers from different backgrounds on the runway. At the end, we all became friends. The cast was a cool balance – it was a really good mix of people with a strong sense of respect and care between all of us.

WHAT'S IT LIKE BEING BACKSTAGE AT A SPORTS BANGER SHOW?

It's colourful, it's all over the place, full of hyped-up energy and laughing. It's so chaotic, and then, when the moment comes, everyone's brains just connect and boom!

At the beginning, when I first started working with Sports Banger, I wanted to play professional, like, 'Ok, this is a fashion show, blah, blah, blah', and every time, Jon would just make jokes about my way of doing stuff, my methods and everything. Jon really doesn't give a fuck, and it's ok for it not to be perfect. Like if we have a long wait between two models walking – who cares? It's always chaotic, but it works. I don't know why it always works, but it always does.

I'VE HEARD THE RUN-THROUGHS NEVER MAKE IT PAST ONE SONG.

Oh god, the fucking run-throughs! They're so important, but every time we try to make them happen, Jon and I just end up shouting at each other, and then everyone goes back to hair and make-up, and then we hug because we've just told each other to fuck off!

WHAT HAS IT MEANT FOR YOU TO BE INVOLVED WITH SPORTS BANGER?

So much! It's brought me a sense of letting go and breaking boundaries creatively. It's given me a sense of faith – like, you can really stay true to your heart and actually make things happen in this industry.

Putting a show together like we do, it's so chaotic, but you find the order in it. It's really given me the confidence to put together other shows because, again, it's always worked out. Working with Sports Banger has just really pushed the boundaries of my vision.

Dom Ridler

Art director and creative producer, Sports Banger

HOW AND WHY DID YOU END UP WORKING WITH SPORTS BANGER?

I worked in fashion when I was a lot younger, in fashion publishing and editorial stuff. Then I went to uni and did art, but I always kept the door open to fashion stuff as well.

I'm good friends with Luis, who ran Tottenham Textiles in the studio next door to Sports Banger, so that's how I first met Jonny. We ended up talking about the direction of the fashion shows and where he wanted to take them. It just felt like there was so much potential there. I ended up going to Jon's first show, and I was blown away by the vibes and the spirit of it. We had a conversation afterwards where it was decided there and then that I was going to work on the next one, which was in six months' time ... and then I've just hung around since then.

HOW LONG AGO WAS THAT?

So this would have been 2019. I'd just graduated from Saint Martins, and I really didn't know a huge amount about Sports Banger.

GIVEN THAT YOU DIDN'T KNOW MUCH ABOUT SPORTS BANGER, WHAT LED YOU TO DECIDE TO WORK WITH JON?

I've been exposed to a lot of fashion, but I immediately felt like there was something very, very different about what was being communicated with Banger. It was rough around the edges but still felt like a really solid vibe. It just felt exciting and a bit subversive. It felt as much about the music or the characters walking down the runway as about the clothes. It was like, a lot of different energies smashing into each other and making something beautiful. At the shows, it was full-blown pots and pans music against a voguing dancer next to some lad with a crowbar ... a fucking dog .... It was carnage. It was raucous. It was brilliant.

AS SOMEONE WHO STUDIED FINE ARTS, WHAT'S YOUR PERSPECTIVE ON HOW SPORTS BANGER MAKES WORK HAPPEN?

There's a lot of like, self-restraint and a lot of refinement in art, generally. With the things that we make at Banger, we just apply the correct message to the correct media. A lot of the time we're not restricted by the tools; we just find the right tool that works to convey that message. Sometimes that's T-shirts, and sometimes it's an object or a print or something else. But we move quickly, and it's very malleable, and it's very reactive. We can create stuff and immediately get it out of our system. It's just like fireworks when an idea starts to roll.

WHAT'S YOUR INVOLVEMENT IN THE CREATIVE PROCESS?

Well, funnily enough, Jon used to actually introduce me as a 'translator', which I always thought was really jokes. One aspect of Jon is that, because he's so impulsive, ideas can often get burned quite quick. Whereas, what I offer is kind of a soundboard, and I can sketch out ideas. So when they come out, we can really quickly mood board something or write something up. We've had the opportunity to really expand a lot of things that have been in his mind for quite a long time and those more difficult projects that always feel a bit 'blue sky', I think we've really managed to actually get to grips with them. It also makes room for new stuff to flow in.

HOW WOULD YOU DESCRIBE YOUR WORKING RELATIONSHIP WITH JON?

It's *very* funny. We seem to laugh a ridiculous amount of the time. It's probably like, 5% serious and 95% screams. We laugh a lot, and that's what we get off on. One of the central tenets of Sports Banger is that things should feel fun, and when you do things you should feel joy.

WHAT ABOUT THE INNER WORKINGS OF WHAT GOES ON AT SPORTS BANGER HQ?

Well firstly, Jon's really good at turning up now, which is great. There were times in the old studio … I think we were so fucking bored of being in that place, neither of us wanted to be there. Then, when we moved here, we suddenly found a new kind of enthusiasm for making stuff. I guess the day-to-day running is very much as you would think, like, we have to sell stuff to be able to make stuff. So a lot of the time we're strategising about how to make cash. I guess, bottom line is we need to pay the rent. So there is that aspect of it, where like, we're just packing T-shirts.

The inner workings of the studio just got a lot more interesting because we've got a pigeon that keeps on turning up. Like, seriously, she comes upstairs into the office, and we feed her – her name's Billie. We think she's from the book gods because she turned up the same day that Jon started writing the introduction. Isn't that beautiful?

IN ANY CLOSE WORKING RELATIONSHIP, YOU START TO DEVELOP QUITE A PARTICULAR WAY OF COMMUNICATING. ARE YOU ABLE TO TAP INTO THE PECULIARITIES OF THE WAY THAT YOU AND JON COMMUNICATE?

We've definitely got a really good shorthand. There's great mutual respect for each other's work but we can also be really cutting and completely bitchy to each other, which really helps with being very straight up about things that we feel, which is unique. When we're trying to work something out, I don't think egos really come into it. I think we're always just trying to think of what would be the best outcome. I've worked with a lot of artists or designers and it always feels like the process can be fraught with the worry that you might bruise someone's ego. Jon and I have got to the point where the feedback can just flow, and it doesn't need to be sugar-coated.

WHAT HAVE BEEN SOME OF YOUR PROUDEST MOMENTS AT BANGER?

The problem is that everything that we work on is always better than the last thing. But I think overall, the Covid Letters project was so mega. That was so close to my heart. We worked in so many different ways with those kids. I even ended up interviewing the kids and making a radio show off the back of it. And then we did the book. That, for me, is an incredible example of what you can do when you have fuck all and there are people who need to say something. It was like, how can we help these kids say something and do it in a special way? And also, a lot of artists at that time weren't doing anything about Covid, and we kind of sat there for a while, like, 'God, no one's doing anything.' And then we were like, 'Hang on, we're not fucking doing anything!' Jon had already started thinking about this idea on his own and then it just snowballed. It's really special. I'm really, really proud of that project. I think it's stunning.

AS SOMEBODY WHO'S DEEPLY IMMERSED IN THE WORLD OF SPORTS BANGER, WHAT WOULD YOU SAY ARE SOME OF THE KEY CHARACTERISTICS THAT MAKE SOMETHING A SPORTS BANGER-WORTHY PROJECT?

You have to be honest about what this is. It isn't really a brand, is it? It's Jon. Sports Banger is him. So I guess a lot of things begin with inspiration from him. There are aspects of community, of partying … joy. There's a bit of attitude, but it doesn't feel toxic or anything. There's a certain authenticity, dare I say, from everything that we do because it's true to Jon and he won't do it unless it is. Ultimately, it all comes from Jon, and that's what makes it feel 'Sports Banger'. What's unique is that there's also so much room for collaborative expression. The initial ideas are born from Jon, but within that is room for a creative conversation, which often lands us miles away from where we first began, but always holds the Banger spirit.

WHAT HAS WORKING WITH SPORTS BANGER DONE FOR YOU?

I think about this a lot. I can be quite particular, and I think the ease and spontaneity of Sports Banger has really loosened me up. It's definitely had an influence on the way I work. There's something to be said for working from your instincts. Now I confidently stand behind stuff, and I don't second-guess things that we do.

Max Allen

Artist and designer, London

MAX, CAN YOU TELL US WHAT IT IS THAT YOU DO?

I'm an artist, mainly working in costume and textiles. At the core, my work is folk art. I make work for and about my community of working-class and queer people – hoping to entertain and amuse, but also to tell stories and challenge. My work can be found on all levels, including as costumes for independent queer performers and large commercial fashion spaces, but it always features details and processes that are specific to me. It's about finding luxury in craft and care.

YOU FIRST BROUGHT GLAMOUR TO SPORTS BANGER IN THE 'POP CULTURE IS TRASH' FASHION SHOW. WHAT BROUGHT YOU AND BANGER TOGETHER?

I was aware of Sports Banger's work from Instagram and was drawn to its clear and subversive use of branding. I didn't know much about the person behind it but I found our social circles overlapping. After being introduced to Jon by Dom Ridler, I found there were many parallels with our ideas, work and intentions.

YOU AND JON BOTH CAME UP THROUGH CLUB CULTURE, RAVING AND WORKING AT CLUBS AND NIGHTS IN AND AROUND LONDON. HOW HAS CLUB CULTURE SHAPED YOUR WORK?

Working in clubs was the only place I could make money when I moved to London. Fashion doesn't pay, and you have to have support and inherent wealth to have any career or even be accepted as part of it. In clubs – specifically, the underground and independent queer clubs of east London – I could turn up in outfits I'd made for myself and earn enough money for rent while having fun and also having my creativity seen and respected by those around me.

We all value the craft and creation of our peers and community over mainstream aesthetics, brands and artists – so we commission and bring industry and income to each other, even beyond the club space.

SPORTS BANGER IS ALL ABOUT USING WHAT YOU'VE GOT AND DOING WHAT YOU CAN. TALK TO US ABOUT YOUR DIY PROCESS?

I work with what's available and take inspiration from what's around me. It's as simple as being poor and only being able to use the cheapest materials, then processing them to become something different. Craft is pretty political in a climate where the working classes have had all their culture and time to create taken away. In a world where all colour and detail and decoration are stripped back to favour grey minimalism, we forget that Britain has a rich cultural heritage of craft, folk costume and creativity.

FOR 'THE PEOPLE DESERVE BEAUTY', YOU DESIGNED HAND-DYED NEON TUNICS WITH A NOD TO MEDIEVAL DRESS. CAN YOU TELL US ABOUT YOUR RELATIONSHIP WITH PERIOD COSTUME AND DESIGN?

The tunic pattern I made is one of the earliest forms of garment making. It's all rectangles – very simple, but it works with the body so fluidly. Using muslin – which is usually seen as quite natural and 'soft' – and dying it acid sunset colours reminiscent of sweetie wrappers and rave lights creates something interesting.

Most of my initial research came from my interest in historical costume and fashion, but without any historical correctness. I love the idea of exploding the V&A and trying to put everything back together with no understanding of the past – how it could look to put an 1830s skirt with a 1970s top and a hat from a pantomime dame.

YOU CELEBRATE MANY BRITISH ICONS THROUGH YOUR WORK. WHAT CHARACTERS INSPIRE YOU?

I'm fascinated with how we show our culture through our clothes – from badges and band T-shirts to logos and designers. From a Radio 6 dad wearing his band T-shirt out to gigs, to young queer kids with their shredded rave uniforms, to demi-bourgeoisie home-owning gay men wearing their Craig Green jackets to Broadway Market. Everyone is desperate to align themselves in some way. I like to use images of pop culture and British icons to play with this idea of our need to align ourselves with culture – twisting images in brazen, unexpected ways: an enlarged picture of Shirley Valentine on a skirt, the Leeds Victoria Quarter on the back of a corset, or papier-mâché badges and jewellery covered with images of Barbara Windsor.

ENTERING YOUR STUDIO FEELS LIKE LANDING ON ANOTHER PLANET – A HYPER-COLOUR SPACE WHERE YOU BRING YOUR WORK TO LIFE. CAN YOU DESCRIBE YOUR STUDIO AND WHAT IT MEANS TO WORK THERE?

I'm lucky to have found a large warehouse for an affordable amount, but it's broken, and gross, and hard to live and work in. It's freezing in the winter, hot in summer, it leaks, etc. But I can do what I want with the walls and space. My spaces always just organically look like myself. I look at pictures from my childhood bedroom and its similar, it shows it's a natural way of how my mind works, I need to get things out my head onto walls and my habitat to silence my brain and find clarity in ideas.

A lot of my design choices come from dropping a cutting from a magazine on the floor next to some fabric, the clashing of ideas and collaging of styles helps me to find new ways to create.

WHAT IS MAX ALLEN'S TIP FROM THE TOP?

Bondaweb! And lots of it!

POP CULTURE IS TRASH - show playlist
Bodysnatch - Euphony (Just 4 U London) - Big City Records
Benton - Brian's Sound - BBS
Top Buzz - Living In Darkness - Basement Records
DMX Krew - Street Boys - Rephlex
Bergsonist - Colonial Revolution - Alergy Season x Discwoman
BE3K - I'm Sexy (Selling It)
TSVI - Darabukka (Lazy Flow vogue crash edit) - Nervous Horizon
STAS - Burning Castle - Babylon Records
Jon E Ca$h - CaSh Beat (Hoods Up) - Black Ops
The Prodigy - Fire (Sunrise Version) - XL Recordings
Shades Of Rhythm - Extacy - ZTT Records

THE PEOPLE DESERVE BEAUTY - show playlist
Henry Buck - 0793 (Heras Records)
Rave 2 The Grave - NRG edit (Jedi Recordings)
Traxman - Playing With A Rubber Band (Dance Mania)
Posthuman - Temptation feat Josh Caffè (DABJ)
Neil Landstrumm - Alt Rocker (Sneaker Social Club)
International Rude Boy - Paragone edit (Formation Records)
Chole Robinson & Dj ADHD - Titch
Beat Dominator - 1.2.3.4.5.6 Bass (Pandisc)
Instra:Mental - Voyeur (Disfigured Dubz)
Dj Deeon - Shake Dat Butt (Dance Mania)
COOP - Wearing it Wrong (Heras Records)
Benton - Primal Pads (Heras Records)
Praga Khan - Injected with a Poison (Profile Records)

Tracklists from two Sports Banger fashion shows. Best played loud.

MAD
BANG

SON
DIE
BANG

MAKING THE MAISON
by Jonny Banger

A few years back, it became clear that we'd outgrown 724 Seven Sisters Road and had to find a bigger place. We knew we'd found our Maison de Bang Bang as soon as we saw a ropey old garage come up for rent through the local council. It was five minutes down the road with two floors, double-height doors, and a small courtyard. Perfect. Squatters took it over while the council were deliberating over our application, which was fine and fair play – I've been to lots of squat parties; it all comes back around.

It was a major effort getting the place into shape, but it's been so inspiring to see the Maison come to life. We built a shop on the ground floor, complete with decks and a Formula Sound mixer, 12-inch drivers hanging from the ceiling, and a 15-inch sub wedged between stacked boxes of stock. The sound's so clear and weighty it knocks your head off. In the studio upstairs, we sit all day surrounded by our whole archive, hand-me-down sewing machines, and shelves full of books and reference materials. DJ and producer friends pass through to play their new music, and we host parties for our record label in the same space where we pack the T-shirts. When we did a project with the photographer Gareth McConnell, we sewed the huge backdrop for the shoot upstairs and set it all up in our workshop next door. After it was done, we cut up the backdrop and made it into a dress and a shirt. Things go round and round, and we use what we've got. Everything under one roof or fuck off. There's beauty in that.

But it isn't some fantasy dream world in Tottenham. It's fucked. The work in this book covers 10 years of a country in steady decline. If this generation wasn't fucked enough already, then Brexit just fully ripped it apart. As I write this, the workers of this country are leading an unprecedented wave of strikes and industrial action. Ambulance workers, nurses, junior doctors, teachers, firefighters, bus drivers, rail workers, civil servants, refuse workers, passport office staff, journalists, traffic wardens (FREE PARKING). Everything is a fucking struggle. Sports Banger started at the bottom and we're still at the bottom. Working on this book has taken a lot and the reality of the creative conditions we have to deal with daily is fucking impossible. It's hard to cover costs, hard to make it work. I'm skint and paying extortionate rent to a private landlord for a one-bed flat in a block of social housing on the high road. It's shit, but I wake up every morning to the sounds of pigeons cooing above me, and that's free.

The most important thing is to surround yourself with like-minded people. It's these relationships that make things happen – even if it's nothing more than just having our voices heard and throwing some magic into the shitstorm. Corporate agencies sniff about and blow smoke up your arse, but they hardly ever come through with real money. Any collabs I've done I negotiate myself, ask for triple and sign with a fluffy pink pen.

I wrote the words for the beginning of this book as a pigeon took up residence in our studio. A year later, I wrote these last words as I found a dead pigeon on my balcony. Just looks like he croaked it. You can see he had a tough life. Fuck it, I Googled it. Apparently it's an omen that foretells violence and civil unrest. Fuck knows.

Everything in this book is political because politics is what we're living every day. That's what really affects our lives, the bastards. There's nothing more urgent than that. We got loads on our hands to get creative with and excited or angry about. Art is so powerful. Clothing is powerful. Raving is political. Find whatever you believe in and go for it. And don't forget to say what you mean, nah mean??!

MAISON DE BANG BANG

Previous, left: Jonny in the Maison's courtyard trying to work out where all the money has gone.
Above, left: Renovations on the Maison. Jonny and Matt Harriman start work on clearing out a giant commercial fish smoker left by the previous tenant.

Above, right: Stripping out the old walls at the Maison.
Below: Matt gives the Margiela treatment to the first batch of Sports Banger 'Maison de Bang Bang' T-shirts.
Opposite: Squatters' notice from the door of the Maison. In the time it took to get the keys, squatters had already moved in.

THIS IS A NON-RESIDENTIAL BUILDING
Section 144, LASPO does NOT apply

This is NOT a "residential building" within the meaning of section 144, Legal Aid, Sentencing and Punishment of Offenders Act 2012 because it was NOT designed or adapted, before the time of our entry, for use as a place to live (ss (3)(b)).

insert reasons why the above applies if not physically obvious:

The provisions of section 144 are therefore NOT APPLICABLE to this building or to our occupation of it.

Part II, Criminal Law Act 1977
(As amended by Criminal Justice and Public Order Act, 1994) DOES APPLY

LEGAL WARNING
TAKE NOTICE

THAT we occupy this property and at all times there is at least one person in occupation.

THAT any entry or attempt to enter into these premises without our permission is therefore a criminal offence as any one of us who is in physical possession is opposed to such entry without our permission.

THAT if you attempt to enter by violence or by threatening violence we will prosecute you. You may receive a sentence of up to six months' imprisonment and/or a fine of up to £5,000.

THAT if you want to get us out you will have to issue a claim for possession in the County Court or in the High Court.

The Occupiers

N.B. Signing this Legal Warning is optional. It is equally valid whether or not it is signed.

FASHION'S FIRST CROWBAR. ▬▬▬▬▬▬▬▬ free party
crowbar that he took down the runway for 'My First Fashion Show'.

MAKING THE MAISON

Opposite: Chunky at the sound check for 'The People Deserve Beauty', February 2022.
Above: Banger pigeons are fed a mix of seeds and nuts – a unique blend that's packed with energy and nutrition. Sunflower seeds go down a storm.

SOLIDARITY WITH STRIKING

SOLIDARITY WITH STRIKING WORKERS

SOLIDARITY WITH STRIKING SOLIDARITY

SOLIDARITY WITH STRIKING

SOLIDARITY WITH STRIKING

MAISON DE BANG BANG

Above: 'Solidarity with Striking Workers' patchwork hoods
hanging at the Maison.
Opposite: THE TOTTENHAM TELFAR. Big and beautiful.

MAKING THE MAISON

Opposite: Actor Jaime Winstone (interviewed on page 228) celebrated her time playing Peggy Mitchell in an 'EastEnders' special by commissioning Sports Banger to make a 'GET OUT MY PUB' skirt suit with brooches by Max Allen.

Above: Emanuelle Soum during rehearsals for 'The People Deserve Beauty' runway show. Rehearsals are often a nightmare and descend into chaos, with everyone losing their heads.
Below: Actor Samantha Morton wears a MAX Banger muslin dress from 'The People Deserve Beauty' collection.

MAISON DE BANG BANG

Above: Jonny holding an artwork commissioned by the London Fire Brigade. The piece, called 'UNDERPAID UNDERVALUED', uses The Prodigy's ant logo in reference to their 1992 track, 'Fire'. The work's name is a nod to the firefighters and the working classes who keep things moving – the worker ants.
Opposite: Sports Banger's 'NASA' hoodie featured in *MASSES* magazine, Spring/Summer 2017.

MAISON DE BANG BANG

Above: CYNICISM MASQUERADING AS OPTIMISM. Dom Ridler attends the BFI London Film Festival dressed in a custom Banger immersion suit commissioned for the UK *Triangle of Sadness* premiere. *Inset:* Director Ruben Östlund and Dom en route to the red carpet. *Opposite:* A riot of models fill the runway at 'The People Deserve Beauty' runway show.

Surrounded by HERAS fencing at a rave in south London, I shouted in a friend's ear 'I love HERAS, great name for a record label!' The ubiquitous brand of portable steel fences was founded in the Netherlands in 1966 and is the first mobile security fence. You see it every day across the UK and Europe at building sites, festivals and raves to restrict public access, divide and exclude. The idea behind the label is that the music sounds like what the fence looks like: hard, obnoxious, industrial, but a design classic. It's built for purpose.

254   MAISON DE BANG BANG

Previous, left: The first two EPs released on HERAS Records:
Neil Landstrumm's 'Doberman' and COOP's 'Wearing it Wrong'.
Previous, right: A record box constructed by Jack Hanson,
made with crowd-sourced (/kindly stolen) HERAS plates.
Above: 'HERAS' socks with fence dimensions made for the
release of 'Wearing it Wrong'.

Still from the video for 'Lightweights' from the 'Wearing it Wrong' EP. During the pandemic, local councils used HERAS fencing to block off outdoor gyms. In this north London park, the public turned the fencing onto its side so they could access the equipment. Upturned fences like these could be found in parks across the UK.

The original working title for this show was 'Honestly, We Can't Afford It'. We held it at the Maison in February 2022. Models queued up in the alleyway outside as the worst storm in decades was about to hit the UK. There were 90mph winds and torrential rain outside. Inside, the show was romantic. The shapes were elegant and full of drama. A dodgy lighting rig and low-hanging laser scanned the runway. This was Banger couture. Half the crowd whistled, the other half cried.

Previous, left: Metal roses and crown made by Jack Hanson using HERAS plates stolen for Sports Banger by obliging members of the public. Faux fur trim provided by designer Emma Brewin.
Previous, right: Eloise Smyth in a 'Slazenger Banger' bikini on the runway. Behind her, dancers carry a Gareth McConnell + Sports Banger satin quilt.

THE PEOPLE DESERVE BEAUTY

In 2022, it was revealed that Downing Street staff held
regular 'Wine Time Friday' drinks during nationwide lockdowns.
In cardboard 'Bastard Masks', Banger dancers mocked the
British establishment on the runway.

THE PEOPLE DESERVE BEAUTY

Every runway look from 'The People Deserve Beauty'. With the country down the toilet and being run by bastards, it felt fitting to give people a bit of beauty.

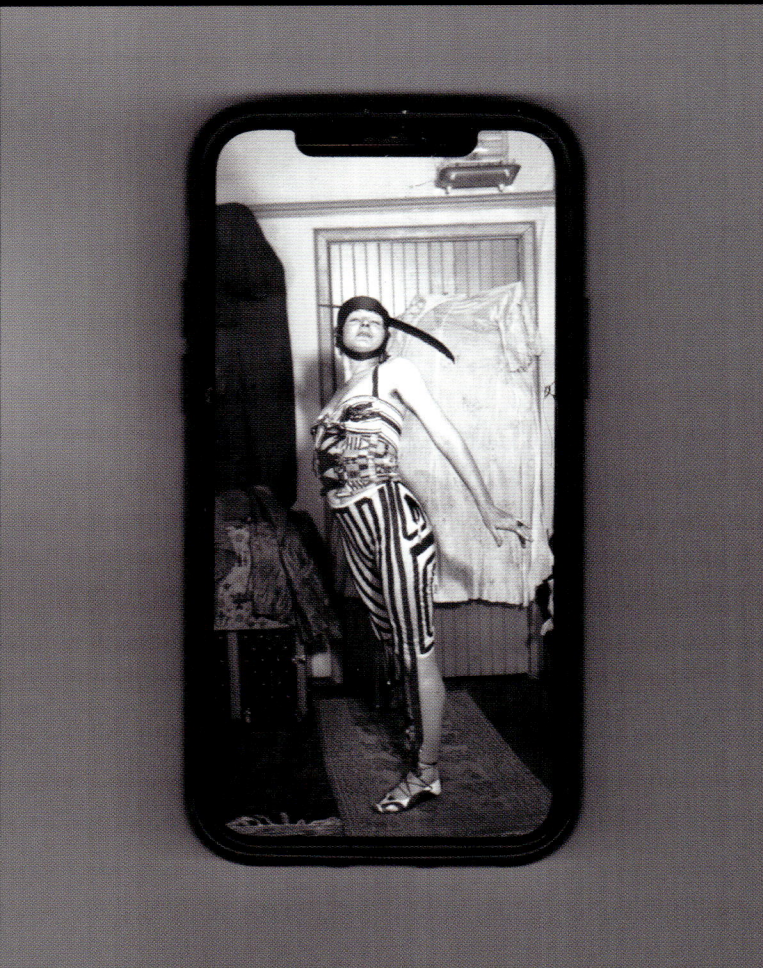
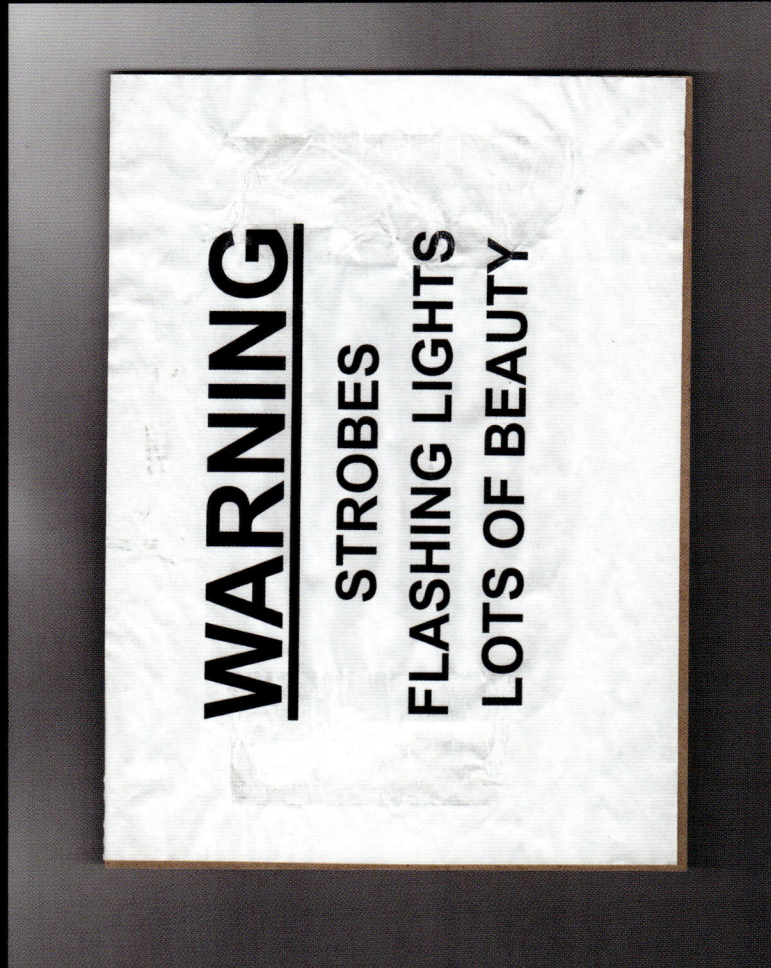

Clockwise from top left: Counterfeit Chanel toilet seat covers and pedestal mats; pages from Jonny's sketchbooks; Banger's venue warning sign; the artist and mother of Dada, Elsa Baroness von Freytag-Loringhoven, who inspired the 'Toilet Bride' look from the show.

THE PEOPLE DESERVE BEAUTY

Made by costume designer Maria Bracher and worn by Emanuelle Soum, the 'Toilet Bride' look closes 'The People Deserve Beauty'. Emanuelle handed out the last of the HERAS metal roses to the euphoric sounds of Praga Khan's 1991 track 'Free Your Body (Injected With a Poison)'.

We were completely skint after moving into our new studio space and didn't really have the money to pull off a runway show. We'd already printed and completely bootlegged a load of unofficial Lucozade NRG T-shirts, hoping they would sell afterwards and cover some costs. As the costs got higher and higher, almost clearing out the bank account, I thought: we're fucked. I hit up a number in my phone saved from years ago as 'Wesley Lucozade' and two days before the show, Lucozade came onboard as an official sponsor. The money covered everything we'd just spent. We printed a giant Lucozade bottle on polysatin to line a skirt-suit, but at the last minute decided to cut it into a dress. Georgie Hobday walked down the runway in it, and the look became one of the stars of the night. After a random turn of events, the Lucozade dress ended up on display at the Museum of Applied Arts in Vienna as part of their exhibition 'The Fest: Between Representation and Revolt'.

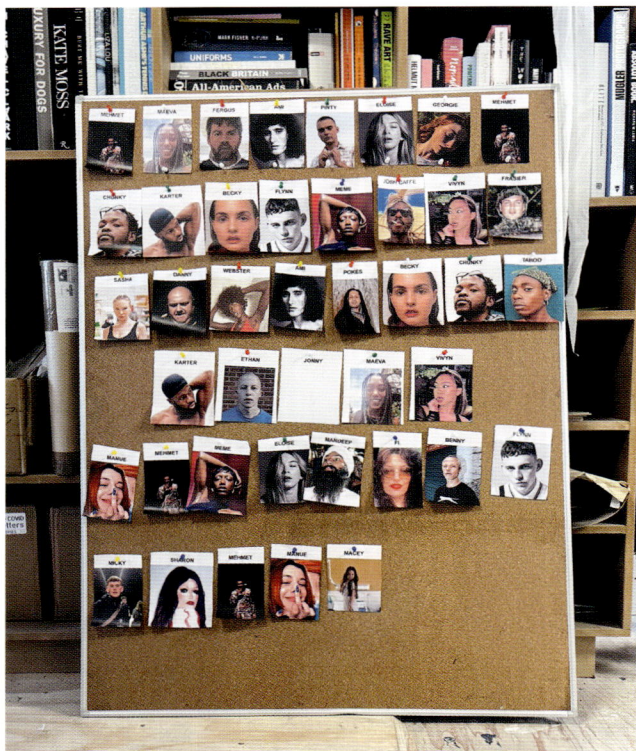

Clockwise from top left: Fittings for the Lucozade 'NRG!' dress; Megan Paran-Rutterford, Jonny, Georgie Hobday and Maison de Bang Bang head of atelier Holly Harris in the studio; patchwork 'POP' jumper by Rough Splinters for Sports Banger; 'The People Deserve Beauty' casting board.

We started work on 'The People Deserve Beauty' as the country was coming out of a long lockdown. We hadn't seen our friends in over a year, and we wanted to bring everyone together again. We had so many incredible artists work with us on this show: Max Allen, Jack Hanson, Anna Lomax, Charlie McCosker, Tom Proper, Emma Brewin, Dan Buck Joyce, Maria Bracher, Emmanuel Soum. When we're collaborating with someone, we start with an idea and then we ask them to take it for a spin. Two heads are better than one. Ten are better than two.

Clockwise from top left: ACME thunderer whistle stamped with 'ACME BANGER LOMAX' branding; dancers rehearse for the runway in cardboard masks of disgraced politicians in a nod to 'Spitting Image'; Emanuelle Soum and Dom Ridler backstage on show day; dancer Karteer donning impossibly long lashes by make-up artist Becca Wordingham.

MAISON DE BANG BANG

Screen-printed denim 'Spitting Image' skirt suit. The 'If we all spit together we'll drown the bastards' quote is from trade union leader Bob Crow (RIP), used on the original 'Spitting Image' T-shirts from the 1980s.

Dear Jonny
Bausch Wells-Next-the-Sea

I thought your "People Deserve Beauth" looked Great! I wished I could have been there. The Spitting Image T-Shirts were a vast improvement on the originals — please send me a video of the show (clip to — .com — So I can see your mischief!)

Thanks very much for the T-shirts. You would be very welcome to come to Norfolk for a visit — I have heaps of subversive books of drawing I have been ripping off for decades you would enjoy.

PIP PIP ROGER
PS I am a FAN.!!

From Roger Law

A letter and drawing from 'Spitting Image' creator and artist Roger Law. Jonny explains: 'We'd already bootlegged the "Bastards" T-shirts when we got given Roger's home telephone number, so we rang him to ask permission. Roger swore merrily and was more than happy for us to help ourselves. The photo attached is Roger at home in Norfolk in his bootlegged "Bastards" T-shirt.'

We were inspired by William Hogarth's theory of the Line of Beauty — the idea that the perfect form is a winding, wavy line. Our line of beauty is a giant inflatable wiggle.

Above: The 'Sports Banger Wiggle', constructed from deadstock T-shirts and an inflatable tube.
Opposite: Two pieces made by Charlie McCosker. On the left, the 'YES Peace' skirt, made from reworked T-shirt offcuts, and on the right, the 'Truth Twisters' skirt made from cut-up Banger protest T-shirts that complete the 'Maiden Britannia' outfit.

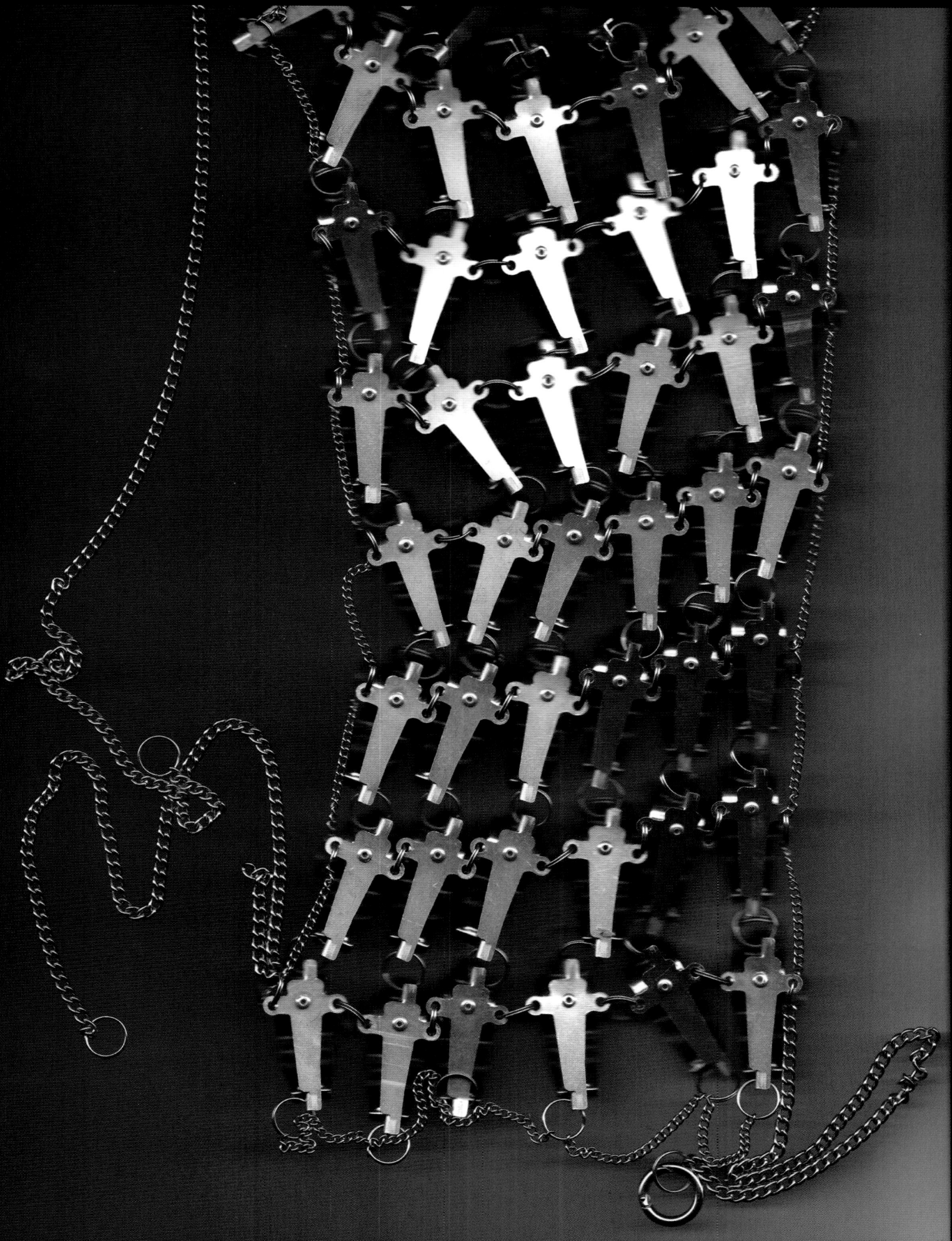

THE PEOPLE DESERVE BEAUTY

Opposite: Ami Benton in the 'Whistleblower' on the runway.
Above: Detail of the reverse side of the 'Whistleblower' made by
Anna Lomax (interviewed on page 51) made from ACME whistles.
Each whistle is riveted onto a specially engineered laser-cut
backplate and then joined using jump rings.

VOGUE

REVIEW

Sports Banger:
Fall 2022 Ready-to-Wear

Luke Leitch
Vogue, 22 February 2022

The audience went demented, the cast danced, and the whistle crew blew at the end of this show. As they did, the adventurous buyer who'd ventured way off schedule to check out Sports Banger turned to me and stated with flat certainty: 'The best thing at London Fashion Week.'

In a city awash with hardscrabble designers, Jonny Banger's Tottenham-based venture is surely amongst the most low-budget of all. What enabled it to present a show as rich as this is the spontaneous philosophy of creative democracy, social enterprise, political criticism, bootleg satire, and hardcore hedonism that combines to draw the like-minded to pitch in. Not unlike the sound systems of the rave culture to which Sports Banger is both adjacent and an overlap, this brand is a big tent – or a muddy field – within which all who contribute to the set list share equal billing.

This season's show, the first since September 2019, was also the official opening of the new Banger studio space acquired courtesy of Haringey Council that Banger deservedly wangled during the pandemic. Along with his food and drink deliveries to healthcare workers, another Banger pandemic wheeze was his exhibition of Instagram-solicited first-wave children's drawings and letters, 'The Covid Letters: A Vital Update' at the Foundling Museum under the co-curation of Turner Prize-winning artist Jeremy Deller, who was at the show. The young lady in the crown, Macie, was a local Covid Letter correspondent, a cystic fibrosis sufferer, who acted as Queen of Tottenham.

The collection was called 'The People Deserve Beauty' because, Banger said afterwards, 'there is not a lot of beauty around right now: more and more of it is being taken away.' The atmosphere was certainly beautiful – during one sudden inter-look lull in the DJ Klose One mixed, HERAS Records (Banger's label) soundtrack, a woman in the audience observed, 'This is so good!' to a just-then silenced room, and the entire audience burst into laughter and cheers. Amongst the most impressive and hilarious of these looks was the Paco Rabanne parodying dress and headdress made from a donation of 1,000 Acme Thunderer whistles by Banger and his long-time co-conspirator, Anna Lomax. Considering they persuaded a company named Essex Lasers to cut the connecting plates and hardware for a trifling amount, the fit of the final product was impressively high-decibel. Another fabulous high-low IP-flouting look was Maria Bracher's cut-out dress and flower headdress; the dress and gloves were cut in counterfeit Chanel shower curtains, and the headdress in counterfeit Chanel toilet seat covers that Banger had acquired from a dodgy Manchester supplier.

Charlie McCosker cut and spliced dead stock Sports Banger T-shirts, socks, and balaclavas – including the classic HM Government Truth Twisters tweet shirt – while Emma Brewin delivered the fur crown. Max Allen, much cheerier about life than at the last show, returned with Elliott Adcock to deliver anarchic hand-dyed collages of overdyed Banger print candy-coloured patches in acid-hermit Saxon shapes, including a draped linen shirt dress with a 10-foot train. Other protagonists included Rough Splinters (patched smiley face pieces) and Gareth McConnell, whose image Dream Meadow XIV featured on the satin sheet that backdropped one Cream-reminiscent raver babe bikini. Other elements were upcycled from unused pieces from Banger's excellent Slazenger collaborations with Sports Direct (including some notable MUD 4 IT festival wellies). The roses tossed into the crowd were made by Jack Hanson from HERAS signs that hundreds of Banger followers on social media had pulled from pieces of that company's industrial fencing and sent him in exchange for free T-shirts.

All of these composite elements, combined and marinated in the power of the bass and the enthusiasm of the audience, were delivered with – sponsor alert – Lucozade-levels of infectious personal energy by a super-diverse cast of Banger-adjacent characters, both old and new. The funniest single moment was probably the Emanuelle Soum choreographed dancers wearing masks depicting the British Prime Minister and his closest Cabinet cohorts as they performed to a completely unrepeatable MC, yet everyone who walked added a specific and vital glimmer to the mosaic kaleidoscope of the whole.

In the fashion arena, companies tend to transmit messages of ideology and spirit – messages related to politics, or social injustice and diversity, or sustainability, or art, or other human freedoms and challenges – chiefly in order to amplify and market their operations as manufacturers of clothing. What's cool about Banger is that here – in a way we haven't seen properly since maybe Katharine Hamnett – that model is flipped: The clothing is the byproduct that services the message that is its end product. And because the message that Banger's wider activities personify – the right to rave, to resist bad government, and to be creatively generous – is so right and infectious, you can only see it attracting more fellow travellers who want to be there, see that, and buy the T-shirt. Especially now he's built a new website. Vibe-wise, Banger is the best.

THE PEOPLE DESERVE BEAUTY

Sharon Le Grand storms the runway in a MAX Banger dress with a 10-foot train.

MAISON DE BANG BANG

THE PEOPLE DESERVE BEAUTY

The party after the Maison de Bang Bang finally opened to the public.

KISS my bASS

This is a collaboration between Max Allen and Sports Banger, the two fashion houses of Tottenham. The collection is inspired by fast cars, soft cocks, hard graphics, Buzz Sweets packets and acid summer skies.

MAISON DE BANG BANG

Previous, left: A MAX Banger poster design, nicked from an old advert from *Max Power*, a British car magazine.
Previous, right: Sunglasses, model's own.
Above: Maëva Berthelot gets her arse out in a MAX Banger T-shirt, hand-dyed panties and jersey stockings.

Above: Detail of ombré dyed MAX Banger garment on printing bed.
Inset: Designer and collaborator Charlie McCosker models another MAX Banger look.
Overleaf: Charlie McCcsker, Pinty, Maëva Berthelot and J. Caesar on the hood of a friend's Fiat Panda 'hot-hatch'.

KISS MY BAS

SEVEN SISTERS IS BURNING
by Jeremy Deller

The first time I met Jon (if you could call it a meeting), he came up to me, said a few words, gave me some T-shirts and ran off. The gift was appropriate, as I'd started out selling T-shirts, and I understood their power. To see someone actually wearing something you've made is a bit of a thrill and probably a little addictive. The next time we met was at Sports Banger's first fashion show, held in Jon's tiny studio on Seven Sisters Road. It was epic in its ambition, with a whole worldview laid out for all to see. Since then, we've become good friends.

Being in an artist's studio can be like walking around inside their mind. Every object has a story, and nothing is there by accident. A studio can also articulate an artist's vision for society. It's an expression of how they see the world and a space for the community they've created. Jon's HQ is just this – a place where, in the spirit of Warhol's Factory, work and life are inseparable. Jon brings people together, and through Banger, he pushes culture forward in unexpected ways. We get a taste of this vision in his fashion shows, which are part manifesto and part total artwork – incorporating performance, music and politics. The shows (both on and off the runway) are populated by the extended group of people who make up the Banger universe. I suspect that for Jon, creating communities is the actual work – the point of everything he does. This community starts at Maison de Bang Bang and radiates out through the food bank, the Mega Raves, and, inevitably, the Instagram feed, to the point where people buy T-shirts to become part of something bigger. I've drawn a diagram to describe what I mean here, as, to me, this extended (and constantly expanding) community seems to be at the heart of the entire Sports Banger project.

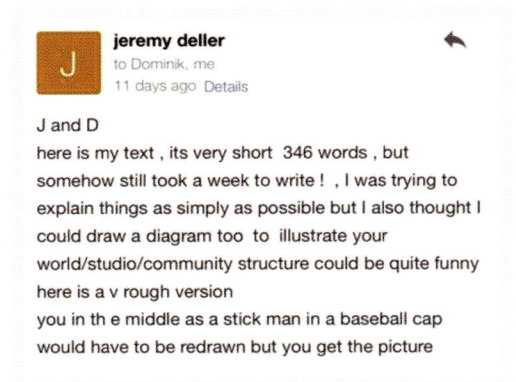

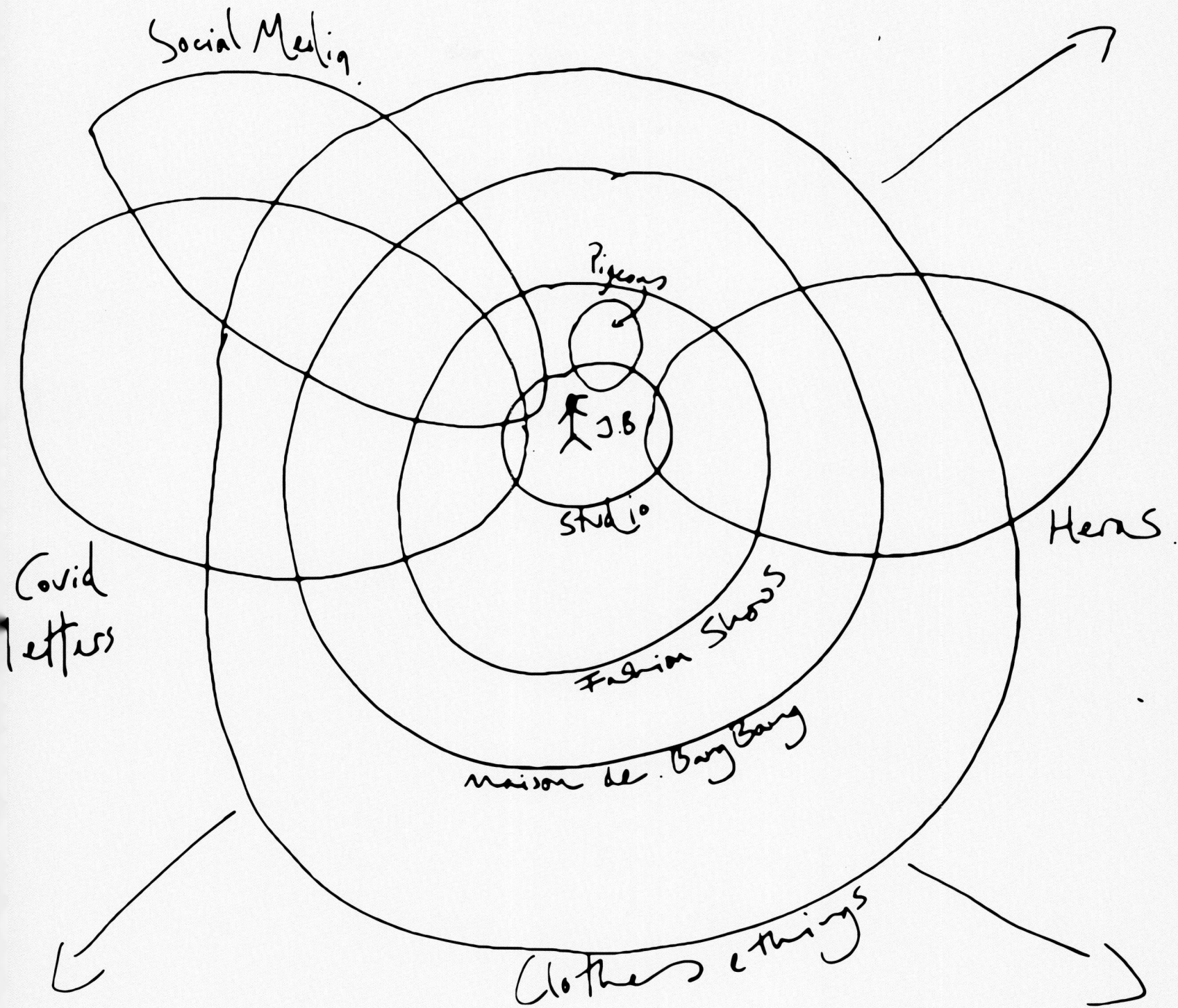

Social Media

Pigeons

J.B

Studio

Fashion Shows

Covid
letters

Hens.

maison de Bang Bang

Clothes & things

The World

The final act is a collaboration with our favourite photographer Gareth McConnell. Gareth sent me a print during lockdown as a gift of solidarity, as we were both fundraising for our local communities. I've got all his books and I find his work fascinating. To see 'The People Deserve Beauty' through Gareth's psychedelic lens is a dream.

MAISON DE BANG BANG

Previous, right: Chunky wears 'Bastards' parka and appliquéd tracksuit bottoms by Sports Banger. Boots by Timberland.
Above: Eloise Smyth wears the 'Whistleblower' head piece by Sports Banger + ACME + Anna Lomax.
Opposite: Emanuelle Soum wears plated crown by Sports Banger + Jack Hanson + Emma Brewin. Inflatable body 'Wiggle' by Sports Banger. Shoes by Pleaser.

'I saw what Jon was doing [during lockdown] and it blew me away. I consider him a kind of 'rave Renaissance man' and I just wanted to reach out with a gift to say "I hear ya brother and I love it".'
– Gareth McConnell

THE FINAL ACT

Opposite: 'Dream Meadow XXVII', 2021, by Gareth McConnell.
Above: Alice Doig wears patchwork dress by Sports Banger.
Shoes courtesy of Vivienne Westwood archive.

Above: Danny Harrison wears 'Bin Bags' tracksuit by Sports Banger. 'Whistle head' by Esther Dillner.
Opposite: Emanuelle Soum wears inflatable body 'Wiggle' by Sports Banger. Shoes by Pleaser.

MAISON DE BANG BANG

Above: Mandeep Dubb wears 'Moving Banger' jumper, leather body belt and overprint tracksuit bottoms by Sports Banger. Boots by Timberland.
Opposite: Alice Doig wears a draped skirt by Sports Banger, plated bustier and metal roses by Sports Banger + Jack Hanson.

MAISON DE BANG BANG

Above: Mikey Boyce wears the 'Bastards' shirt and shorts by Sports
Banger + Max Allen. Metal roses by Sports Banger + Jack Hanson.
Opposite: Emanuelle Soum wears the 'Toilet Bride' dress by Sports
Banger + Maria Bracher. Metal roses by Sports Banger + Jack Hanson.
Shoes courtesy of Vivienne Westwood archive.

For me, the figures are reminiscent of some kind of allegorical deities ... perhaps residents in Mu Mu Land and waiting for the KLF to arrive in an ice cream van ... that with a bit of Fischli & Weiss "Rat and Bear" thrown in .... I kinda want to see a film of them out shopping in Lidl or trekking across a glacier....' – Gareth McConnell

MAISON DE BANG BANG

Dom Ridler wears the 'Bin Bags' tracksuit by Sports Banger. 'Whistle head' by Esther Dillner. Trainers by Reebok. Eloise Smyth wears the 'Whistleblower' dress & headpiece by ACME + Banger + Anna Lomax. Shoes courtesy of Vivienne Westwood archive.

This is serious couture. It takes a day to sew a small section . I'm just finishing the top section. Then I'll do the fluffy fringe bit, then I'll do the perimeter edges

If I have time I might try to lengthen it slightly .

Hi I know this is a massively long shot, but my grandad is a retired NHS GP, he came over from Pakistan and has worked in the uk for over 50 years.

He really liked the NHS hoodies, but I didn't manage to get him

Hi
I recently bought a Sports Banger t shirt, however am not satisfied so would like a refund please.
Please can you send me the address I should return it to.
Thankyou, Joe

To: Jon Wright

RE: Refund
14 December 2013 17:33

I posted it off today, thanks. Didn't like the design as much when on me compared to in the photos

Good or bad, big or small, these are the labels, platforms and media brands young people mentioned most often to us during our research:

Our @livityuk fashion report launches this week and @sportsbanger was one of the most influential brands mentioned by our audience

HYPEBEAST
NIKE
RAF SIMONS
H&M
depop
YEEZY
PYREX
PUMA
UNIQLO
COS
LV
ebay
BALENCIAGA
American Apparel
VETEMENTS
Levi's
RALPH LAUREN
Off-White™
BANGER
asos
carhartt
GUCCI
HOODLAB

DO YOU WANT TO BE YOUR OWN PERSON?

Subject: Solidarity t-shirts
To: hello@sportsbanger.com
<hello@sportsbanger.com>

Hiya,

I've been given your details by one of our members about free solidarity t-shirts for striking workers?

Not sure if you're aware, but along side the royal mail strikes there are 40,000 CWU members in BT are out on strike on the 30th & 31st of this month. Around 900 of those are my members i⬛⬛⬛⬛⬛⬛⬛⬛. Of course not expecting 900 t-shirts but having a few would be great to hand out on picket lines!

How do we go about getting hold of these?

Many thanks

Political Officer
CWU ⬛⬛⬛⬛

Sent from Samsung Mobile on O2
Get Outlook for Android

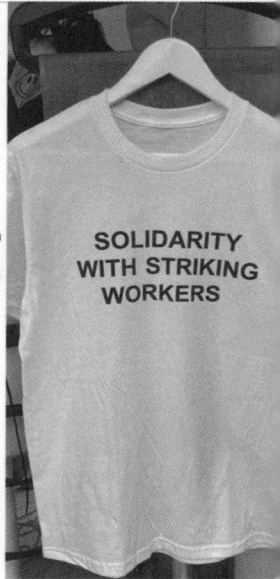

SOLIDARITY WITH STRIKING WORKERS

Today 15:14

My thoughts are with you during this stressful time 🙏

Fuck you

Mate I'm being serious

Fuckin hell

Fuck you

For once actually being nice

FUCK YOU

Fuck you
Delivered

Thank you, he's so happy 😂

THE FOUNDLING MUSEUM

Foundling Museum ✔ @Foundli... · 1h
'..the rudest and shoutiest art show in London' – Time Out

GMP City Centre ✔
@GMPCityCentre

Man queueing for limited edition trainers got passerby to queue for 2nd pair + hands over £260. Man distracted + passerby runs off with cash

13/04/2016 07:16

was doing my ward rounds at the hospital today wearing my banger nhs tee and when i walked onto one of the longer term wards this old lady started clapping then this other one did then one kissed me
16:26

t was well nice 16:27

Little Miss Trouble lives in Uptonogood Cottage surrounded by fields and trees and more fields and more trees, and even more fields.

Her nearest neighbours live miles and miles away and there is a very good reason for this.

Send me a pic and I'll send you a sports banger x @tommyjeans @tommyhilfiger tshirt
16:06

Do you remember about 8 years ago he gave you his business card?
16:07

I bloody well do.... still in my warrant card holder!!! 😂😂😂
16:09

PROPERTY OF THE
J O N N Y
BANGER
16:10

⬛⬛⬛⬛.com
Sun 11/11/2018, 4:13 AM

⬛⬛⬛⬛ year). It's first years and all from different backgrounds and few I've spoked to feel intimidated by notion of art schools and fashion industry whatever but just want them to believe in them self push what they wanna say not latest article on dazed and that and just know that through that they can make a big impact by accommodating to any bullshit. Sorry if sounds lame but lot of them never been exposed to all this and I want them to just believe in why they're here in salford not csm and that.

As I said no rush but let me know and if u need anything from my side whatever let me know. The module it's from is contextual context

Ami Benton

Runway model and cabaret performer, London

YOU WORE THE WHISTLEBLOWER – AKA THE WORLD'S HEAVIEST DRESS – AT BANGER'S 'THE PEOPLE DESERVE BEAUTY' SHOW. WHAT WAS THAT LIKE?

Do you know what? It was actually amazing. Jonny messaged me saying, 'We've got this outfit, and we can only imagine you wearing it.' And then he added, 'Oh, it's a dress made of 1000 whistles.' For me, being in the cabaret scene, I'm used to dancing in *really* heavy headdresses and feather showgirl backpacks, and my job is to make it look effortless. But when it came time for the final fitting of the whistleblower dress, I must admit it was a bit of a shock to the system because wow, it was really heavy. The team were so nice and said that if it was too heavy, they could adjust the whole thing – they even had to put cushioning on my shoulders to make sure it didn't cut into me too much. But I was like, there's no way that I'm going to say no to wearing this masterpiece down the runway. My thought process was, even if it took me 10 minutes to walk down the runway, I was going to own it with power and grace regardless. When I came out, the response from everyone was like, 'Oh my god, this dress!' And I just felt amazing – so amazing that I forgot how heavy it was. The heaviness actually helped because it created a really performative moment, I felt like a statuesque goddess gliding down the runway.

I even had someone recognize me at Glastonbury that year for being the model who wore the Sports Banger 'Whistle' dress, which was just mad!

HOW DOES WALKING FOR SPORTS BANGER COMPARE TO WALKING FOR BRANDS LIKE JEAN PAUL GAULTIER?

They're two different ends of the spectrum. You've got Gaultier, which is the crème de la crème of haute couture fashion and then you've got Sports Banger, which is so underground and current. I must say, both are very humble and personable designers. Gaultier's final haute couture show was such a huge moment in my career – wearing classic archive looks from his past collections and sharing the runway with '90s and current supermodels like Erin O'Connor and Bella Hadid. Then there's Sports Banger, which is completely underground, so up-and-coming and forward-thinking. Walking his runway is like the best night out you will ever have, and you're sharing the runway with all his best mates, which makes the whole experience backstage and on stage such a hoot. It's also really cool to be part of something that is actually creating a stamp in the fashion world. At first, I didn't realize all the hype he'd caused, but now everyone's talking about Sports Banger.

WHAT'S JONNY LIKE TO WORK WITH?

Jonny is a legend. He's full of fun and doesn't take himself, or the brand, too seriously. But you can tell how much the brand and his team mean to him by all the work he puts into everything. He has ultimate respect for you as a model and a human, which I really appreciate. Being a model in the industry, you sometimes end up working for people who treat you like a mannequin, so it's really refreshing to work with like-minded creatives. With Jonny, you don't really feel like you're working for him – you feel like he's your mate.

Celeste Kennedy Doig

Producer, Sports Banger

HOW DID YOU COME TO BE INVOLVED WITH JONNY AND SPORTS BANGER?

I can't quite remember where I met Jonny, it was either at a rave or at Notting Hill Carnival. He's best friends with my cousin Ruairi [Klose One] and he was always at ours for Christmas dinner. For years I was just Klose One's cousin but I think I have finally made it into the world as Celeste.

I first worked with Sports Banger when I offered to help out at the second fashion show as a runner. Quite soon I was working on the next show, when Josh Caffé walked through the crowd in the tiny, packed studio with giant butterfly wings as the 'Giz a Fiver Fisting Fairy' to the sounds of Paranoid London. If someone isn't squeezing sideways through a door into a packed room it's not a Sports Banger show.

AND WHAT IS IT THAT YOU DO WITH SPORTS BANGER EXACTLY?

I would say I am the in-house producer. I help to make any of the many mad projects that Jonny and Dom conjure up come to life. There's so many jobs – you just have to get your hands dirty. I'll even organize bin collections, get invoices paid and do some washing up. Over the last year or so, I produced the incredible photoshoot with Gareth McConnell, the MEGA RAVE at Fabric, Sports Banger opening Shangri-La at Glastonbury, and 'The People Deserve Beauty' fashion show.

For the last show, we used a neighbour's community space as back-of-house. We had 20 hair and make-up stations, almost 30 models, the styling area and a makeshift photo studio upstairs. Safe to say it was chaos. After the show, we were all so happy and excited, and rushed backstage to get changed and then go grab a drink next door. One of the ladies who runs the space stormed in, totally furious and started screaming at us to clean up immediately. There was white powder all over the desks – she thought it was drugs, but it was Sharon Le Grand's make-up lol.

Sports Banger's approach to production is very DIY. I never have an assistant leading up to any of the projects we do. (Although I really hope to change this one day!) From casting to call sheets, it's a very hands-on role that allows me to be creative and resourceful and I feel very privileged to move through the projects in this way.

WHAT ARE THE MAJOR DIFFERENCES BETWEEN PRODUCING FOR A LUXURY FASHION BRAND WITH LOTS OF RESOURCES AND MONEY, AND A BRAND LIKE SPORTS BANGER?

Working on fashion shows for luxury brands is an incredible experience. There are so many roles in a fashion show, from production to casting to styling to the atelier. Each of these sections has teams of people ensuring the deadlines are met and there are enough hands to make these things happen. A major factor is budget – a lot of these fashion shows have substantial budgets that can make the impossible possible.

At Sports Banger, it's an entirely different ball game. First of all, the team is tiny and the budget is non-existent. From the start, we're all involved in the conversation, from casting to location to the collection. It feels so exciting to have creative input. Originally, we were going to put on 'The People Deserve Beauty' at the studio and have the runway extending out the door but due to an extreme weather warning, we moved it next door to Matt's studio, which not long before had been a completely derelict fish smokehouse. The place was a state, with a skip full of rubbish, half a roof and a dead fox. (We had to burn a lot of incense to get rid of that smell.) Matt made the best and most simple lighting rig I've ever seen. The show was pure chaos, which reflects Sports Banger and the people behind it so well. The audience was filled with friends and family and the looks on their faces made it all worth it.

I'M SURE THERE ARE MANY, BUT CAN YOU TELL US ABOUT A MEMORABLE MOMENT IN YOUR TIME WITH SPORTS BANGER?

When we worked on the shoot with Gareth McConnell, we were two models short so I asked my sister Alice and her boyfriend Mikey to fill in. Alice ended up being so incredibly photogenic that an image of her ended up on 300 billboards all over the UK. (Jon managed to blag the billboards for free.) Another highlight was when we did a MEGA RAVE three-room takeover at Fabric on the Friday before Notting Hill Carnival – arguably the most important weekend of the year. Jonny and Ruairi asked me if I could host my night Bubble Like Soup in Room 3. Having grown up in Trinidad I can't describe the feeling of hearing Soca in Room 3 at Fabric the Friday before Carnival.

Neil Landstrumm

Music producer, Edinburgh

HOW DID YOU FIRST CONNECT WITH SPORTS BANGER?

I started seeing the T-shirts at gigs, and as Banger's presence on Instagram started permeating, the tentacles reached into my network. I also started chatting to Loefah from Swamp 81, and there was always this crossover between those guys and Sports Banger – the style and the clothes and everything. I'm not massive on the social media kind of thing, I hold back from that, but I started following them. I noticed my music playing in a couple of their stories and made a mental note to reach out.

At the time, I happened to have a few tracks that sort of distilled down my entry into the UK rave scene – the type of hardcore that was around in 1990/1991, before jungle was jungle and all that kind of stuff. I saw Sports Banger was launching a label, so reached out, and it all fell into place organically from there.

CAN YOU REMEMBER SOME OF THE EARLY T-SHIRTS THAT STOOD OUT FOR YOU?

The early ones. It was the 'FREE TULISA', the 'Upside-Down Reebok' logo … the Pat Butcher one and the Nigella one … maybe Fuck Boris. He's a brilliant artist, you know? He weaves together all these areas that he's interested in: rave culture, streetwear, that social conscience kind of stuff… it's a really interesting blend of all these things, and I love the fact that it's independent, surfing the outer limits of branding while bootlegging. I think it's genius – it's just really, really clever, and it's deep, too. It's much deeper than I think some people see on the surface.

WHAT'S YOUR VIEW ON HOW SPORTS BANGER FITS INTO THE LINEAGE OF RAVE?

It's definitely like the early nineties, in the mould of a social youth movement, and the kind of DIY punk feeling of *get off your arse and do it yourself.* The wider problem with dance music now is that it's just entirely hedonistic and has completely lost all connection to why it originally started. Sports Banger kind of bridges that. Like the Mega Raves – they're just very inclusive, which is brilliant. They're very fun. People aren't afraid to have a good time and let themselves go. That's what was brilliant about acid house and early rave culture – it really did bring people together, all these disparate groups. In Scotland, it was football casuals – pretty violent, nasty people – but when they were brought into rave culture, it just softened them up. There was unity through the music. I know all that stuff's clichéd to say, but it did actually happen. That kind of feeling is what Banger taps into; it's just really good fun.

THE COMMUNITIES FORMED THROUGH RAVE CULTURE CAN BE SO STRONG – AND A POWERFUL VEHICLE FOR SOCIAL CHANGE.

Sports Banger is almost like a beacon for fairness in society, and Jon is opportunistic in the sense that he reacts to current events, which is really clever, like the NHS thing. But it's done with the greatest integrity and honesty – it's done with love and care. If you know Jon, you see where it comes from … what happened to his mum …. The same thing happened to me with my brother, and we bonded over that, and we both have this great admiration and respect for the NHS.

WHAT'S IT LIKE PLAYING AT THE MEGA RAVES?

The Mega Rave 4 at The Cause – with Paranoid London, 187 Lockdown, Josh Caffé, Tasha, Klose One, Jay Carder, Jerome Hill and KT – is my favourite one I've done so far. Just interesting party music, none of it po-faced or too serious, and quite extravagant. It was Halloween, so there was a real interesting mix – some people were dressed up, some had just come from work. Some people go to the raves just because it's Sports Banger – they don't really know much about electronic music or rave. So Jon also pulls people in who are new to this, like the NHS workers who come along for free.

WHAT DOES IT MEAN TO YOU TO BE INVOLVED WITH SPORTS BANGER?

It's an absolute honour for me to be on HERAS 001. I'm so proud of that record, and it's gone on to do really well. So that's a real sort of feather in my cap, and I've got the record up on my studio wall.

I love what Jon does, and we bounce ideas off each other. You know, it's just really nice to be a part of that story and the way it's unfolded.

The Sports Banger crew are a really nice bunch. There's no bullshit. Everybody gets something out of it, financially, which is great, but nobody's really doing it for that. It's a counterpoint to all the superficial stuff that appears on social media – no authenticity, just people using social media to their advantage. I'm really honoured to be a part of it.

Jeanie Crystal

Performance artist and co-founder of FABOO TV, London

WHAT (AND WHO) IS FABOO TV? HOW DID IT COME TOGETHER, AND WHAT'S IT ALL ABOUT?

I founded Faboo alongside my friend Josh Quinton, who's an animator. It started as a party because we felt there was a space missing in the London nightclub scene. We wanted to mix things up and throw parties with a real range of genres. I would curate the nights so you could see and hear anything from a dance hall DJ to a drag opera singer to a punk band – sometimes, people would just grab the microphone and start doing god knows what. No one knew what they were gonna see. It was a vibe. We released DIY films to advertize the party and really went in on the production, which encouraged people to go wild on their outfits. There were some serious looks thrown. It was a real spectacle and fusion of artists, musicians, dancers, queens, and ravers.

When the lockdown hit (and obviously nightlife just stopped), Josh moved into my horrible studio in cable street, and we decided to turn the party into an online show that platformed some of our favourite people and artists. We had no money, so just took things out of skips for sets and shot everything on our phones. Everyone worked for free on it, and it became a way of staying connected to our community.

When everything reopened, from the success of the show, we got offered a shop in Camden for free. We filled it with all our favourite DIY designers and gave them one hundred per cent of the profits. It became a community hub and hang out, like the parties, but now it was about seeing the hand of the artist on all the objects in the shop.

So now Faboo really combines all these things – we're a party, a TV collective, a production house and an occasional space for artists to sell their stuff.

FABOO COLLABORATED WITH SPORTS BANGER ON AN 'ALTERNATIVE XMAS MESSAGE' VIDEO. CAN YOU TELL US ABOUT IT? AND WHY DO YOU THINK BANGER AND FABOO ARE SUCH A GOOD MATCH?

Ha! It was a kinky hot mess with Jon dressed as Santa being tied up by some tarty Christmas angels while everyone sang 'shake your bum, wiggle your tits, it's CHRISTMAS BITCH!'

Christmas is such a fucked time of year for so many people with the stress of buying stuff and all the family traumas people are forced to deal with. The video was about doing something silly and filthy to counteract all the faux love and peace messaging. Also, it was a chance to rip down those robbing Tory bastards with some satirical animations from Josh.

For me, it's always made sense to work with Sports Banger. My dad was a market trader, and Jon has this very particular sense of humour, work ethic, empathy, and creativity that I think comes from that working-class culture (along with a good dose of glamour and subversion). I think Faboo and Sports Banger are very much aligned – we're both gobby queens!

AS A FELLOW RABBLE-ROUSER, CAN YOU TELL US ABOUT GETTING SHIT DONE?

Well, I can't do anything without the community of people that are part of Faboo. It's a highly collaborative process. And when it comes to parties, or the online show that we do, or the pop-up boutiques, I curate the right people around me, and then everyone gets busy with what they're good at. It's an egalitarian way of working because everyone knows they're putting in for the greater good. In this case, if it's us making a space within a system that doesn't represent us or doesn't necessarily platform us the way we like to be platformed, whether it be like, queer, working-class, trans, Black people … it's all hands on deck when it comes to Faboo because it's quite an authentic kind of expression of the underground queer community.

There definitely is no formula! It's like, I have an idea, and then somehow, it just happens. But I sometimes think we never really know what the outcome is going to be, particularly when it's art making. So if it's a video or an event, we just get everyone that we feel most comfortable with and respect in a room. Then we just turn the camera on with a very, very loose idea … and then something is born out of the chaos.

WHAT IS THE FUTURE VISION FOR FABOO?

Faboo is constantly in flux, depending on what's happening around us and within our community. I'm currently in a band called Jeanie and the White Boys, and my mate and collaborator Eliza Rose, who I worked with on the video for her single 'B.O.T.A. (Baddest Of Them All)'. A DIY release going to number one [in the UK singles chart] is practically impossible, so we are making moves and disrupting the status quo, which is the energy Faboo thrives off. With the recent passing of Vivienne Westwood, a Faboo hero, it also feels natural that the future vision is a record label that centres queer punk artists, that's what I'm plotting anyway, but god knows something always seems to pop up!

Holly Harris

Pattern cutter, Sports Banger

WHAT WAS YOUR INITIAL IMPRESSION OF SPORTS BANGER?

I had no idea what Sports Banger was until I met Jon. He walked into my old place of work [Tottenham Textiles], telling us he was renting the shop next door – it all seemed very exciting and I liked the tee's he was making, I wanted to be involved and know more! A few months down the line and I asked to be his Saturday shop girl, that's when I really started to understand what Sports Banger was all about.

WHAT'S THE WEIRDEST THING YOU'VE HAD TO MAKE?

We've made some really crazy things. I think one of my favourites was when I made the sock for the 'Wiggle' inflatable pool toy. It's made from old T-shirts stitched together into a 3D spiral. We had a right laugh putting it together. Was a great relief to me when we inflated it and it worked! We've tried to make various wiggles a few times now and 'dressed' a model in a new colourful version for the last show.

CAN YOU DESCRIBE THE STUDIO SETUP?

Do you know what, it's such an improvement from the shop on Seven Sisters Road, which was really dirty and had no real space for doing anything. When we got into this space, I was so happy when Matt built us a proper pattern-cutting table. We've set up all the machines, it looks great! It's usually me, Jon, Dom and Celeste in the space – we have such a laugh. When it comes to designing and making, it's a real team effort and can often be so fluid. I love it.

WHAT IS THE BIGGEST CHALLENGE OF WORKING WITH SPORTS BANGER?

It's probably cash flow, actually, but that's more in terms of the whole business. We have so many ideas, and there are so many things we want to do … although Jon does have this amazing way of getting money in at the very last minute.

WHAT'S IT LIKE SEEING YOUR CREATIONS ON THE RUNWAY?

Well, most of the time, you're kind of so in it that you don't realize how impactful it all is. Especially with the last show, there was so much energy backstage, and I was finishing off some pieces like 20 minutes before call time and then it was straight into getting models changed. I don't think I realized how brilliant the last show was until we watched it back together a few days afterwards. I was like, 'Oh my god, this is amazing. I can't believe we did this.' Sports Banger has such an impact on everybody and I love that, we really do make a right bang in our shows.

Contributors

THE AUTHOR

Jonny Banger (b. 1984, Colchester) is an artist, raver and the founder of Sports Banger, a London-based clothing brand and rag-tag collective that interrogates British pop culture, class and politics through fashion shows, raves, exhibitions and community projects. In 2019, Jonny authored his first book, *Diary of a Bootlegger*, which was published by Rough Trade Books. In 2020, he channelled profits from T-shirt sales into setting up a food bank at a north London primary school and delivering a programme to distribute free meals to healthcare workers across London; he received a Haringey Heroes Award from the Mayor of Haringey for these projects. Also in 2020, Jonny exhibited over 200 government letters defaced by kids and young people from across the UK at London's Foundling Museum (where he was made a Fellow later that year). He also published the works in *The COVID Letters: A Vital Update*, self-published under the Sports Banger imprint in 2021. Jonny has been invited to speak about his work at the Design Museum (London), Royal College of Arts (London), Bound Art Book Fair (Manchester), Forwards Festival (Bristol) and at various colleges and social initiatives across the UK. Sports Banger's clothing has been exhibited at the London College of Fashion, the Museum of Applied Arts (Vienna) and in other independent venues. Sports Banger won the Innovation & Excellence Award at *DJ Magazine*'s Best of British Awards 2020. Jonny presents a monthly show on Rinse FM under Sports Banger's music label HERAS Records. He lives in Tottenham, north London, and loves pigeons.

THE ESSAYISTS

Jeremy Deller is an English conceptual, video and installation artist. He won the Turner Prize in 2004.

Anastasiia Fedorova is a writer, curator and researcher based in London.

Nathalie Khan is a fashion historian and curator.

THE INTERVIEWEES

Max Allen
Artist and designer, London

Artwork (aka Arthur Smith)
Music producer and DJ, New York

Ami Benton
Runway model and cabaret performer, London

Chunky
Musician, MC and DJ, Manchester

Jeanie Crystal
Performance artist and co-founder of FABOO TV, London

Celeste Kennedy Doig
Producer, Sports Banger

Holly Harris
Pattern cutter, Sports Banger

Caro Howell
Director of the Foundling Museum, London

Klose One
HERAS label manager, Sports Banger

Neil Landstrumm
Music producer, Edinburgh

Anna Lomax
Visual Artist, London

Dom Ridler
Art director and creative producer, Sports Banger

Eloise Smyth,
Actor, London

Emanuelle Soum (aka Elle Miyake Mugler)
Choreographer and performance artist, Paris

Totally Enormous Extinct Dinosaurs
(aka Orlando Higginbottom)
Musician, Los Angeles

Sumitra Upham
Curator and head of public programmes at the Crafts Council, London

Jaime Winstone
Actor, London

Member of free party crew Odyssey Soundsystem,

Picture Credits

Manchester, 110–11
Matthews, Patrick, 166–7
Max Power, 278
May, Theresa, 39, 169
MC Chunky, 87–9, 93, 110–11, 145,
     162–3, 242, 285
MC Taboo, 192, 196
McConnell, Gareth, 272, 299;
     photographs of 'The People Deserve
     Beauty', 284–96
McCosker, Charlie, 268, 272
McQueen, Alexander, 127, 228
Mega Aid, 210, 213
Mega Raves, 12–13, 53, 57, 95, 132, 134,
     162–3, 282, 299
Mella Dee, 162–3
Meme Gold, 32, 57, 87–90, 110, 143, 145,
     152, 195
metal, in fashion design, 191, 196, 207,
     257–8, 270–1
Mindwarp raves, 7
Miyake, Faze, 84–5
modelling, 298–9
The Mona Lisa of Tottenham, 61, 63
Moncler, 110, 183, 194
money: judge's wig made from, 188–9,
     194, 196; in shoes, 156–61
Moss, Kate, 189, 194
Mother Pigeon, 201
Mr Shuffle, 117
'MUD', 121
Mugler, Thierry, 192, 194

N   NASA, 249
     Nasty, Marcus, 196
     National Pigeon Service, 82
     NHS, 38–9, 70–6, 173, 225, 297, 300; 1%
          pay rise, 173; copyright, 74; junior
          doctors' dispute, 38, 70–1, 76–77,
          216, 237; T–shirts and logo, 53,
          69–70, 72, 105, 109, 179, 190, 194,
          196, 210–12, 216–17, 222
     Nike, 38, 61, 69–70, 72
     Nite Dykez, 38
     Norfolk, 98
     'Not Bad for a Woman', 125
     'Not for Sale', 127
     Notting Hill Carnival, 168–9, 299
     Novelist, 144, 152

O   Odyssey Soundsystem, 96–8, 106
     Orgreave, Battle of, 124
     Östlund, Ruben, 250
     Outlook Festival, 110

P   padlock, 96
     pandemic, 38, 106, 133, 255; Covid
          Letters project, 216–21, 223–4, 226,
          272; 'Wine Time Fridays', 259
     lockdowns, 111
     Paranoid London, 12–13, 202, 205, 208
     Paran-Rutterford, Megan, 87–9
     'PAT ON THE BACK', 124
     PayPal, 7
     'The People Deserve Beauty',10, 104,
          232–3, 247, 251, 256–64, 265,
          298–9; casting boards, 264; Gareth
          McConnell's photographs of, 284–96;
          Vogue review, 272
     'Phone Thieves', 30–3, 116
     piano tracksuit, 94
     'Pigeon Park' fashion show, 172

pigeons, 7, 82, 111, 243; tracksuit,
     198–201
Pintando, Mutando, 208
'Pirate Radio is Good for Your Mind', 120
policing, 100–1, 106
'Pop Culture is Trash' fashion show, 16–17,
     133, 174–9, 192, 196, 232–3; casting
     boards, 190; Vogue review, 194
posters, 73
The Prodigy, 248
'Propaganda' (song), 98
Proper, Tom, 21
protests, 164–5, 169

Q   Quinton, Josh, 302

R   R&S Records, 127
     Ralph Lauren, 15, 124
     rap, 110
     raves, 52–3, 95, 99; illegality, 96, 98–103,
          106
     RAVING SHOES, 124
     'The Real Thing', 38
     Rebelle, Josie, 121
     Reebok, 42–3, 46–7, 51, 110, 111, 118,
          121; Classics, 156–9
     refugees, 119
     Ridler, Dominik, 57, 230–1, 250, 265, 296
     Rinse FM, 21, 42, 110
     Robinson, Keith, 106
     Rolls Royce, 192
     Rose, Eliza, 10, 127
     Rose, Ruby, 75
     Rough Splinters, 264, 272
     'RUNNER' (T-shirt), 121

S   Saatchi, Charles, 34
     Sanders, Bernie, 39
     Sarca, Ancuta, 151, 152, 194
     school meals, 133, 155, 172, 210
     School Records, 21, 110
     screen printing, 45–6
     Seryah, 192
     Seven Sisters Road studio, 60–1, 80,
          84–5, 133, 142–3, 152, 205, 208,
          234–8, 282
     Seven Sisters station, 80
     Sharp, Pat, 124
     'shit mix' jar, 61, 66
     'Shocker', 44
     Shogs, Hannah, 213
     'SHUT/DOWN', 79
     Sid the Snail (Tottenham landmark), 61,
          63, 122
     Singh, Yung, 162–3
     Skepta, 42–3, 78–9
     Skream, 37, 143, 152–3
     Slazenger, 61, 86–93, 110, 123, 139, 148,
          152, 272; Banger Classic, 156–7,
          160–1; pigeon tracksuit, 198–201
     Slim, 192
     Smile & Wave, 116
     Smith, Arthur see Artwork (Arthur Smith)
     Smyth, Eloise, 16–17, 133, 184, 227, 257,
          286, 296
     Snowbombing (festival), 55, 124
     Soum, Emanuelle (Elle Miyake Mugler),
          57, 144, 187, 194, 229, 247, 263,
          265, 272, 287, 295
     sound systems, 106, 133
     Souza, Tania, 119
     'Spitting Image', 266–7

Sports Direct, 76–7
squatters, 239
St Clement, Pam, 124
stickers, 33
strikes, solidarity with, 127, 138, 244
Swaffham, 98
Swamp 81, 21, 52, 110

T   'Take Pills and Kick the Tories Back to
          Hell',166–7
     TANK magazine, 36
     Tasha, 162–3, 300
     'Team Nigella', 34–7, 116, 300
     techno, 52
     Temujin, 162–3
     tennis, 86, 87, 91–2, 117
     Thatcher, Margaret, 124
     Three Lions, 123
     The Three Stooges, 172
     toilet seat, 262–3
     Tommy Hilfiger, 41, 126, 202, 206,
          208–9
     Top of the Pops, 78–9
     Totally Enormous Extinct Dinosaurs, 50
     Tottenham see Seven Sisters Road studio
     Tottenham Textiles, 148–9, 152, 182, 194,
          230, 303
     Triangle of Sadness, 250
     'Truth Twisters', 73, 269, 272
     T-shirt designs, 21, 52, 113–28, 137, 300
     Twitter: unauthorized Cabinet Office tweet,
          173

U   UK Tek, 106
     'Under The Counter', 69–75
     'Underpaid, Undervalued', 248
     Union Jack, 172
     unions, 127
     Unity23 free party, 100, 107
     Upham, Sumitra, 109

V   Vetements, 39
     Vibe Bar, 21
     Vienna: Museum of Applied Arts, 264
     Vogue, 152, 225; reviews, 194, 208,
          272

W   Wallis, Gary, 127
     warehouse parties, 99
     Warwick, Dame Cathy, 72
     Watson, Gavin, 194
     'Wearing it Wrong' EP, 252, 255
     Webster, 192
     Welcome to Bangtazia, 95
     Whalley, Quinn, 208
     'Whistleblower', 270–2, 286, 296, 298
     Who Are You, Polly Maggoo? 196–7
     'Wiggle', 268, 287, 291, 303
     Windross, Norris 'da Boss,' 21
     Winstone, Jaime, 152, 228, 246
     Wordingham, Becca, 16-17, 265
     'The World is Ours to Share', 108, 119
     Wright, Billy, 201

Y   Yankah, Ellie, 119
     'YES, PEACE', 119
     Yotka, Steff, 225
     'You're a Keeper', 120

Z   Zed Bias, 116
     Ziu, Leila, 200
     ZOMBY, 117

Thanks

Special thanks to Dom Ridler for the insane amount of work and tobacco navigating this. Thanks to Jane and Tristan at Thames & Hudson for entrusting us to make this book – we missed every deadline lol. Thank you Emma Capps for giving me the confidence to write. Alfie Allen and Joel for the design (this is the second book we've done – wanna make it a trilogy?). Matt Harriman for everything and more, the adventure continues (DJ Smash Hits 4 life). Bianca my love, you bring the mayhem, I'll bring the chaos – fireworks on tap. Rolling round, windows down, Klose One sound. Anna Lomax, a continued inspiration, blow your whistle, let's go. Ollie Grove, always happily furious when I put your phone number online. Sam McFadden (do you know what we do yet?). Tom Proper, let's go bash some billboards. Jeremy Deller, because art is for the people and art is magic. Luke Leitch, top words and friendship. The female bosses Katy Ellis and Katie Thiebaud, my adopted rave mums. Artwork, for the kindness and pisstakes. Loefah, for believing and making me feel a part of something. Tasha, you are the best (and your sets should come with a hazard warning). Celeste, you're always right – big up the whole family. Lisa, oi oi, my original HERAS sister, love you. Emanuelle, yes bish, my French queen, thank you for joining two beautiful worlds and trusting us – bigger, louder. Eloise, me lil sis, u set rooms on fire and it makes me proud. Orlando, let the doves fly – I'll meet you in LA. Frazier for dragging me out of London to shit in the woods. Dan Buck Joyce, without you there's no video. Big up Marcus Barnes for gathering all our mates' interviews. Lizzie Newell, thanks friend (who's going to listen?). Benton, they said the Wright brothers would never fly. Caro Howell, you gave a home to a project no one else would touch and even got the government to pay for it lol. Sumitra, thank u for kicking a door open so I could speak – kinda life-changing. Hettie Judah, u got ur own section on my bookshelf but none signed yet. Tommy D my bro, forever awesome tapes from Hull. Arms out wide, Tyneeeeeeeside. Vibbidy Vibes OG Stone House rock stars rolling. Wee Man and the whole Odyssey Soundsystem crew. Morgane and Spiral. Younie for the electrics and teaching me the way of the PLUR. Benny Ill for teaching me the way of the samurai. Chris Stead, your work is stunning and so is the Pigeon Park collective. Danny 187, forever Britain's Next Top Model. Neil Landstrumm, you gave HERAS wings. Johnnie Optimo, your encouraging words never left. Lasha, Ryan and all the FOLD family, what a gaff, thank u for what you have built, I learn something every time. Henry Buck, give us the album. Teddy Bones, see u 2moro, 11am. Paul Woolford for splitting the atom. Mr Future from a faraway place, Mat Playford. Chunky – daaaasss wassup mic brother. Claus in the house. Jake Hardy for tech support. SGT Pokes, always salute my friend. Andy Neas bro, what a time, allergy kids unite. Gareth McConnell, a friendship made, throw some flowers on it, let's fuck some shit up. Max Allen, the only book I want is yours. Chloé Robinson, you deserve it all. Paranoid London, imagine us fuckers never meeting. Big up Quinn, Dels, Josh Caffé, Clams. Pow Pow Alex Pow (RIP). Shouts to Peter Doig, everything on ice. The magnificent David Hoyle. Charlie McCosker, Jack Hanson, Devon Analogue, Trish Lad, Jeanie Crystal. Susie Crome and Cassie. Meriel and Lois and the Club Mexicana gang. Olu and Priceless. Anna Wall. Thanks Rhiannon Isabel for always repping us in shoots. Big ups to Andreas Wavey Garms, we done it our ways. Out to Pat. Eliza Rose, the baddest. Meme Gold, runway pube stroker. Ryan Hawaii – art art art. Bluetoof and Jossy Mitsu, you's killing it. Jack 'wang-a-welly' Walmsley. Big up Oneman. Out to the Vibe Bar crew. Shouts Hannah Shogs, Jessie, Luke Button, Mia Mouse, Fergus of Essex, Mella Dee the Don from Donny. D.ablo, see you in September. Nia Archives, bang ur head. Melanie Blatt. Jaime Winstone. OG logo design by Josh Stika. Gav Watson. Will RS, ello mate. Will Skillers. Bobby Skillz and Floyd El Fresh. Pinty. Elk. Russel Porter report. Dirty Dike. James Rompa. Marcus Nasty, it's a raffle thing. Maëva Berthelot to the world. Daisy, Dusty Knuckle. Ravi cares. Meatball Molly, put an elbow on it. Jake IRIS (RIP). Mark 'Supercar' Suchopar (RIP). Soft Core, ya know. Jay Carder, harder. Odisy. Mushy Manchester. Duncan Petro. Zed 'the boss' Bias. Skream (the OG). Kimi Faux Naif and the Fabric crew. Daz Rarekind and Ewan, Daps, Steve Clear and Big P. Uncle Jim (Nause Corp). Snail. Disorda. 2Kold. Si Bonobo. Pavan. Dave Illaman. Mr Tumnus. Big Fun Dan and Lani. Lula. Praf. Uncle Will and Paula. Skepta. Novelist. Emerald. Migz. Rinse FM family, Geeneus. Man like Morgan. Casisdead, let's do it. DJ Ron, the Sarsaparilla Kid. Daniel Avery. Rup and Verity. Lois, thank you for letting me sleep on the floor, honorary south London. Thank you Holly Harris and Megan Paran-Rutterford for all ur work (no laughing in the studio). Pete Fowler. James Endeacott and the family. Emma Brewin and exhaust-sniffer Grape. Footsie, yes king. Clint 419, dun it. The torn Banger lettering on this book bootlegs one of the most iconic typographic covers in publishing history – big up Tony Palladino. Lemn Sissay. Roger 'Spitting Image' Law. Jamie Brown (giz a lamp). Haroun Hayward (giz a painting). Nina at Rough Trade Books, you started all this word stuff. Olive, do ur hair orange again. Freddie Rough Splinters. Luis Tottex. Fanx to Zsolt, Lily, Fifth Column, Holly and Alex at Orto Print. Khaly and Buildhollywood. Garry Blackburn of Leatherhead. Rob A'ce. Thanks Lottie and Matilda. Yes Daseplate, I watched you build it (viva la trolley bashers). Taboo, an icon. Sharon Le Grand, a legend. Hannah Holland, family foundling. Out to Mandeep. Mehmet Mustard, who's upset ya. Stuart at The Cause. Steff Yotka. Ruthie Toots, where's roof? Maria Bracher, costume legend. Plastician. LCY. Alexandra Amiri. Lecos Marks, I'm doing it, I'm doing it. Charlie Smith and family. Thank you Chris and thank you Dad for the hustle and belief in community for good. Original Camden girl Irene. Love to my brother Steve and Will and Charbs. Big up to our pigeons Billie, Piper, Ghost, Swoosh, Nicotine, Ice, Pollock, Krays, Blues Brothers … angels watching over us. All my Colchester CCC crew. Queen Macie. All the Banger pirates on the high seas. Big up Shaun Roberts – 'live the shit out of life', and people, check your poo. Special mentions to Jan 'Aset' Francis and Sonic Sonia, peace girl, x.

This book is dedicated to my Mum and Auntie Val.

778 illustrations

FRONT COVER Artwork by Sports Banger.
BACK COVER Sports Banger peace graphic. Designed by Sports Banger.

First published in the United Kingdom in 2023 by
Thames & Hudson Ltd, 181A High Holborn,
London WC1V 7QX

First published in the United States of America in 2023 by
Thames & Hudson Inc., 500 Fifth Avenue,
New York, New York 10110

Sports Banger © 2023 Thames & Hudson Ltd, London

Introductions and captions © 2023 Sports Banger
'Why Bootlegging Will Never Die' © 2023 Anastasiia Fedorova
'Modern Metal Is Trash' © 2023 Nathalie Khan
'Seven Sisters Is Burning' by Jeremy Deller

For image copyright information see p. 306

Project Manager: Dom Ridler
Managing Editor: Emma Capps
Design: Alfie Allen and Joel Wilson
Interviews: Marcus Barnes

British Library Cataloguing-in-Publication Data
A catalogue record for this book is available from the British Library

Library of Congress Control Number 2023939136

ISBN 978-0-500-02619-9

Printed and bound in China by
Toppan Leefung Printing Limited

FSC MIX
Paper from
responsible sources
FSC® C104723

Be the first to know about our new releases,
exclusive content and author events by visiting
thamesandhudson.com
thamesandhudsonusa.com
thamesandhudson.com.au